Lecture Notes in Economics and Mathematical Systems

(Vol. 1–15: Lecture Notes in Operations Research and Mathematical Economics, Vol. 16–59: Lecture Notes in Operations Research and Mathematical Systems) For information about Vols. 1–29, please contact your bookseller or Springer-Verlag

Vol. 30: H. Noltemeier, Sensitivitätsanalyse bei diskreten linearen Optimierungsproblemen. VI, 102 Seiten. 1970.

Vol. 31: M. Kühlmeyer, Die nichtzentrale t-Verteilung. II, 106 Seiten. 1970.

Vol. 32: F. Bartholomes und G. Hotz, Homomorphismen und Reduktionen linearer Sprachen. XII, 143 Seiten. 1970. DM 18,–

Vol. 33: K. Hinderer, Foundations of Non-stationary Dynamic Programming with Discrete Time Parameter. VI, 160 pages. 1970.

Vol. 34: H. Störmer, Semi-Markoff-Prozesse mit endlich vielen Zuständen. Theorie und Anwendungen. VII, 128 Seiten. 1970.

Vol. 35: F. Ferschl, Markovketten. VI, 168 Seiten. 1970.

Vol. 36: M. J. P. Magill, On a General Economic Theory of Motion. VI, 95 pages. 1970.

Vol. 37: H. Müller-Merbach, On Round-Off Errors in Linear Programming. V, 48 pages. 1970.

Vol. 38: Statistische Methoden I. Herausgegeben von E. Walter. VIII, 338 Seiten. 1970.

Vol. 39: Statistische Methoden II. Herausgegeben von E. Walter. IV, 157 Seiten. 1970.

Vol. 40: H. Drygas, The Coordinate-Free Approach to Gauss-Markov Estimation. VIII, 113 pages. 1970.

Vol. 41: U. Ueing, Zwei Lösungsmethoden für nichtkonvexe Programmierungsprobleme. IV, 92 Seiten. 1971.

Vol. 42: A. V. Balakrishnan, Introduction to Optimization Theory in a Hilbert Space. IV, 153 pages. 1971.

Vol. 43: J. A. Morales, Bayesian Full Information Structural Analysis. VI, 154 pages. 1971.

Vol. 44: G. Feichtinger, Stochastische Modelle demographischer Prozesse. IX, 404 Seiten. 1971.

Vol. 45: K. Wendler, Hauptaustauschschritte (Principal Pivoting). II, 64 Seiten. 1971.

Vol. 46: C. Boucher, Leçons sur la théorie des automates mathématiques. VIII, 193 pages. 1971.

Vol. 47: H. A. Nour Eldin, Optimierung linearer Regelsysteme mit quadratischer Zielfunktion. VIII, 163 Seiten. 1971.

Vol. 48: M. Constam, FORTRAN für Anfänger. 2. Auflage. VI, 148 Seiten. 1973.

Vol. 49: Ch. Schneeweiß, Regelungstechnische stochastische Optimierungsverfahren. XI, 254 Seiten. 1971.

Vol. 50: Unternehmensforschung Heute – Übersichtsvorträge der Züricher Tagung von SVOR und DGU, September 1970. Herausgeben von M. Beckmann. IV, 133 Seiten. 1971.

Vol. 51: Digitale Simulation. Herausgegeben von K. Bauknecht und W. Nef. IV, 207 Seiten. 1971.

Vol. 52: Invariant Imbedding. Proceedings 1970. Edited by R. E. Bellman and E. D. Denman. IV, 148 pages. 1971.

Vol. 53: J. Rosenmüller, Kooperative Spiele und Märkte. III, 152 Seiten. 1971.

Vol. 54: C. C. von Weizsäcker, Steady State Capital Theory. III, 102 pages. 1971.

Vol. 55: P. A. V. B. Swamy, Statistical Inference in Random Coefficient Regression Models. VIII, 209 pages. 1971.

Vol. 56: Mohamed A. El-Hodiri, Constrained Extrema. Introduction to the Differentiable Case with Economic Applications. III, 130 pages. 1971.

Vol. 57: E. Freund, Zeitvariable Mehrgrößensysteme. VIII, 160 Seiten. 1971.

Vol. 58: P. B. Hagelschuer, Theorie der linearen Dekomposition. VII, 191 Seiten. 1971.

Vol. 59: J. A. Hanson, Growth in Open Economies. V, 128 pages. 1971.

Vol. 60: H. Hauptmann, Schätz- und Kontrolltheorie in stetigen dynamischen Wirtschaftsmodellen. V, 104 Seiten. 1971.

Vol. 61: K. H. F. Meyer, Wartesysteme mit variabler Bearbeitungsrate. VII, 314 Seiten. 1971.

Vol. 62: W. Krelle u. G. Gabisch unter Mitarbeit von J. Burgermeister, Wachstumstheorie. VII, 223 Seiten. 1972.

Vol. 63: J. Kohlas, Monte Carlo Simulation im Operations Research. VI, 162 Seiten. 1972.

Vol. 64: P. Gessner u. K. Spremann, Optimierung in Funktionenräumen. IV, 120 Seiten. 1972.

Vol. 65: W. Everling, Exercises in Computer Systems Analysis. VIII, 184 pages. 1972.

Vol. 66: F. Bauer, P. Garabedian and D. Korn, Supercritical Wing Sections. V, 211 pages. 1972.

Vol. 67: I. V. Girsanov, Lectures on Mathematical Theory of Extremum Problems. V, 136 pages. 1972.

Vol. 68: J. Loeckx, Computability and Decidability. An Introduction for Students of Computer Science. VI, 76 pages. 1972.

Vol. 69: S. Ashour, Sequencing Theory. V, 133 pages. 1972.

Vol. 70: J. P. Brown, The Economic Effects of Floods. Investigations of a Stochastic Model of Rational Investment. Behavior in the Face of Floods. V, 87 pages. 1972.

Vol. 71: R. Henn und O. Opitz, Konsum- und Produktionstheorie II. V, 134 Seiten. 1972.

Vol. 72: T. P. Bagchi and J. G. C. Templeton, Numerical Methods in Markov Chains and Bulk Queues. XI, 89 pages. 1972.

Vol. 73: H. Kiendl, Suboptimale Regler mit abschnittweise linearer Struktur. VI, 146 Seiten. 1972.

Vol. 74: F. Pokropp, Aggregation von Produktionsfunktionen. VI, 107 Seiten. 1972.

Vol. 75: GI-Gesellschaft für Informatik e.V. Bericht Nr. 3. 1. Fachtagung über Programmiersprachen · München, 9.–11. März 1971. Herausgegeben im Auftrag der Gesellschaft für Informatik von H. Langmaack und M. Paul. VII, 280 Seiten. 1972.

Vol. 76: G. Fandel, Optimale Entscheidung bei mehrfacher Zielsetzung. II, 121 Seiten. 1972.

Vol. 77: A. Auslender, Problèmes de Minimax via l'Analyse Convexe et les Inégalités Variationelles: Théorie et Algorithmes. VII, 132 pages. 1972.

Vol. 78: GI-Gesellschaft für Informatik e.V. 2. Jahrestagung, Karlsruhe, 2.–4. Oktober 1972. Herausgegeben im Auftrag der Gesellschaft für Informatik von P. Deussen. XI, 576 Seiten. 1973.

Vol. 79: A. Berman, Cones, Matrices and Mathematical Programming. V, 96 pages. 1973.

Vol. 80: International Seminar on Trends in Mathematical Modelling, Venice, 13–18 December 1971. Edited by N. Hawkes. VI, 288 pages. 1973.

Vol. 81: Advanced Course on Software Engineering. Edited by F. L. Bauer. XII, 545 pages. 1973.

Vol. 82: R. Saeks, Resolution Space, Operators and Systems. X, 267 pages. 1973.

continuation on page 159

Lecture Notes
in Economics and
Mathematical Systems

Managing Editors: M. Beckmann and H. P. Künzi

193

Jati K. Sengupta

Optimal Decisions under Uncertainty

Springer-Verlag
Berlin Heidelberg New York 1981

Author
Prof. J. K. Sengupta
University of California, Department of Economics
Santa Barbara, Calif. 93106, USA

ISBN-13: 978-3-540-10869-6 e-ISBN-13: 978-3-642-87720-9
DOI: 10.1007/978-3-642-87720-9

2142/3140-543210

To

KRISHNA

With love and admiration

PREFACE

The theory of optimal decisions in a stochastic environment has seen many new developments in recent years. The implications of such theory for empirical and policy applications are several. This book attempts to analyze some of the important applied aspects of this theory and its recent developments.

The stochastic environment is considered here in specific form, e.g., (a) linear programs (LP) with parameters subject to a probabilistic mechanism, (b) decision models with risk aversion, (c) resource allocation in a team, and (d) national economic planning. The book attempts to provide new research insights into several areas, e.g., (a) mixed strategy solutions and econometric tests of hypotheses of LP models, (b) the dual problems of efficient estimation and optimal regulation, (c) input-output planning under imperfect competition, and (d) linear programs viewed as constrained statistical games.

Methods of optimal decision rules developed here for quadratic and linear decision problems are applicable in three broad areas: (a) applied economic models in resource allocation, planning and team decision, (b) operations research models in management decisions involving portfolio analysis and stochastic programming, and (c) systems science models in stochastic control and adaptive behavior.

Some results reported here have been published in professional journals before, and I would like to thank the following journals in particular: International Journal of Systems Science, Journal of Optimization Theory and Applications and Journal of Mathematical Analysis and Applications.

I am most deeply indebted to my wife for her utmost support. But for her conviction it would have been impossible to complete the work.

J.K.S.

CONTENTS

CHAPTER 1

OPTIMAL DECISIONS: THEORY AND PRACTICE

Rules for optimal decisions using some form of quantitative models have been developed and applied in several disciplines including economics, management science, cybernetic and social systems. Two types of model formulations have been most common e.g. static and dynamic, or deterministic and stochastic. In the former case the role of time is explicitly introduced in the specification, whereas in the latter the probabilistic variations in data are of great interest.

The theory of decision-making in a stochastic environment has many facets that are different from deterministic theory. Some of these aspects are: (a) the information structure available, (b) the forms of probability distribution, (c) the conditional nature of the state observed, (d) the criteria of optimality accepted and (e) the types of validation tests adopted.

The first aspect deals with the question of the relative cost and value of a particular kind of quantitative information in selecting or updating an optimal solution. Pertinent questions here are of the following types: When is information incomplete? What are the gains from cooperation or otherwise in team decisions? How can one optimally discriminate between two channels of information?

The second aspect deals with the robustness of any optimal solution selected. How sensitive is the optimal solution to any departure from the assumption of normality? When is a mixed strategy preferable over a pure strategy? In what situations posterior distributions may help improve the optimal strategies?

The third aspect is concerned with the forecasting component, distinct from the regulating component of the optimal solution vector. This aspect is particularly important in dynamic environments, when the conditional means and conditional variances of the state variable may change our time, due to the underlying stochastic process and hence Kalman-filtering and other techniques of state estimation and forecasting have to be built into the system.

The fourth aspect deals with the criteria of acceptability of an optimal solution. Unlike deterministic systems, we have here several plausible criteria that are applied in empirical studies. These criteria share however some common features e.g., (a) a measure of rish aversion, (b) an assumption about the underlying probability distribution and the existence of its parameters and (c) an ordering among feasible solutions whether optimal or not.

The fifth aspect deals with the emprical validation of an optimal solution in terms of the observed pattern of behavior. When samples are available for the two sets of solutions, the observed and the optimal, statistical testing of a null hypothesis proves to be useful in suggesting a direction. If the null hypothesis is that the two solutions are identical and it is rejected in a statistical sense, one has to analyze the details of the specification to locate possible sources.

A linear stochastic model is used in this book as a basic quantitative framework, by means of which the above aspects are operationally discussed and applied. Linear models in stochastic programming and stochastic control are frequently utilized here to illustrate the informational and other apsects of the theory and applications.

Recent developments in stochastic LP models are discussed in their operational aspects in Chapter 2 with particular reference to the following: (a) when would mixed strategy solutions be preferable over pure strategy solutions? (b) How could sample and other information be utilized in updating a particular optimal solution selected? (c) How would one perform a statistical test on K optimal solution vectors, each one being the optimum for a particular sample unit?

The concept of rish aversion and the notion that an optimal solution must minimize in some sense the cost of risk have been most critical in optimal decision theory under risk. It is purported to contribute towards equilibrium, stability and boundedness of solutions. It is not frequently recognized however that there are several measures of risk aversion, used in various applied fields with very differing implications. Chapter 3 provides a critical survey and appraisal of the operational measures available. In particular the survey distinguishes between univariate and multivariate measures and between parametric and non-parametric measures.

Allocation of resources and selection of an optimal output-mix have provided a central issue in the economic theory of decentralization e.g. among firms within an industry or, among members of a team. The informational aspects of a team decision have used quadratic objective functions to derive optimal linear decision rules. The operation of such decision rules in stochastic environment raises important issues, some of which are treated in Chapter 4. The issues dealt with explore the consequences of complete and incomplete cooperation, of selecting mixed strategy solutions and of Stackelberg strategies under games.

In macroeconomic planning and policy, the use of Leontief-type input-output model is very widespread. The implications of using this as a linear stochastic model are explored in Chapter 5 with particular reference to risk aversion, imperfect competition and stabilization policy. It is argued that in a stochastic environment such a model may lead to linear decision rules that have destabilizing characteristics.

A stochastic LP model may be viewed as nonzero-sum in two distinct ways either through stochastic parameters or through mixed strategies defined over the primal and dual variables respectively. Those formulations are analyzed in Chapter 6 to show the implications of more than one type of mixed strategy solutions. Since a mixed strategy solution is considered to be more risk averse than a pure strategy solution, it is potentially applicable over a wider environment. This is followed in Chapter 7 by brief comments on the trends of applied research in the field of optimal decisions under uncertainty.

CHAPTER 2

LINEAR PROGRAMMING UNDER UNCERTAINTY

1. Introduction

Conventional methods of introducing risk and uncertainty into a linear programming (LP) model, where some parameters are random generally ignore the following cases: (a) the mixed strategy solutions, (b) the possibility of informational improvement and search, and (c) statistical testing of the LP model viewed econometrically.

Our objective here is to illustrate the applications of linear programming under uncertainty to these cases and thereby demonstrate the usefulness of the methods of stochastic linear programming. Since we intend to emphasize the applied aspects, we consider a somplified framework of an LP model: max $z = \theta' x$, $x \varepsilon R$ where the constraint set R is assumed nonstochastic, in most cases, and the vector θ is assumed to be generated by a probabilistic mechanism. Here x is an n-element column vector and the set R may be specified for example by:

$$R : \{x | Ax \leq b, \ x \geq 0\} \tag{1.1}$$

where the m-by-n matrix A and the m-element column vector b are suitable constants, fixed and nonrandom. For different applications, several specialized interpretations of the above LP model will be found useful. In production applications, the decision vector x is output, z is profit and parameters A and b represent the input coefficients and the resource vector respectively. If net returns (θ) per unit of output is known or estimated suitably, the firm's decision problem is to maximize profit, given the sct S of parameters (A, b, θ). In many resource allocation problems e.g. agricultural production where b represents resources like land, the b-vector is also the decision variable along with outputs x and further there exists market prices (r) at which the resources may be bought or sold. In this case, the LP model appears as:

$$\max_{\{b,x\}} \quad z = \theta' x - r' b \tag{1.2}$$

subject to the constraint set R. More implicitly, the choise of resources b_i may be subject to a budget constraint:

$$q_i C = b_i, \quad q_i \geq 0, \quad \Sigma q_i = 1 \tag{1.3}$$

where C is the total budget and the proportion q_i determines the resource level b_i. These allocation ratios q_i are then the decision variables in the LP model

$$\max_{\{q,x\}} \quad z = \theta'x - r'b \text{ subject to } x \in R \tag{1.4}$$

It is clear that in case of (1.2), the model can be written as a Lagrangian problem

$$L = L(x, r) = \theta'x + r'(b - Ax) \tag{1.5}$$

where nonnegative vectors x and r are to be optimally chosen. If the nonnegativity conditions on x and r are ignored and the parameters θ, b, A are assumed normally and independently distributed, then the conditional distribution of profit L, $p(L|x, r)$ is also normal. The joint distribution $p(L; x, r)$ may then be expressed as:

$$p(L; x, r) = (L|x, r)\, p(x, r) \tag{1.6}$$

where $p(x, r)$ is the joint probability of the decision vectors x and r. In case of pure strategies, $p(x, r)$ is degenerate, since x, r are nonrandom; but $p(x, r)$ is nondegenerate for mixed strategies. If only the θ-vector is random and A, b are fixed, then the probabilistic relation (1.6) would appear as:

$$p(z; x) = p(z|x)\, p(x) \tag{1.7}$$

where $x \in R$ and R is a deterministic set of constraints. Thus, optimizing over the joint distribution $p(z; x)$ would not be identical with that over the conditional distribution $p(z|x)$, unless $p(x)$ is degenerate or constant independent of x. The choice of decision vector x is of course further restricted in the decision space to lie in the nonnegative orthant. This may be interpreted in two ways: either as truncation in the space of distribution of profits $p(z; x)$ or, as transformation to a new set of coordinates. The latter case is related to stochastic programming [18, 23]. Let x_0 be a fixed goal e.g. a vector with positive elements and define $y = x - x_0$ as a distance from this point. The new decision vector is now y, instead of x and hence the transformed LP problem is:

$$\max_{y} z(y) = \theta'y$$

$$\text{where } y \in R(y);\ R(y) = \{y|Ay \leq b\} \tag{1.8}$$

Since the restriction sets R or R(y) will be assumed deterministic or nonrandom in most cases, except those specifically mentioned, we would assume a simplified representation as follows:

$$x'e = 1,\ x \geq 0;\ r'e = 1,\ r \geq 0$$

$$y'e = 1;\ y \text{ free in sign} \tag{1.9}$$

where e is a vector with each element being unity.

There is a basic distinction in stochastic LP models between two types of distribution problems, one in the population and the other in the sampling space. This may be easily illustrated when θ only is random as in (1.1) with a deterministic set R where $x \in R$. In the population there is a prior distribution of θ, but in the sample space there is a posterior distribution of θ given the sample observations. Even if θ is unknown constant, its sample estimate $\hat{\theta}$ has a sampling distribution $p(\hat{\theta}|\theta)$, depending on the form of the estimator. Let there be K estimators $\hat{\theta}(k)$ based on N observations each, leading to K optimal vectors $x(k)$ and the associated profits $z(k)$, $k = 1,2,\ldots,K$. How do we choose between them? This is the problem of K distributions. The active approach of stochastic linear programming [18] provides one type of solution thus: for any decision vector $x(k)$ or, equivalently any allocation vector q defined in (1.3), it considers the distance between the sampling distribution $p_k = p(\hat{\theta}(k)|\theta)$ and the population distribution $p = p(\theta)$ and $x(0)$ is taken to be the optimal, if it has among others the smallest distance. The choice of distance measure is of course not unique. Nonparametric measures based on Kolmogorov-Smirnov statistics or, parametric measures based on Mahalanobis distance in multivariate statistics have been used in stochastic LP models [20, 21], where the latter uses the normality assumption.

From an informational viewpoint, it is convenient to consider the objective function $\theta'x$ in a quadratic form dependent specifically on the state of the environment $s \in \Omega$, where Ω is an index set:

$$\begin{aligned} \theta &= \theta(s) = p(s) - v - R'x \\ \theta'(s)x &= p(s)'x - v'x - x'Rx \end{aligned} \tag{2.1}$$

Here only price $p(s)$ depends on the random environment s but the cost parameters v, R' are fixed and deterministic. This type of quadratic response function has been used in theory of team decisions [11, 13], where resources are to be optimally allocated in a random environment. If one assumes a perfect forecast $\hat{p}(s)$ of $p(s)$ for every s in the future, then the optimal linear decision rule (LDR) is

$$(R + R')x(s) = \hat{p}(s) - v - \lambda(s)e \tag{2.2}$$

where $\lambda = \lambda(s)$ is the Lagrange multiplier associated with the constraint set R given in the form (1.9) and the notation $x = x(s)$, $\lambda = \lambda(s)$ is used to indicate the dependence of the optimal solution on the forecast for each $s \in \Omega$. Denoting the right-hand side of (2.2) by the state vector $c(s)$, the inverse of $(R + R')$ by M and the state of information used in the forecast by H_τ, $\tau < s$, the optimal solution (2.2) can be expressed as a control vector:

$$x(s) = Mc(s),\ H_\tau,\ \tau < s \text{ given}$$
$$E(x(s)|I_\tau) = ME(c(s)|H_\tau),\ \tau < s \qquad (2.3)$$
$$\text{Var } \{x(s)|H_\tau\} = MV_cM'$$

where E is expectation over $s \in \Omega$, var $\{x(s)|H_\tau\}$ is the conditional variance-covariance matrix of x(s) and V_c is the conditional variance-covariance matrix of c(s), given the information available up to time $\tau < s$. It is clear that if c(s) is normally distributed $N(\bar{c}, V_c)$ with conditional mean $\bar{c}$ and variance-covariance matrix V_c, the optimal solution vector x(s) would also be normally distributed $N(M\bar{c}, MV_c'M')$ with a conditional mean $M\bar{c}$ and a covariance matrix MV_cM'. This specification (2.3) is in accorance with control-theoretic formulation i.e.

$$x(s) = \bar{x} + \varepsilon(s) = M(\bar{c} + \gamma(s)) \qquad (2.4)$$

where $\varepsilon(s)$; $\gamma(s)$ are noise elements and $\bar{x}$, $\bar{c}$ may be the signals. This control-theoretic formulation in stochastic programming is useful in two important directions. First, this may be viewed as an econometric model and indeed LDR have been so used in applied work [19, 24]. These LDR (2.4) can be statistically estimated by least squares or generalized least squares, provided the data on the pair (c(s), x(s); $s \in \Omega_\tau$) are available, where Ω_τ is the set of observations or information available. Such estimates of LDR would provide approximate optimal solutions, $\hat{x}$ say. The usefulness of such approximate regression solutions, from the informational and computational viewpoints may be considered in suitable practical situations.

Secondly, the sequential aspects of information improvement when the normality assumption does or does not hold may be explicitly analyzed in this framework. This may be particularly imporant in time-series data, when the forecasting process can incorporate optimal filtering characteristics, as in Kalman-Bucy filtering theory [25]. The fact that the noise elements $\gamma(s)$ of the state vector may generate those of the optimal control vector x suggest the need for corrective actions, if the forecasts $\hat{c}$ of c(s) are not perfect. Besides, there may be two other errors present e.g. the errors of measurement and the errors of the system. We would consider the implications of some of these errors on the specification of the optimal solution vector of a stochastic LP model.

2. Mixed Strategy Solutions

One may describe the mixed strategy solutions in stochastic LP models in at least three ways: (1) as a zero-sum or nonzero-sum game, (2) as a method of mixing two or more pure strategy solutions, or (3) as a Bayesian problem defined by (1.7), when the probability p(x) of the decision vector is nondegenerate. We consider in this section the third case, with an example to illustrate the application of second case.

For the second case, consider the LP problems (1.8) and assume that y has no constraints that are binding. Assume two pure strategy vectors y(k), k = 1, 2 such that the conditional distribution $p(z|y(k))$ of profits is normal $N(\mu(k), \sigma^2(k))$ with mean $\mu(k) = m'(k)\, y(k)$ and variance $\sigma^2(k) = Y'(k)\, V(k)\, Y(k)$ where m(k), V(k) are the means and variance-covariance matrices of the conditional distribution of θ given y(k). Assume the decision-maker (DM) to be a risk-averter and suppose he wants to ensure in each case he chooses y(1) or y(2) that his ruin probability is less than 0.001. Then, in each case k = 1, 2 he must maximize the risk-adjusted utility level u(k):

$$u(k) = m'(k)\; y(k) - 3.0\; [y'(k)\; V(k)\; y(k)]^{\frac{1}{2}} \tag{3.1}$$

Assuming y(k) to be nonzero, the optimal solution $y^0(k)$ must satisfy the stationarity condition:

$$y^0(k) = \frac{1}{3}\,\sigma(k)\; V^{-1}(k)\; m\,(k),\; k = 1,\, 2 \tag{3.2}$$

A mixed strategy however is defined by $\lambda y(1) + (1 - \lambda)\, y(2)$, where λ is a constant lying between zero and one, which denotes the proportion of time y(1) is chosen as a pure strategy. Since the mean and variance associated with $\lambda y(1)$ are $\lambda m'(1)\, y(1)$ and $\lambda^2 y(1)'V(1)y(1)$, the combined utility level is μ_T is:

$$u_T = \lambda\mu(1) + (1 - \lambda)\;\mu(2) - 3.0\;(\lambda^2\;\sigma^2(1) + (1 - \lambda)^2\;\sigma^2(2))^{\frac{1}{2}} \tag{3.3}$$

which assures a ruin probability less than 0.001. The optimal solutions λ^0, $y_T^0(k)$ in this case are

$$\begin{aligned} \lambda^0 &= \frac{1}{3}\;[q(\mu(1) - \mu(2))]\;(\sigma_0^2)^{-1} + \sigma^2(2)(\sigma_0^2)^{-1} \\ y_T^0(k) &= \frac{1}{3}\;\sigma_0\;(V^{-1}(k)\; m(k)),\; k = 1,\, 2 \end{aligned} \tag{3.4}$$

where

$$q = [(\lambda^0)^2\;\sigma^2(1) + (1 - \lambda^0)^2\;\sigma^2(2)]^{\frac{1}{2}}$$

$$\sigma_0^2 = \sigma^2(1) + \sigma^2(2)$$

It is clear that λ^0 will take a value zero, if $\mu(1) = \mu(2)$ and $\sigma^2(2) = 0$, in which case the pure strategy $y_T^0(2)$ is preferable. Further, since the sum of risks, $\sigma(1) + \sigma(2)$ associated with the pure strategies would tend to be greater than the risk $\sigma_0 = \sqrt{(\sigma^2(1) + \sigma^2(2))}$ for the mixed strategy, the risk-adjusted utility level u_T^0 would be higher in the mixed strategy case i.e., $u_T^0 > u^0(1) + u^0(2)$, if $\mu(1) = \mu(2)$. Also, since $(t_1 + t_2)\sigma_0 > t_1\,\sigma(1) + t_2\,\sigma(2)$ is likely to hold for all positive $t_k = V^{-1}(k)\; m(k)$, we have that optimal output $y_T^0(k)$ in mixed strategy case is higher than that $(y^0(k))$ of the pure strategy case for each $k = 1, 2$. The incentive for the decision-maker (DM) to consider completely mixed (i.e., $0 < \lambda < 1$) instead of pure strategies thus depends on two important factors: how large is the difference of two conditional means $\mu(1)$ and $\mu(2)$ and by how much the combined risk σ_0 exceeds the sum, $\sigma(1) + \sigma(2)$ of two individual risks. A third factor, depending on the covariance of responses of two individual strategies may also be important if the two strategy choices $y(1)$, $y(2)$ are not statistically independent.

Thus the incentive problem for the DM essentially consists in choosing an optimal value of λ by maximizing u_T in (3.3) subject to

$$\mu(k) \geq \mu^0(k),\; k = 1, 2$$

$$\sigma^2(k) \leq \sigma^{02}(k),\; k = 1, 2$$

where $\mu(k) = m'(k)\; y^0(k)$, $\sigma^{02}(k) = y^0(k)'V(k)y^0(k)$ are the means and variances of returns in the pure strategy cases. The generalization of this framework form two to three or more strategies may be worked out in a straight forward manner. Also, by varying the ruin probability level, one may generate a whole set of optimal mixed strategies, each appropriate to the risk class to which the DM belongs.

This case can easily be generalized to the case (1.6) when besides θ, the other parameters b, A are also random. Assume that the conditional distribution $p(L\;x = \bar{x},\; r = \bar{r})$ of profits is normal, given that x and r are at their mean, further the elements of θ, A and b are assumed to be statistically independent. Then the 0.001 ruin probability level can again be specified by

$$\mu(L) = \bar{\theta}'\bar{x} + \bar{r}'(\bar{b} - \bar{A}\bar{x}) - 3\sigma_L \qquad (4.1)$$

where $\sigma^2 = \bar{x}'V\,\bar{x} + \bar{r}'V\,\bar{r} + \bar{r}'\hat{S}\,\bar{r}$, $\hat{S}$ is a diagonal matrix with diagonal elements $s_{ii} = \bar{x}'V_i\bar{x}$ where V_i = variance-covariance matrix of a_i, the i-th column vector in matrix A and the mean values of θ, b, A are denoted by $\bar{\theta}$, $\bar{b}$, $\bar{A}$ respectively. However, the expression σ_L which is the square root of variance σ_L^2 of L makes the optimization problem highly nonlinear in this case. We may therefore adopt a slightly different and approximate approach. Instead of the expression $3\sigma_L$ in the objective function (4.1), we introduce it through a constraint as

$$9.0\ \sigma_L^2 = \alpha_0^2 \tag{4.2}$$

and maximize instead the utility function:

$$u_0(1) = \bar{\theta}'\bar{x} + \bar{r}'(\bar{b} - \bar{A}\bar{x}) \tag{4.3}$$

where α_0 is a suitable positive constant. The constraint (4.2) so imposed as to ensure that the probability of ruin is equal to or, less than 0.001. Using λ_0 as the Lagrange multiplier for (4.2), the optimal values of $\bar{x}$, $\bar{r}$ must satisfy the stationarity condition

$$\begin{aligned} \bar{A}'\bar{r} &= \bar{\theta} - 18\ \lambda_0(V_\theta + \sum_{i=1}^{m} \bar{r}_i^2\ V_i)\bar{x} \\ \bar{A}\bar{x} &= \bar{b} - 18\ \lambda_0\ (V_b + \hat{S})\bar{r} \end{aligned} \tag{4.4}$$

If the elements of matrix A are nonrandom, so that $\hat{S}$ and V_i are null matrices, then the expressions (4.4) become simpler as follows:

$$\begin{aligned} A'\bar{r} &= \bar{\theta} - 18\ \lambda_0\ V_\theta\bar{x} \\ A\bar{x} &= \bar{b} - 18\ \lambda_0\ V_b\bar{r} \end{aligned} \tag{4.5}$$

It is easy to identify these as Cournot-Nash reaction curves in $(\bar{x}, \bar{r})$ space and the condition for an equilibrium is that the coefficient matrix

$$M = \begin{bmatrix} A' & 18\ \lambda_0\ V_\theta \\ 18\ \lambda_0\ V_b & A \end{bmatrix}$$

is of full rank i.e., m + n. The equilibrium solution need not however be stable, unless the stopes of the two reaction curves satisfy appropriate conditions of stability. Note that the equilibrium values of mean strategies $\bar{x}$, $\bar{r}$ may be interpreted in two ways: either as a pair of dual strategies of one player or, as two strategy vectors, one for each player. In either case the system (4.5) of linear reaction curves has a natural interpretation: θ and b have to be replaced by their respective risk-adjusted values $\theta^* = \bar{\theta} - 18\ \lambda_0\bar{x}$, $b^* = \bar{b} - 18\ \lambda_0\ V_b\bar{r}$. Furthermore, λ_0 could vary due to variation of α_0^2; this would be clear if we write (4.2) more flexibly as

$$9.0\ \sigma_L^2 \leq \alpha_o^2$$

The variation of the equilibrium solution in the $(\bar{x}, \bar{r})$ space, consequent on varying λ_o would thus reflect the impact of risk aversion on the choice of optimal strategy vectors by the two players [22].

Next we consider the case (1.7), when only θ is random and the probability distributions $p(z|x)$, $p(x)$ are both normal i.e.,

$$p(z|x) \sim N(\bar{\theta}'x,\ x'V_\theta x)$$

$$p(x) \sim N(\mu_x,\ V_x) \qquad (4.6)$$

As a rule for an optimal choice of the decision vector x, we adopt the maximum probability criterion (MPC), according to which we maximize the joint probability $p(z|x) \cdot p(x)$ with respect to x. Since this is equivalent to maximizing its logarithm, we obtain the nonlinear program:

$$\max f(x) = -\tfrac{1}{2}[\ln (x'V_\theta x) + (x'Cx)\ (x'V_\theta x)^{-1}$$

$$+ \ln |V_x| + (x - \mu_x)'V_x^{-1}\ (x - \mu_x)] \qquad (4.7)$$

Subject to $x \in R$

where R includes constraints on the control space x including normalization conditions, $C = (\theta - \bar{\theta})(\theta - \bar{\theta})'$ and $|V_x|$ denotes the determinant of V_x which is assumed to be a fixed constant. Some special cases of the nonlinear program (NLP) above may be easily interpreted. First, if a sample mean estimate $\hat{\theta}$ of θ is used, such that C is a null matrix by the unbiasedness condition $\hat{\theta} = \bar{\theta}$, then the optimal strategy x must satisfy the stationarity condition:

$$[V_\theta + V_x^{-1}\ (x'V_\theta s)]x = (x'V_\theta x)\ V_x^{-1}\ \mu_x \qquad (4.8)$$

If we set $x'V_\theta x = \alpha$, $\alpha > 0$ by a normalization convention, then (4.8) reduces to

$$x = \alpha[V_\theta + \alpha V_x^{-1}]^{-1}\ V_x^{-1}\ \mu_x = \alpha[V_\theta + \alpha I]^{-1}\ \mu_x \qquad (4.9)$$

if V_x is an identity matrix. Expanding the right-hand side of (4.9) and retaining up to quadratic terms, one obtains:

$$x = [I - \frac{V_\theta}{\alpha} + \frac{1}{\alpha^2}\ V_\theta V_\theta]\ \mu_x$$

Up to linear terms this gives

$$x = [I - \frac{V_\theta}{\alpha}]\,\mu_x \tag{4.10}$$

which says that optimal policy would be to set x not at the mean level μ_x but at the level determined by (4.10), which is of course approximate up to linear terms. Again, if V_θ is null i.e. there is no variability in parameter θ, then it follows from (4.9) that it is optimal to set x at the mean level i.e. $x = \mu_x$ and this is true for any nonzero α and any nonsingular V_x.

A second case arises when C is not null i.e. $\hat{\theta}$ is not equal to $\bar{\theta}$ but the normalization condition $x'V_\theta x = \alpha_0 > 0$ is imposed before f(x) in (4.7) is maximized. In this case the optimal decision vector x is:

$$x = [I + \frac{V_x C}{\alpha_0}]^{-1}\,\mu_x$$

Expanding the right-hand side up to linear terms, decision vector x, that is approximately optimal turns out to be

$$x = [I - \frac{V_x C}{\alpha_0}]\,\mu_x$$

This is comparable to the case (4.10) above. Also, if the normalization condition $x'Cx = \beta_0 > 0$ is imposed before the function f(x) in (4.7) is maximized and there is no normalization on the term $x'V_\theta x$, then the optimal vector x satisfies the condition:

$$x'V_\theta x = 1/\beta_0 = (x'Cx)^{-1}$$

A third case arises ehen the term lnp(x) is taken out from the objective function and two control vectors x_1, x_2 say are considered and log $p(z|x_i)$ is maximized for i = 1,2. This is made however subject to a normalization condition

$$(x_i - \mu_x)'\,(x_i - \mu_x) \leq 1,\ i = 1,\ 2 \tag{5.1}$$

this leads to the nonlinear program

$$\max f(x) = -\tfrac{1}{2}\ln(x_i'V_\theta x_i) + \lambda_i[1-(x_i - \mu_x)'(x_i - \mu_x]$$

where λ_i is the Lagrange multiplier associated with the i-th constraint (5.1) and it has been assumed that C is null i.e. an unbiased estimate $\hat{\theta} = \bar{\theta}$ of θ is used.

If the optimal λ_i's are not zero, the optimal solutions x_1, x_2 would be:

$$x_1 - \mu_x = -(x_1' V_\theta x_1)^{-1} (V_\theta x_1)$$

$$x_2 - \mu_x = -(x_2' V_\theta x_2)^{-1} (V_\theta x_2) \qquad (5.3)$$

Denoting $x_i' V_\theta x_i$ by $\alpha_i > 0$ in (5.3) and following the method of expansion used in (4.10) we obtain up to linear terms:

$$x_1 = (I - \alpha_1 V_\theta)\mu_x$$

$$x_2 = (I - \alpha_2 V_\theta)\mu_x$$

Hence x_1 is nearer to μ_x in the sense of minimum absolute value, $x_i - \mu_x$ if $\alpha_2 > \alpha_1 > 0$. Thus, although x_1, x_2 satisfies the equality

$$(x_i - \mu_x)' (x_i - \mu_x) = 1$$

for each i, the variance-covariance matrix V_θ of θ determines their optimal degree of nearness to the mean parameter μ_x.

These special cases thus serve to emphasize the relative merits of choosing the control vector x near the mean μ_x. When x is a pure strategy, p(x) is degenerate; then the problem of maximizing f(x) in (4.7) can be rewritten as:

$$\max f(x) = - \frac{1}{2} (x'Cx)(x'V_\theta x)^{-1}$$

subject to

$$x'V_\theta x = \alpha$$

Applying to first order conditions $\partial f(x)/\partial x = 0$ and $\partial f(x)/\partial \alpha = 0$ one obtains

$$[\lambda\alpha V_\theta - C]\, x = 0 \qquad (5.4)$$

$$x'Cx = \lambda\alpha^2$$

$$f(x) = - \tfrac{1}{2} \lambda\alpha \qquad (5.5)$$

where λ is the Lagrange multiplier associated with $x'V_\theta x = \alpha$. It is clear that λ must be an eigenvalue of the problem (5.4) and since V_θ and C are symmetric, the eigenvalues must be real and by condition (5.5), the smallest eigenvalue has to be chosen.

In the general case however when p(x) is nondegenerate, the nonlinear program (4.7) cannot be explicitly solved. However, if θ and x are scalars, the solution can be explicitly computed as follows:

$$x = \frac{1}{2}\,[\mu \;\pm \sqrt{(\mu_x^2 - 4\sigma_x^2)}]$$

assuming that $\sigma_x^2 > x^2$ which is a sufficient condition for a maximum. The two optimal values from (5.6) are

$$x = (\mu_x - \frac{\sigma_x}{\mu_x} - \frac{\varepsilon}{2}) \text{ and } \frac{\sigma_x}{\mu_x} + \frac{\varepsilon}{2}$$

where ε is a positive quantity derived from (5.6). Thus the optimal x is set equal to not the mean μ_x but to a level deviating from it.

Note that the calculation of optimal mixed strategies by this method can be given a recursive interpretation [15]: either as a method of revising an initial optimal x when later observations are available, or as an adaptive method of revising the conditional distribution $p(z|x)$ before applying the maximum probability criterion. Such recursive methods are closely related to the duality theory of simultaneous prediction and control [16, 21].

One practical difficulty in applying the MPC is of course the lack of knowledge of the prior distribution p(x) of the decision vector x. One might therefore suggest an alternative approach, where vectors $x_1, x_2, \ldots, x_N$ are selected in the decision space, where x_i is an n-element column vector having a probability

$$p(x_i) = p_i \geq 0, \quad \sum_{i=1}^{N} p_i = 1 \tag{6.1}$$

p_i. In the randomized decision space spanned by the N vectors x_i, this probability p_i has two practical interpretations. It denotes the proportion of times the vector point x_i is selected. Alternatively, it is the probability of selecting one of our N points $x_1, x_2, \ldots, x_N$ in an equi-probability sampling experiment. In the theory of optimal design [3,4], any choice of the set $(p_1, p_2, \ldots, p_N)$ satisfying (6.1) is called spectrum of the design and given a specific choice, one could use the ruin probability criterion for instance to determine an optimal vector point x_i. For the case N = 2 this can be very simply illustrated. For instance the objective junction in this case would be

$$f = p\bar{\theta}'x_1 + (1 - p)\bar{\theta}'x_2 - 3(p\sigma_1^2 + (1 - p)\sigma_2^2)^{\frac{1}{2}} \tag{6.1}$$

where $\sigma_i^2 = x_i' \, V_\theta \, x_i$ and $p_1 = p$, $p_2 = 1 - p$. The optimal values of x_i and p which would simultaneously maximize $f = f(x_1, x_2, p)$ in (6.1) are then:

$$x_i^* = [(\sigma_2^2 - p^*(\sigma_2^2 - \sigma_1^2)^{-\frac{1}{2}} \, V_\theta^{-1} \, \bar{\theta} \qquad i = 1,2$$

$$p^* = \frac{1}{(\sigma^2 - \sigma^2)^2} \{\sigma_2^2 - \frac{4}{9} (\mu_2 - \mu_1)^2\} \tag{6.2}$$

where the condition $\sigma_2^2 > \sigma_1^2$ is needed for sufficiency and the terms $\sigma_i^2 = x_i^{*\prime} \, V_\theta \, x_i^*$ and $\mu_i = \bar{\theta}' x_i^*$ are now evaluated at the optimal values. For feasibility the optimal value p^* must also satisfy $0 \leq p^* \leq 1$. Hence one may set $\mu_2 \geq \mu_1$ and normalize one of the two variances σ_2^2, σ_1^2 to unity. Setting $\sigma_2^2 = 1.0$ it is clear that $p^* = 1.0$ (i.e. a pure strategy solution), whenever $\mu_1 = \mu_2$ and $\sigma_1^2 = 0$. Otherwise any increase of σ_2^2 tends to increase the optimal value of p^*. Furthermore, the optimal values x_1^*, x_2^* have the separability property

$$x_1^* = k \, x_2^*$$

for some appropriate constant k different from zero.

Note however that the solution (x_1^*, x_2^*, p^*) above is a maximax solution in the sense

$$f(x_1^*, x_2^*, p^*) = \max_x \; \max_p f(x_1, x_2, p)$$

But since other values of p exist in the spectrum of the design (6.1) one could also define maximin strategies $\tilde{x}_1^*$, $\tilde{x}_2^*$, $\tilde{p}^*$

$$\begin{aligned} f(\tilde{x}_1^*, \tilde{x}_2^*, \tilde{p}^*) &= \max_x \; \min_p f(x_1, x_2, p) \\ &\leq f(x_1^*, x_2^*, p^*), \quad \tilde{p}^* \neq p^* \end{aligned} \tag{6.3}$$

provided they exist in a nontrivial sense. The maximin strategies have the Bayesian interpretation: the DM first considers the worst that can happen in his selection of any subset among N points (i.e. he chooses $\tilde{p}^*$) and then in the second stage maximizes the resulting objection function. Thus, the first stage specifies in some sense the desired degree of diversification and the second stage optimizes the level of output activity and their substitution.

3. Informational Efficiency

We consider now the quadratic decision model (2.3) where the state of environment is specified by the state variable c(s), which is an n-dimensional random variable. If the state of environment c(s) is completely known to the DM or it is perfectly forecast with no error, then the optimal decision is specified by the LDR (2.3). However, in general the state of environment is not completely known and hence we may assume, after Chu [5] who has extended Radner's work here, that limited information about the state of environment is available to him in terms of data y:

$$y = h(c) \tag{7.1}$$

where the function h = h(c) is called the information function. It will be assumed for simplicity that it is of the linear form:

$$y = Hc + \delta \tag{7.2}$$

where y is an m-dimensional column vector with $0 \le m \le n$ and δ is the noise component of the information channel assumed to be statistically independent with zero mean and covariances V_τ. Two information structures are then distinguished: complete when m = n, and null, when m is zero, where m denotes the rank of the matrix H which is of dimension m-by-n. H is assumed fixed and nonrandom.

To derive explicit results, we have to assume specific distributions of the vector random variables of the problem, which are three in number: δ = noise in the information channel, γ = disturbance of the state or system noise and ε = the random component associated with the control variable. These random variables would be assumed to be independent Gaussian in the following sense:

$$\begin{aligned} &f(c) \sim N(\bar{c}, V_c) \\ &f(y\ c) \sim N(Hc, V_\tau) \\ &f(y,c) = f(y|c)f(c) \\ &f(y) \sim N(H\bar{c}, S_\tau),\ S_\tau = HV_cH' + V_\tau \\ &f(c|y) = f(y|c)f(c)/f(y)\ \text{(Bayes rule)} \end{aligned} \tag{7.3}$$

where $f(\cdot)$ denotes the density function, V_τ denotes the variance-covariance matrix of δ dependent on information indexed by τ, where τ may denote for example the sample observations. It is assumed that V_τ does not depend on current or future x.

Two lines of attack are now possible, since controls x have to be set as a function of the measured variable y through the information channel H in (7.2). First, one may maximize the conditional density f(c|y) with respect to c for given H and given the prior distribution f(c) of c. This generates a conditional estimate $\hat{c}$ of c. The optimal LDR is then

$$\hat{x} = M\hat{c} \tag{7.4}$$

Secondly, we may maximize the probability density f(y,c) in a sequential sense to obtain a minimum variance estimate $\tilde{c}$ say. Then the optimum decision rule is

$$\tilde{x} = M\tilde{c} \tag{7.5}$$

Maximizing the logarithm of $f(c|y)$ i.e.

$$\ln f(c|y) = \ln f(y|c) + \ln f(c) - \ln f(y)$$

under the assumptions (7.3) leads to the result

$$\begin{aligned}\hat{c} &= \bar{c} + V_c H' S_\tau^{-1} y \\ &= \bar{c} + H'(HH')^{-1} y, \\ &\quad \text{if } V_c = I,\ V_\tau = \phi \text{ (null)}\end{aligned} \tag{7.6}$$

thus, if there is no system noise and no noise in the information channel and the vector c is homoscedastic, then

$$\begin{aligned}\hat{x} &= M(\bar{c} + y), \text{ if } H = I_n \text{ (complete information)} \\ &= M\bar{c}, \text{ if } H = \phi \text{ (null): null information}\end{aligned}$$

It is clear that in the general case (7.6), optimal decision vector $\hat{x}$ can be decomposed into two parts $\bar{x}(1)$ and $\bar{x}(2)$ where

$$\begin{aligned}&\bar{x}(1) = M\bar{c},\ \bar{x}(2) = M\, V_c H' S_\tau^{-1} y \\ &\hat{x} = \bar{x}(1) + \bar{x}(2)\end{aligned} \tag{7.7}$$

and $\bar{x}(1)$ represents the null information case. The component $\bar{x}(2)$ may therefore be viewed as improvement due to the sequential information contained in channel H and the covariances V_c, and V_τ.

In the second case (7.5), Bayesian methods generate the sequential estimate $\tilde{c}$ as follows:

$$\tilde{c} = [H'V_\tau^{-1}H + V_c^{-1}]^{-1}\,[H'V_\tau^{-1}y + V_c^{-1}\,\bar{c}]$$

By adding the subtracting $H'V_\tau^{-1}\,H\bar{c}$ to the right-hand side we get

$$\tilde{c} = \bar{c} + [H'V_\tau^{-1}H + V_c^{-1}]^{-1} H'V_\tau^{-1}(y - H\bar{c})$$

$$= \bar{c} + K_\tau(y - H\bar{c}) \quad (7.8)$$

where

$$K_\tau = [H'V_\tau^{-1}H + V_c^{-1}] H'V_\tau^{-1}$$

It is easy to show that

$$E\tilde{c} = [H'V_\tau^{-1}H + V_c^{-1}]^{-1} [H'V_\tau^{-1} H\bar{c} + V_c^{-1} \bar{c}]$$

$$E(\tilde{c} - \bar{c}) = 0$$

$$\text{Var } (\tilde{c} - \bar{c}) = (H'V_\tau^{-1} H + V_c^{-1})^1$$

For a fixed time point $\tau = t$, one may use the subscript t in y, $\tilde{c}$ and $\bar{c}$ in (7.8) and then (7.8) becomes

$$\tilde{c}_{t+1} = \tilde{c}_t + V_{t+1} H'V_t^{-1} (y_{t+1} - H\tilde{c}_t) \quad (7.9)$$

where

$$V_{t+1} = (H'V_t^{-1} H + V_t^{-1})^{-1}$$
$$V_o = V_c$$
H: constant matrix assumed time-independent

thus the optimal LDR

$$\tilde{x}_{t+1} = M\tilde{c}_{t+1} \quad (7.10)$$

can be recursively improved. Note that (7.9) admits of a Kalman-filter interpretation. Thus, if T is the sample size and T is zero, the optimal estimate of c is on using the prior distribution f(c):

$$\tilde{c} = \bar{c} \text{ with } \text{Var}(\tilde{c}_o) = V_o$$

After a single observation T = 1 and using (7.8), the optimal estimate is:

$$\tilde{c}_1 = \tilde{c}_o + V_1H'V_\tau^{-1} (y_1 - H\tilde{c}_o)$$

where V_1 is the error variance after the first observation and under (7.9):

$$V_1 = [H'V_\tau^{-1} H + V_0^{-1}]^{-1}$$

After two observations (T = 2), the optimal estimate is:

$$\tilde{c}_2 = \tilde{c}_1 + V_2 H' V_\tau^{-1} (y_2 - H\tilde{c}_1)$$

where the error variance V_2 is given by

$$V_2 = [H'V_\tau^{-1} H + V_1^{-1}]^{-1}$$

Hence after (t + 1) observations, the estimate $\tilde{c}_{t+1}$ is obtained from (7.9). Thus, the sequential improvement of the optimal LDR: $\tilde{x}_{t+1}$ may be related to three sources: the original error component ε of the control variable, the error in estimating $\tilde{c}_t$ in the previous time point and the error represented by $(y_{t+1} - H\tilde{c}_t)$. The matrix K_τ in (7.8) may be interpreted as the gain matrix in Kalman-Bucy filtering theory [15] and in suitable cases [16] an optimal choice of this matrix is possible.

If $V_c = V_\tau = I$ (identity matrix), then the optimal LDR becomes

$$\tilde{x} = M\bar{c}, \text{ if } H = \phi \text{ (null information)}$$
$$= \tfrac{1}{2} M(\bar{c} + y), \text{ if } H = I \text{ (complete information)}$$

Thus the value of improvement in information may be sequentially incorporated in the LDR approach under the Gaussian assumption (7.3) on the random variables. In case however the normality assumptions (7.3) do not hold, the optimal LDR mentioned above would only hold approximately, the degree of approximation depending on types of nonnormal distributions. However, since under mild conditions of central limit theorem, a wide class of nonnormal distributions converge to normality, any nonnormal density in this class can be expanded in Edgeworth series in terms of Hermite polynomials [10] and thereby the optimal decision rules, possibly nonlinear in form can be derived in principle. Alternatively, nonlinear filtering theory [15, 25] can be applied.

When sample observations are available in time series form and decisions are to be sequentially made using a stochastic LP model, two other types of information design appear to be useful in applied models. In the first case we take a quadratic approximation of the ruin probability criterion but use it in a sequential sense. In the second case, we use the theory of optimal search to maximize the probability of detecting the target value, when there is a specified convex function representing cost of search [26].

In the first case we have the problem, first analyzed by Bracken and Soland [1] that the coefficient vector c in the objective function $z = c'x$ is the unknown mean vector of a multivariate Gaussian process and we have T observations c_t and their sample mean estimates $\hat{c}_t$. Using the n-dimensional vector $\hat{c}_t$ based on earlier information, the profit function is $\hat{z}_t = \hat{c}_t' \hat{x}_t$. This profit function is successively revised by the LDR:

$$\hat{z}_{t+1} = \hat{z}_t + \alpha(z_t - \hat{z}_t) \tag{8.1}$$

where α is a suitable correction factor to be optimally chosen; $z_t = c_t' x_t$ is realized profits whereas $\hat{z}_t$ is the estimated profit related to z_t by

$$z_t = h \hat{z}_t + \varepsilon \tag{8.2}$$

where ε is the stochastic component with zero mean and constant variance σ_ε^2 and independently distributed. Note that when T observations are available on the pair $(z_t, \hat{z}_t)$, the relation (8.2) may be directly estimated by linear regression and if the estimated coefficient h differs from 1.0, the estimated forecast $\hat{z}$ will differ from z. Using (8.2) in (8.1) we obtain the recursive process

$$\hat{z}_{t+1} = (\alpha(h - 1) + 1)z_t + \alpha\varepsilon$$

the mean (m_{t+1}) and variance (σ_{t+1}^2) of which are given by:

$$\begin{aligned} m_{t+1} &= \beta m_t \quad , \quad \beta = \alpha(h - 1) + 1 \\ \sigma_{t+1}^2 &= \beta^2 \sigma_t^2 + \alpha^2 \sigma_\varepsilon^2 \end{aligned} \tag{8.3}$$

The decision problem now is how to choose α so that decisions $\hat{x}_t$ are successively improved. The criterion for improvement is assumed to be of a quadratic form:

$$u_{t+1} = m_{t+1} - \tfrac{1}{2} \sigma_{t+1}^2 \tag{8.4}$$

which differs from the ruin probability criterion (3.1) in that it is strictly quadratic. Maximizing (8.4) we obtain the optimal values $\hat{x}_t^0$, α^0 as:

$$\begin{aligned} \hat{x}_t^0 &= \beta_t^{-1} V_t^{-1} \mu_t, \quad \beta_t = \alpha_t^0 (h - 1) + 1 \\ \alpha^0 &= \alpha_t^0 = [\sigma_\varepsilon^2 + \sigma_t^2 (h - 1)^2]^{-1} [m_t - \sigma_t^2] (h - 1) \end{aligned} \tag{8.5}$$

where $\hat{c}_t$ is assumed to be a Gaussina process with mean μ_t and variance-covariance matrix V_t. Note that the element h can be interpreted as an information channel, although it is a scalar case. If h = 1 (i.e. complete information), then α_t^0 is zero; hence no updating of decision rules is needed and $\hat{x}_t^0 = V_t^{-1} \mu_t$. But if h = 0 (null information), the optimal α is given by

$$\alpha_t^0 = (\sigma_t^2 - m_t)(\sigma_\varepsilon^2 + \sigma_t^2)^{-1}$$

It is clear that we need $\sigma_t^2 > m_t$, if the optimal value α_t^2 has to lie between zero and one. However if a fixed value of α_0, $0 < \alpha_0 < 1$ is used instead of the time-varying one given by (8.5), the system (8.3) of linear difference equations can be solved as

$$m_t = m_o \beta^t; \; \sigma_t^2 = A_1 \beta^{2t} + A_2$$

where (8.6)

$$A_1 = \sigma_o^2 - \alpha_o^2 \sigma_\varepsilon^2 (1 - \beta^2)^{-1}$$

$$A_2 = a^2 \sigma_\varepsilon^2 (1 - \beta^2)^{-1}$$

$$\sigma_o^2 = \text{initial variance}, \; m_o = \text{initial mean}$$

It is clear that $\beta < 1$, if $h < 1$ in which case m_t tends to zero as $t \to \infty$. This means that for a large t, we may minimize the variance term σ_{t+1}^2 to obtain

$$\alpha^0 = \alpha_t^0 = [\sigma_\varepsilon^2 + \sigma_t^2 (1 - h)^2]^{-1} \sigma_t^2 (1 - h)$$

where, of course we have to replace the time-varying term σ_t^2 by an average $\bar{\sigma}^2$ when we seek a replacement of α_t^0 by a constant optimal value, say α_0.

The value of improvement in information through the adaptive behavior (8.5) may thus be estimated in terms of the difference of α_0 in (8.6) and α_t^0 in (8.5). Such adaptive behavior can also be interpreted as learning algorithms in the context of stochastic LP problems [19].

Next we consider the information basis of search and related models of market organizations [14] under conditions of imperfect market information. A seller in such a market has incomplete information on the demand function

$$x = g(c), \; c = p - v \tag{9.1}$$

where x is quantity, c is price over unit cost and g(c) has a negative slope. If the demand functions were known completely, the seller could determine optimal x by maximizing profit

$$z = c'x, \ x \in R \tag{9.2}$$

where x belongs to a feasibility set R of production or supply constraints assumed to be known. Under incomplete information he has however got to spend resources to search for the unknown value of c which may be fixed or time-varying. Thus there is a cost of search and the associated process of learning about the demand function g(c). First, we consider the static case when the unknown value of c is not time-varying but it can take two values c(1) and c(2) with certain probabilities. There is a fixed amount of budget to find the target value of c and let u_1, u_2 denote the proportion of the budget spent in searching in the two cells and $d_j = d(u_j)$ be the probability of detecting it. We assume the value of search $W = W(d_j)$ to be proportional to d_j and of an exponential form:

$$W(d_j) = \beta_j d_j \ , \ \beta_j > 0$$

$$d_j = [1 - \exp(-\alpha_j u_j), \quad \alpha_j > 0 \tag{9.3}$$

There are two motivations for this form. First, it assumes the detection probability to be exponential, which is quite conventional in theory of optimal search [26]. Second, if u_j, the search effort is measured in time, then the detection probability has a nonnegative domain. Like the central limit theorem, positive random variables tend to be distributed in the limit like an exponential distribution.

Here β_j is the factor of proportionality and α_j denotes the effectiveness index of search effort. The decusion problem is: how to allocate search effort between the two cells c(1), c(2) in order to maximize the probability of detection?

This leads to the nonlinear program:

$$\max_{u_j} \Pi = \sum_{j=1}^{2} c(j)'x(j)d_j$$

subject to (9.4)

$$x'(j)e(j) = 1, \ x(j) \geq 0$$

$$\sum_{j=1}^{2} u_j = 1, \quad u_j \geq 0$$

where e(j) is an n-dimensional fector with each element unity. The constraints of (9.4) are normalizing conditions, of which the first one stipulates $\sum_{i=1}^{n} x_i(j) = 1$ for each j. If instead of maximizing the probability of detection, we maximize the value of search effort, we would replace d_j in the objection function above by $W(d_j) = \beta_j d_j$ and solve the resulting nonlinear program. A simpler case which is easier to analyze arises when the vectors c(j), x(j) are scalars, c_j, x_j and there are n values of j. In this case we have the model analogous to (9.4) as follows:

$$\max \Pi = \sum_{j=1}^{n} c_j x_j \, [1 - \exp(-\alpha_j u_j)]$$

$$\text{subject to} \qquad (9.5)$$

$$\Sigma x_j = 1, \; x_j \geq 0$$

$$\Sigma u_j - 1, \; u_j \geq 0$$

Assuming the existence of interior solutions, the optimal values u_j^o, x_j^o are easily calculated as:

$$u_j^o = \frac{1}{\alpha_j} [-\ln (\frac{c_j - \lambda^o}{c_j})^+]; \; \Sigma u_j^o = 1$$

$$x_j^o = \frac{s^o}{c_j \alpha_j} \exp(\alpha_j u_j^o); \; \Sigma x_j^o = 1$$

$$\lambda^o = \Sigma c_j x_j^o (1 - \exp(-\alpha_j u_j^o)) \qquad (9.6)$$

$$s^o = \Sigma \alpha_j c_j x_j^o u_j^o \exp(-\alpha_j u_j^o)$$

$$\text{all } j = 1, 2, \ldots, n$$

where λ and s are Lagrange multipliers associated with the two equality constraints and the notation $\ln(\beta)^+$ means $\ln\beta$ if β is positive, but otherwise it is zero.

Likewise, in the two cells case (9.4), the optimal interior solutions, if they exist are given by

$$u_j^o = \frac{1}{\alpha_j} \ln(q_j)^+, \; q_j = [c_i(j) - \lambda^o(j)]/c_i(j)$$

$$x_j^o(j) = \frac{s^o}{c_i(j)} \exp(\alpha_j u_j^o)$$

$\Sigma u_j^o = 1$, $x^o(j)'\ e(j) = 1$; all $j = 1, 2$; all $i = 1, 2, \ldots, n$
where $c_i(j)$, $x_i(j)$ are the i-th components of vectors $c(j)$, $x(j)$ and $\lambda(j)$ is the Lagrange multiplier associated with the j-th equality constraint.

Two characteristics of the model (9.5) which is based on the criterion of maximum probability of detection may be noted. First, the elements x_j, u_j of vectors x and u may be interpreted as probabilities i.e. as mixed strategies except when x_j, u_j takes the value 1.0 for a particular j. In the latter case, they define pure strategies. Since the model is linear in x, it is clear that

$$x_1^o = 1,\ x_2^o = 0 \text{ if } c_1 > c_2 > 0,\ \alpha_1 = \alpha_2 \text{ or, } \alpha_1 > \alpha_2,\ c_1 = c_2$$

This game-theoretic formulation suggests that if u_j were strategies controlled by an opponent player he would choose u_j to minimize the probability of detection. Thus minimix solutions can be characterized in terms of min max $\Pi = \Pi(u,x)$, where the control variables u of the opponent may be interpreted in terms of strategies chosen by the rival firms or other customers of the market.

Second, the criterion of maximum probability of detection may be replaced by a trade-off analysis followed in reliability programming [18]. For instance, let γ_j be the probability level associated with a search effort u_j:

$$1 - \exp(-\alpha_j u_j) = \gamma_j,\ 0 < \gamma_j < 1$$

then

$$u_j = -\ln(1 - \frac{\gamma_j}{c_j\, x_j})/\alpha_j$$

This implies that increasing the reliability level γ_j would necessitate an increase in search effort u_j for a fixed level of x.

Since the probability of false targets i.e. the probability of non-detection is $\exp(-\alpha_j u_j)$, another appropriate objective function is the minimization of the loss probability

$$\min_u L = \Sigma\, r_j x_j \exp(-\alpha_j u_j)$$

where $r_j x_j$ is the loss associated with the probability of non-detection.

In the general case the situation would be dynamic and the possibility of improving decision vectors x(t) at time t through search efforts denoted by vectors

$u(t-1)$ in the earlier period must be directly admitted into the framework. Let the detection probability at time t be

$$d(t) = 1 - \exp[-\tfrac{1}{2} u'(t) D u(t)]$$

where D is a suitable positive definite matrix. The state of the system denoted by the n-dimensional vector $x(t)$ is assumed to follow the recursive sequence

$$\begin{aligned} x(t) &= Ax(t-1) + Bu(t-1) \\ x(0) &= x_0 \end{aligned} \qquad (9.7)$$

where A and B are suitable constant matrices. The decision model is then of the form:

$$\text{Max } \Pi = \sum_{t=1}^{T} [c'(t)\, x(t)\, \{1 - \exp(-\tfrac{1}{2} u'(t) D u(t))\}]$$

subject to (9.7) and appropriate normalization conditions on $x(t)$ and $u(t)$. Ignoring the normalization constraints, and assuming the existence of solutions, they must satisfy the stationarity conditions

$$\begin{aligned} & A'\lambda(t+1) - \lambda(t) - c(t)\, d(t) = 0 \\ & B'\lambda(t+1) - c'(t)\, x(t)\, (1 - d(t))\, D\, u(t) = 0 \\ & x(t) - Ax(t-1) - Bu(t-1) = 0 \end{aligned} \qquad (9.8)$$

These equations are however heavily nonlinear. Some numerical methods have to be applied to solve it. Two situations can be analyzed here. First, the case when $u(t)$ is zero i.e. $d(t)$ is zero may be compared with an optimal $u(t)$ solved from (9.8). Any improvement if any could be attributed to search effort. Thus the information value of search can be estimated. Second, the steady state of the system, if it is on the optimal trajectory can be easily analyzed as follows:

$$(A' - I)\, \bar{\lambda} = \bar{c}\bar{d}$$

$$B'\bar{\lambda} = \bar{c}'\bar{x}\, (1 - \bar{d})\, D\bar{u}$$

$$(I - A)\, \bar{x} = B\bar{u}$$

where bar over a variable denotes the steady-state values. If the matrix A is assumed to be diagonal, $\hat{A}$ with diagonal elements positive but less than unity (i.e. the system 9.7 is stable), then one may write

$$\bar{\lambda} = -(I - \hat{A})^{-1} \bar{c}\bar{d}$$

$$\bar{x} = (I - \hat{A})^{-1} B\bar{u}$$

$$\bar{u} = \frac{D^{-1}B'\bar{\lambda}}{\bar{c}'\bar{x}(1-\bar{d})}$$

this shows that any increase in $\bar{u}$ which implies an increase in $\bar{d}$ tends to increase (decrease) $\bar{x}$, the output of the system but reduces (increases) its shadow cost $\bar{\lambda}$. Increasing the diagonal elements of the system matrix $\hat{A}$ has a multiplier effect on $\bar{x}$ and $\bar{\lambda}$, the former being positive and the latter negative. So long as $\bar{d} < 1$, an increase in $\bar{d}$ can be secured, for fixed $\bar{x}$, $\bar{\lambda}$ by increasing $\bar{u}$. The optimal values of $\bar{u}$ and $\bar{d}$ however depend on both $\bar{x}$ and $\bar{\lambda}$ i.e. the output and shadow prices of the system. Any increase in the diagonal elements of D tends to reduce the search effort $\bar{u}$.

4. Econometric Tests

In applied and empirical work on LP and quadratic programming models, three types of econometric tests have been considered in the literature. The first type [7, 20] solves K LP problems, one for each firm say in an industry using observed values of the triple $(\theta(k), A(k), b(k))$ for $k = 1, 2, \ldots, K$ and obtains optimal values $x^o(k)$, $z^o(k)$ of output and profits. These values are then assumed to be generated by a random sample of size K. The actual and observed values of output and profits are denoted by $x^a(k)$, $z^a(k)$. Statistical tests are then performed to compare the difference between z^a and z^o over K samples. Several variants of this method are applied as follows:

(a) the diffrence between z^a and z^o is tested by student's t-test, assuming the distributions of z^a, z^o to be normal over K samples [7, 20]. Extensions to cases when normality fails to hold have also been considered [23].

(b) the gap between z^a and z^o or the relative share of large firms in total profits, $[z^a(k) - z^o(k)]/\Sigma z^o(k)$ has been interpreted as monopoly profits and this has been regressed on other instrument variables like the inequality of distribution of strategy resources [12, 17]. The testable hypothesis in agricultural applications for example would be the extent to which the skewness in distribution of relative profits $z^o(k)/\bar{z}^a$ can be explained by that of land ownership, where $\bar{z}^a$ denotes the average of observed profits $z^a(k)$.

(c) the variability in optimal $z^o(k)$ or relative profits $z^o(k)/\bar{z}^a$ has been regressed with respect to the regressor variables such as prices included in $\theta(k)$, various input quantities included in b(k) and outside variables like technology and exogenous policy variables like taxes and subsidies [17, 17]

(d) the variability in relative profits between large and small enterprises has been related to unequal degrees of risk aversion, the latter being measured in terms of weights on the variance of input costs and gross returns [27]. For instance, the linear profit function $z = \theta'x$ has been replaced by a quadratic expected utility function

$$f = \bar{\theta}'x - \frac{\lambda}{2} x'V_\theta x$$

where θ is assumed to be normal $N(\theta, V_\theta)$ with mean θ and variance-covariance matrix V_θ and $\lambda > 0$ is the risk aversion parameter. Using a vector y of Lagrange multipliers for the constraints (1.1) and assuming the existence of interior optimal solutions, the optimal decision vector x^o can be written as a supply function

$$x^o = (\lambda V_\theta)^{-1} [\bar{\theta} - A'y^o] \qquad (10.1)$$

Assuming that such an optimal supply function $x^o k)$ can be realistically assumed for each of K farms, Weins [27] has attempted to estimate the risk aversion parameter λ. His attempt is based on two institutional assumptions: the first is that the observed market input prices are approximately equal to the vector y^o of imputed costs used in (10.1) and the second is that the optimal supply function (10.1) is approximately equal to the observed supply response on the average i.e.

$$\frac{1}{K} \Sigma x^o(k) = \frac{1}{K} \Sigma x^a(k)$$

It is then found by statistical tests that the estimates of the risk aversion parameter λ for large farms (i.e. large in terms of land holdings) differs significantly from that of small farms.

The second type of econometric tests is based on the linkages between LP models and regression models [21, 23]. If the K samples are from a homogeneous population, one could estimate by linear regression the production response function:

$$x^o = Mb + \varepsilon, \ \varepsilon\text{:error} \qquad (10.2)$$

from K observations on the pair $(x^o(k), b(k))$ where $x^o(k)$ is the optimal output vector for k-th unit satisfying the basis equation

$$M(k)^{-1} x^o(k) = b(k); \; x^o(k) \geq 0 \tag{10.3}$$

where it is assumed that M(k) is nonsingular (i.e. the assumption of nondegeneracy) and the stochastic component ε is assumed to be homoscedastic with zero mean and unit variance and distributed independently of b(k). Note that the linear regression model (10.2) has to be conditionally interpreted:

$$E(x^o|b) = Mb; \; E(\varepsilon|b) = 0 \tag{10.4}$$

In other words, the input vector b has to be a nonstochastic regressor.

Some variants of this method are as follows:

(a) If the statistical fit of the linear regression model is good, as mentioned by R^2, the multiple correlation coefficient and other theoretical aspects, then the production function estimate

$$x^o = \hat{M}b \tag{10.5}$$

can be used as an average which is representative of the industry comprising K and other similar units. This is then the optimal production behavior for the representative firm, a concept first used by Alfred Marshall.

(b) If the observed series $x^a(k)$ and the optimal series $x^o(k)$ have close correspondence, then the optimal production response (10.5) would also be close to the observed production behavior. However, the production response (10.5) would be "the best practice" function, since it uses only optimal input-output data. This would be different from an average production function, based on observed input-output data. The best practice function is also called production frontier in economic analysis.

(c) The linear regression (10.5) can also be given an informational interpretation. Assume for instance that K farms can be stratified into two groups such that the inverse of the optimal basis takes two forms: M(1) and M(2) which differ only in two columns. Hence the output vectors $x^o(1)$, $x^o(2)$ of two groups can be written as conditional expectations

$$E(x^o(i)|b(i) = M_1(i)b_1(i) + \sum_{k=2}^{m} M_k(i)b_k(i)$$

$$\text{all } i = 1, 2$$

where $M_k(1) = M_k(2)$ for all $k = 2, 3, \ldots, m$ and $M_1(1) \neq M_2(1)$, $M_k(i)$ being the k-th column vector of firm i. If the part $\sum_{k=2}^{m} M_k(i)b_k(i)$ is not much different between the two firms, then the two production response equations may be combined as

$$E(x^o|b) = \sum_{k=2}^{m} M_k(0)b_k + M_1(1)d_1b_1(1) + M_1(2)d_2b_2(2) \qquad (10.6)$$

where d_1 and d_2 are dummy variables defined as

$$d_1 = \begin{cases} 1, & \text{if } b_1(1) \text{ is used} \\ 0, & \text{otherwise} \end{cases} \quad \text{and } d_2 = \begin{cases} 1, & \text{if } b_1(2) \text{ is used} \\ 0, & \text{otherwise} \end{cases}$$

Similarly, if there are more strata, additional dummy variables could be introduced. This would increase R^2 and hence increase the explanatory part of the regression (10.6)

Thus, in case of G independent strata let μ be the overall population mean vector and let μ_g be the mean vector in g^{th} stratum, $g = 1, 2, \ldots, G$ where N_g is the number of farms in g^{th} stratum and $N = \sum_{g=1}^{G} N_g$. Then

$$\mu = \frac{1}{N} \sum_{g=1}^{G} N_g\mu_g = \sum_{g=1}^{G} (\frac{N_g}{N}) \mu_g$$

$$NV = \sum_{g=1}^{G} N_gV_g + \sum_{g=1}^{G} N_g(\mu_g - \mu)(\mu_g - \mu)'$$

where the variance-covariance matrices are V and V_g for the population and the different strata i.e.

$$\mu_g = \frac{1}{N_g} [x^o(i)|b(i);\ i = 1, 2, \ldots, N_g]$$

$$V_g = \frac{1}{N_g} \sum_{i=1}^{N_g} [(x^o(i) - \mu_g)(x^o(1) - \mu_g)' \mid b(i)]$$

$$V = \frac{1}{N} \sum_{g=1}^{G} \sum_{i=1}^{N_g} [x^o(i) - \mu)(x^o(i) - \mu)' \mid b(i)]$$

It is clear that

$$\sum_{g=1}^{G} \frac{N_g}{N} \operatorname{tr} V_g < \operatorname{tr} V$$

where tr. denotes the trace of a matrix and the inequality is strict, if μ_g's differ between strata and from the overall mean response. Thus, stratification helps to decrease the variability of the mean estimate $\hat{u}_g$ by choosing homogeneous strata where the strata mean responses are very different. The dummy variable method (10.6) thus provides an improved estimate, when the K samples have heteroscedastic variance structure.

In case of heteroscedastic variance structure, other types of estimation methods e.g. switching of regimes, or truncated normal cases have also been discussed in the literature [20].

The third type of econometric test is designed to estimate efficient production functions and compare efficiency of two or more firm-groups, when there may be systematic differences in efficiency across firms in an industry [21]. Denoting the output vector $x^o(k)$ of observations by x_k, the input vector $b(k)$ of observations by b_k and the response coefficient matrix M by M_k, the system (10.2) can be written as

$$x_k = M_k b_k + e_k \qquad k = 1, 2, \ldots, K \tag{11.1}$$

where it is assumed that there are K firm groups each with N_k observations and e_k is the stochastic component with zero means but a heteroscedastic variance-covariance matrix. Note that if the homogeneity postulate fails, the efficient production function (i.e. the production frontier) tend to differ from the average production function and then the stochastic components e_k will contain systematic differences in efficiency also. Several variants of estimation methods have been considered for such situations [21, 23].

(a) the estimates $\hat{M}_k$ have bee obtained under the constraint that the errors $\hat{e}_k$ are constrained to one side of the estimated production surface:

$$\hat{M}_k b_k - \hat{e}_k = x_k, \ \hat{e}_k \geq 0 \tag{11.2}$$

where the hat denotes the estimated quantities. It is clear that only the efficient firms will be on the production frontier and satisfy the equality

$$\hat{x}_k = \hat{M}_k b_k = x_k$$

For all other firms, outputs will be smaller in at least one component. The criterion function for estimation may be the squared sum of errors [23]. However this would not be robust. Hence the Tchebychev criterion of minimizing the absolute sum of deviations may be preferred. An alternative suggestion is to apply the estimate known as the minimum-norm quadratic unbiased estimates, usually applied in models known as mixed-effects models [23].

(b) An alternative measure of efficiency, which does not assume any specific production function concept like (11.1) is obtained as the maximum of a ratio of weighted outputs to weighted inputs subject to the condition that similar ratios for other firms be less than or equal to unity [2]. In more precise form, let x_{ik} and y_{sk} be the n outputs and m inputs of the k-th firm, then one maximizes

$$h_o = \sum_{i=1}^{n} u_i x_{io} / \sum_{s=1}^{m} v_s y_{so}$$

subject to (11.3)

$$\sum_{i=1}^{n} u_i x_{ik} \leq \sum_{s=1}^{m} v_s y_{sk}; \; k = 1, 2, \ldots, K$$

$$u_i, v_s \geq o, \; s = 1, 2, \ldots, m; \; i = 1, 2, \ldots, n$$

It is assumed that the observed outputs x_{ik} and y_{sk} are all positive and known i.e. they imply optimal behavior under the given environment. The optimal values of the weights u_i, v_s are determined by solving the above linear functional fractional program (11.3), for which an equivalent LP model can be easily formulated. Note that the data on all the K firms are used here as a reference set, where the efficiency of one member of this set is to be rated relative to others. Hence the subscript zero is used in the objective function of (11.3) to represent the firm whose efficiency is rated. However this firm is any one of the reference set, hence each firm's efficiency measure is related to others.

Thus given the data set (x_{ik}, y_{sk}) of K firms, a particular firm with (x_{io}, y_{so}) is efficient if and only if in terms of (11.3)

$$h_o^* = \max h_o = 1$$

Two limitations of this method of measuring efficiency must be noted. First, it is dependent on the reference set, so that changes in the total number of firms in the reference set may change the efficiency measure; also in many cases, each of the K firms may be efficient by this test. Second, the stochastic character of the output and input data (x_{ik}, y_{sk}) is altogether ignored. If the inputs and outputs are normally distributed, then instead of (x_{ik}, y_{sk}), the sample means $\bar{x}_{ik}$, $\bar{y}_{sk}$ based on N_k observatons may be used and a stratification method based on their variances employed to cluster firms into different reference sets. Efficiency comparisons may then be more meaningful.

(c) A somewhat different but related measure of efficiency in LP model may be applied using the concept of the coefficient of resource utilization developed by Debreu [6]. Here we have a basic set of resources denoted by an n-dimensional vector z, which belongs to a convex set R_{min}. The convex set R_{min} describes the minimal physical resources to achieve a given utility or satisfaction level for the decision-makers. For any fixed point z^o in the non-negative orthant, the minimum of the distance from z^o not belonging to R_{min} measures the dead loss associated with z^o with z^o not belonging ro R_{min}. Since R_{min} is assumed to be a closed bounded and convex set, a set of prices denoted by vector p would exst by the separating hyperplane theorem; hence the distance from z^o to R_{min} may be measured by $D(x^o, z)$:

$$D(z^o, z) = p'(z^o - z), \ z \in R_{min}, \ z^o \notin R_{min}$$

This price vector however is not unique and there may exist several such intrinsic price vectors for any $z \in R_{min}$. Let z^* be a vector collinear with z^o but belonging to R_{min}:

$$z^* = \rho z^o, \ z^* \in R_{min}$$

By convexity of the set R_{min} we have

$$p'(z^* - z) \geq 0 \text{ i.e. } \frac{p'z}{p'z^*} \leq 0$$

hence

$$\max_{z \in R_{min}} (p'z/p'z^o) = \rho$$

Where ρ is called the coefficient of resource utilization of the system, describing its economic efficiency.

In our context the economic system consists of K LP models, one for each firm or decision-maker. If the resources b(k) are freely transferable and the technology set A(k) is available to the other firms, then the industry chould choose from an enlarged set (A, β) where A = (A(1), A(2), ..., A(K)) and

$\beta = U(\sum_{k=1}^{K} b(k))$ where U is any allocation of the total resource vector. The set R_{min} may then be constructed from this enlarged set and the distance $(z^o - z)$ measured.

As an example, assume that there are two groups of firms K= 2, for each of which we have the optimal production response

$$z(k) = M(k)b(k)$$

where we have used the notation z(k) instead of $x^o(k)$ in (10.3) and assumed that this optimal basis equation holds on the average, so that the mean of the stochastic component ε in (10.2) is zero. Let Π(k) = c'(k)z(k) be the optimal objective function, where c(k) is the average price coefficient vector, assumed to be positive.

Now if c(1) = c(2) = c(0) and Π(1) > Π(2), then one can apply Farkas' theorem on the inequalitiies Π(1) ≥ Π(2) and c(0) ≥ 0 to derive a nonnegative scalar h such that

$$z(1) = z(2) + he,\ h \geq 0 \tag{11.4}$$

where e is an n-dimensional vector with each element unity. Again if b(1) = b(2) = b(0) ≥ 0 and Π(1) ≥ Π(2) then there must exist a nonnegative scalar r say, such that,

$$\lambda(1) = \lambda(2) + re,\ r \geq 0 \tag{11.5}$$

where λ(k) is the shadow price vector of the k-th LP problem.

Now assume that β = b(1) + b(2) and θβ is used to produce output z(1) and (1 - θ)β is used for z(2), where $0 \leq \theta \leq 1$. Total profit for the industry is

$$\Pi(\theta) = \theta c(1)'z(1) + (1 - \theta)c(2)'z(2)$$

If $\Pi_1(\theta) > \Pi_2(\theta)$, where $\Pi_k(\theta) = \theta c'(k)z(k)$, $\theta_1 = \theta$, $\theta_2 = 1 - \theta$ and $\beta \geq 0$, then by

Farkas theorem there must exist a nonnegative vector h, $h \geq 0$ such that

$$M'(1)\ c(1) = \frac{1-\theta}{\theta} M'(2)c(2) + \frac{h}{\theta}$$

ie

$$\lambda(1) \geq \frac{1-\theta}{\theta} \lambda(2) > \lambda(2)$$

$$\text{if } 1 > \theta > \tfrac{1}{2}$$

Thus, resource reallocations between firms or transfer of knowledge about technology may lead to Pareto-optimal improvements. A statistical test of these improvements may therefore be performed by setting up the null hypotheses:

(i) $H_0 : \lambda(1) = \lambda(2)$
(ii) $H_0 : z(1) = z(2)$
(iii) $H_0 : \Pi(1) = \Pi(2)$

In the first two cases, Hotelling's T^2-test may be applicable if it can be reasonably assumed that the quantities $\lambda(k)$, $z(k)$ are distributed like multivariate normals. Then one can test the null hypothesis H_0: $z(1) = z(2)$ by T^2-statistic based on (N - 1) degrees of freedom

$$\frac{T^2}{N-1} = N(z(1) - z(2))'S^{-1}(z(1) - z(2)$$

where S is an m-by-m matrix (since the basis is m-dimensional) denoting the corrected sum of squares and cross products of terms in $(z(1) - z(2))$ for samples of size N. This assumes homoscedasticity. However, if the normality assumption holds only approximately, an approximate T^2-test known as T_v^2-statistic due to James [20] may be used:

$$T_v^2 = [z(1) - z(2)]' \left[\frac{S(1) + S(2)}{N}\right]^{-1} [z(1) - z(2)]$$

where S(k) is the unbiased estimate of variance-covariance matrix of vectors z(k) based on a sample size of N.

A similar test can be applied for the scalar case H_0: $\Pi(1) = \Pi(2)$. Note however that the test in the scalar case may not sufficiently discriminate among the differences in two output vectors or two shadow price vectors [20, 23].

5. Concluding Remarks

Two concluding remarks may be made. Note that in many cases we did not explicitly require nonnegativity on the decision vector. This is particularly true in all cases where estimation aspects were emphasized. For applications in economic cases, either such nonnegativity conditions would have to be explicitly introduced, in which case the computational problems would increase, or suitable modifications in the model have to be introduced.

Secondly, we have emphasized in our development several criteria of choice between risky prospects e.g. probability of the posterior distribution. These are intended to be illustrative rather than exhaustive.

REFERENCES

1. Bracken J. and R.M. Soland: Statistical decision analysis of Stochastic Linear programming problems. Naval Research Logistics Quarterly, 13 (1966), 205-226.

2. Charnes, A., W.W. Cooper and E. Rhodes: Measuring the efficiency of decision-making units. European Journal of Operations Research, 2 (1978), 429-444.

3. Chernoff, H.: The efficient estimation of a parameter measurable by two instruments of unknown precision, in J.S. Rustagi ed., Optimizing Methods in Statistics. Academic Press: New York, 1971, 1-27.

4. Chernoff, H.: Sequential Analysis and Optimal Design. Society for Industrial and Applied Mathematics: Philadelphia, 1972.

5. Chu, K.C.: Designing information structures of quadratic decision problems. Journal of Optimization Theory and Applications, 25 (1978), 139-160.

6. Debreu, G.: The coefficient of resource utilization. Econometrica, 19 (1951), 273-292.

7. Desai, D.: Increasing income nd production on Indian farms: possibilities with existing resource supplies on individual farms, in Selected Readings from Indian Journal of Agricultural Economics, Bombay, 1965.

8. Fox, K.A. and T. Wang: Estimating the effects of institutional and technological changes upon agricultural development: A comparison of multiple regression and programming approaches, in K.A. Fox et. al. eds., Economic Models Estimation and Risk Programming, Ch. 10, Springer Verlag: Berlin, 1969.

9. Just, R.E.: An investigation of the importance of risk in farmers' decisions. American Journal of Agricultural Economics, 56 (1974), 14-25.

10. Kendall, M.G. and A. Stuart: The Advanced Theory of Statistics, vol. 1, Hafner Publishing, New York, 1967.

11. Marschak, J: Economic Information, Decision and Prediction. Selected Essays: vol. 3. D. Reidel Publishing Company: Dordrecht, Holland, 1974.

12. Nugent, J.B.: Linear programming models for national planning: demonstration of a testing procedure. Econometrica, 38 (1970), 831-855.

13. Radner, R.: Allocation of a scarce resource under uncertainty: An example of a team, in C.B. McGuire and R. Radner eds. Decision and Organization: A volume in Honor of Jacob Marschak. North Holland, Amsterdam, 1972, pp. 217-236.

14. Rothschild, M.: Models of market organization with imperfect information: A survey. Journal of Political Economy, 81 (1973), 1283-1308.

15. Sage, A.P. and J.L. Melsa: Estimation Theory with Applications to Communications and Control. McGraw Hill: New York, 1971.

16. Schweppe, F.C.: Uncertain Dynamic Systems. Prentice Hall: Englewood Cliffs, NJ, 1973.

17. Scott, M.F., J.D. MacArthur and D.M.G. Newberry: Project Appraisal in Practice. Heinemann Educational Books: London, 1976.

18. Sengupta, J.K.: Stochastic Programming: Methods and Applications. North Holland, Amsterdam, 1972.

19. Sengupta, J.K.: Adaptive decision rules for stochastic linear programming. International Journal of Systems Science, 9 (1978), 97-109.

20. Sengupta, J.K.: Testing and validation problems in stochastic linear programming. Journal of Cybernetics, 9 (1979), 17-42.

21. Sengupta, J.L.: Selecting an optimal solution in stochastic linear programming. International Journal of Systems Science, 11 (1978), 33-47.

22. Sengupta, J.K.: Constrained nonzero-sum games with partially controllable strategies. Journal of Optimization Theory and Applications, 31 (1980).

23. Sengupta, J.K.: Decision Models in Stochastic Programming. To be published: American Elsevier and North Holland, ca. 1981.

24. Sengupta, J.K. and R.I. Sfeir: The adjustment of output-inventory process under linear decision rules. Journal of Economic Dynamics and Control, 1 (1979), 361-381.

25. Smith, H.W. and F.T. Man: Computation of suboptimal linear controls for nonlinear stochastic systems. International Journal of Control, 10 (1969), 645-655.

26. Stone, L.D.: Theory of Optimal Search. Academic Press: New York, 1975.

27. Weins, T.B.: Peasant risk aversion and allocative behavior: a quadratic programming experiment. American Journal of Agricultural Economics, 58 (1976), 629-635.

CHAPTER 3
RISK AVERSION IN DECISION MODELS

1. Introduction

Risk aversion has formed an integral part in most applied decision models under uncertainty, where the latter is generated by a probabilistic mechanism. This mechanism is not completely known, so that the environment under which decisions are to be made is random. However, the source of randomness may differ from one application to another, hence the decision-making response may vary. For example, in micro-economic models, consumer's or producer's response behavior is analyzed under conditions of price or cost parameter uncertainty and this behavior is compared with the case when there is no uncertainty. In engineering systems having a number of channels, the reliability levels may vary between channels and the noise elements may vary: the decision problem is one of maximizing the system reliability. In quality control, a sample inspection plan seeks to determine an acceptable quality level (AQL) of a product lot by minimizing thecost of making wrong decisions, where the latter involves producer's risk (α) and consumer's risk (β). The probability that a sampling plan will reject AQL is called the producer's risk α i.e. the Type I error, whereas the probability that the plan will accept fraction-defective levels (FDL) is called consumer's risk β i.e. the Type II error. Usually, if the lot quality is equal to or better than AQL quality, p_a is equal to or greater than $(1 - \alpha)$, where p_a denotes the probability of acceptance which is usually 0.95 i.e. $\alpha = 0.05$. Similarly, if the lot quality is equal to or worse than FDL quality, p_a is equal to or less than β, the Type II decision error and p_a is usually 0.10.

Measures of risk aversion are thus related to the source of uncertainty, the specification of the decision model and the system objective which is optimized. For example, the model may be one of linear programming (LP): $\max z = c'x,\ x \in R$ where x is the decision vector and $R:\{x|Ax \leq b,\ x \geq 0\}$ is the constraint set and the parameters (c, A, B) are unknown but subject to a probability generating mechanism. This is a stochastic LP model for which suitable equivalent programs can be derived that are deterministic but nonlinear and inclusive of risk aversion measures. Another example is the linear quadratic Gaussian (LQG) model in stochastic control which leads to linear decision rules under certain conditins. These decision rules have recursive or adaptive properties (e.g. Kalman filters) in the sense that they can be sequentially updated by incorporating posterior knowledge about means and variances when the information sequence is increasing.

The aversion to risk and uncertainty by the decision-maker (DM) may again vary depending on the organizational framework, its hierarchy and the types of information channels and data used. In team decision models of a production-allocation system, the individual and aggregate risks and their perceptions may vary depending on the degree of cooperation or non-cooperation among members. In collective risk theory for an insurance company, the flow of individual premiums and claim payments belonging to different risk classes may be viewed as two continuous and aggregative streams and the company's objective may be to maximize the probability that its aggregate capital S_t at any time t is not zero or negative i.e.

$$\max \text{Pr. } (\min S_t \geq 0, \ t = 1, 2, \ldots, T)$$

where Pr. denotes probability. In game theory models, mixed strategy solutions may be preferred over pure strategies by a player, when the opponent's reaction functions are incompletely known. In two-person nonzero sum games, mixing pure strategies may be adopted as a policy not to reveal his own reaction to the uncertain environment. Mixed strategies have also been used as randomized solutions in stochastic programming problems e.g. if the objective function is partly concave and partly convex, it may be preferable to use mixed rather than pure strategies as optimal solutions.

Our objective here is to provide a selective survey and critical appraisal of the major concepts of risk aversion as applied to economic and other operational decision models. For convenience of presentation, the measures of aversion to uncertainty and risk due to fluctuations or randomness in the environment may be classified into six groups as follows:

A. Parametric Measures e.g., concepts of relative and absolute risk aversion due to Arrow, concepts of conditional and unconditional certainty equivalence, mean-variance characteristics of portfolios etc.

B. Probability-based Measures e.g., probability of ruin, stochastic dominance of one distribution over another, Mahalanobis distance and other measures of distance between two or more distributions of the objective function and probability of detection in the search for the true parameter, etc.

C. Nonparametric Measures e.g., Kolmogorov-Smirnov type distance functions for comparing alternative distributions, stochastic goal programming based on minimizing Tchebychev-type norms, safety first rules, etc.

D. Informational Measures e.g., entropy-based concepts, uncertainty of alternative channels of communication and value of information, Kalman filter and other adaptive behavior, etc.

E. Measures of Risk Sharing and Diversification e.g., mixing pure strategies in the theory of insurance under collective risk, measures of diversity in distribution of species in ecology and measures of product diversity in monopolistic competition under uncertainty, etc.

F. Multivariate Measures e.g., size and shape of the distribution of the multi-criteria objective function, measures based on informational manifold theory and on multiple classification procedures, etc.

1.1 Parametric Measures

One of the most important measures that has found wide applications is the Arrow-Pratt measure (r_A) of absolute risk aversion:

$$r_A = -\partial^2 u(x)/\partial u(x) \tag{1.1}$$

which is easily defined, once we accept the existence of a real-valued utility function u(x) defined on x, the wealth or income. A relative measure is obtained by multiplying (1.1) by x. Arrow argues that the absolute measure is a nonincreasing function of wealth and in portfolio model this implies that risky investment is not an inferior good [1, 3]. This hypothesis of individual's aversion to income or wealth risks has been applied both empirically and analytically in international trade [3], financial decisions [54], agricultural production [52] and other allocation decisions [40].

Two operational implications of this concept of absolute risk aversion appear to be most important. One is the notion of certainty equivalence of a lottery which has consequences represented by the random variable $\tilde{x}$. For all monotonic utility functions $u(\tilde{x})$ defined on the space of $\tilde{x}$, a decision-maker (DM) is said to be risk averse, if he prefers $u(E(\tilde{x}))$ over $E(u(\tilde{x}))$, where E is expectation over the nondegenerate distribution of the random variable $\tilde{x}$ and it is assumed that it is finite or bounded. The certainty equivalent of the lottery is then defined by an amount $\hat{x}$ such that

$$u(\hat{x}) = E[u(\tilde{x})] \tag{1.2}$$

he is indifferent between the lottery and the amount $\hat{x}$ for certain. If the scalar utility function is monotone increasing, it follows that

$$u(E(\tilde{x}) - \pi) = E(u(\tilde{x})) \tag{1.3}$$

where π is a positive risk premium

$$\pi = E\tilde{x} - \hat{x}$$

and it is unique. It follows that if the scalar utility function is concave (convex), it implies risk aversion (risk proneness) with a positive (negative) risk premium.

Two points may be noted about the certainty equivalence notion. The consequences $\tilde{x}$ of the lottery may be an n-element vector rather than a scalar; the vector π of risk premiums [14] is not unique in this case, although an approximate risk premium vector π with n-elements may be computed as

$$\underline{\pi} \cong -\tfrac{1}{2}(\underline{u}')^{-} \text{ tr. } [UV] \tag{1.4}$$

where $\underline{u}'$ is a row vector with n-elemets $u_i = \partial u(\underline{x})/\partial x_i$, U is a Hessian matrix $U = \partial^2 u(\underline{x})/\partial x_i \partial x_j$ of order n and V is the variance-covariance matrix of the random elements of the problem and $(\underline{u}')^{-}$ denotes the generalized inverse of the n-element row vector $\underline{u}'$. The absolute risk aversion matrix R_A corresponding to (1) now becomes

$$R_A = [-u_{ij}/u_i]$$

where u_{ij} are the elements of the Hessian matrix U and u_i is an element of the vector $\underline{u}$. Note however that the multivariate measure of risk aversion still assumes the existence of a scalar utility function. If the utility function is a vector, as in a team decision problem and each member has a positive risk aversion at different levels, how can one define a risk aversion measure for the aggregate team that will retain some consistency over the preference maps of members? This is an open question for research.

However if the utility vector u(j) of each member j = 1, 2, ..., M can be assumed to be multivariate normal N(m(j), V(j)) with mean vector m(j) and variance-covariance matrix V(j), then one can characterize the difference d = u(i) - u(j), i $\neq$ j in terms of a multivariate statistic D^2 known as Mahalanobis distance:

$$D^2 = [\{u(i) - m(i)\} - \{u(j) - m(j)\}]'[V(i) + V(j)]^{-1}$$
$$[\{u(i) - m(i)\} - \{u(j) - m(j)\}]$$

provided the random utility vectors u(i), u(j) are statistically independent. This distance function D^2 may be applied in the sample or observation space and then this becomes Hotelling's T^2 statistic. For example, assume there are K observations on the random vector u(j) for each member j and we want to test the null hypothesis that m(i) = m(j). We form the T^2 statistic based on degrees of freedom K - 1 as follows:

$$\frac{T^2}{K-1} = K\,\bar{d}'\,S^{-1}\,\bar{d} \tag{1.5}$$

where

$$\bar{d} = (\bar{d}_k),\ \bar{d}_k = K^{-1}\sum_{t=1}^{K} d_{tk}$$

$$S = (S_{ks}),\ S_{ks} = \sum_{t=1}^{K} (d_{tk} - \bar{d}_k)(d_{ts} - \bar{d}_k)$$

d_{tk} are observations on vector $d = u(i) - u(j)$

this test statistic is related to Fisher's F distribution

$$\frac{K-p}{p}\,\frac{T^2}{K-1} \sim F_{p,\,K-p}$$

with degrees of freedom p and K - p, where p is the dimension of each utility vector u(j). The critical region will be $T^2 > T^2(f,p,\alpha)$, where $T^2(f,p,\alpha)$ denotes the tabular value of T^2 with degrees of freedom $f = K - 1$ and the level of significance α. If the null hypothesis is rejected at the given significance level α_0 say, then the mean utility vectors for two sample groups i and j are different. The intensity of this difference is then measured by the noncentrality index λ^2, where

$$\lambda^2 = K(m(i) - m(j))'\,[V(i) + V(j)]^{-1}\,(m(i) - m(j))$$

thus, a multivariate measure of risk aversion can be developed for the case when u(j) is a random vector for each j = 1, 2, ..., N if we just stratify the group into g strata or risk classes such that within a given strata the null hypothesis based on (1.5) is not rejected and then apply to each strata a method of deriving a vector efficient point u* say. If such a point $u^* \in R$ exists, where R is a suitable convex set assumed to be closed and bounded, then from Kuhn-Tucker theory it follows that there exist nonnegative weights $w_r \geq 0$ such that an aggregate utility function

$$u(j) = \sum_{r=1}^{p} w_r u_r(j) \tag{1.6}$$

in a scalar form can be defined for each j = 1, 2, ..., N and maximization of u(j) will characterize the vector efficient point u*. Using this scalar utility function (1.6) for a homogeneous strata defined above, one could develop a measure corresponding to (1.4) and the associated risk premium vectors.

Note that the utility function becomes a profit function when we apply this type of risk aversion model (1.1) in production and resource allocation problems with multi-inputs and multi-outputs. This then leads to stochastic linear and quadratic programming models that have been extensively applied [36, 42].

A second point about the risk aversion measure r_A in (1.1) is that it can be used to characterize conditional rather than unconditional certainty equivalence. Thus for any decision or act α, given the state of the world $w \in \Omega$, denote the utility function $u(\tilde{x})$ in terms of the conditional variable $u(\tilde{x}_\alpha(w))$. Then the certainty equivalent $\hat{x}_\alpha(w)$ defined by

$$u(\hat{x}_\alpha(w)) = E[u(\tilde{x}_\alpha(w))] \tag{1.7}$$

depends on the fact that the state of the world w or, the action α conditional on w is given. Note that the expectation operator E in (1.7) is over the states of actions α induced by the states of the world $w \in \Omega$.

This concept of conditional certainty equivalence is particularly useful in linear quadratic Gaussian control problems leading to linear decision rules. The latter can be sequentially updated and improved as more and more information becomes available over time [38].

A second important use of the risk aversion measure r_A in (1.1) is the risk preference function for odering of random lotteries. Let μ and σ be the mean and standard deviation of a random variable x. A scalar function $g = g(\mu, \sigma)$ is called a risk preference function, if for every pair of random variables x_1, x_2 with means μ_1, μ_2 and variances σ_1^2, σ_2^2 it holds that x_1 is preferred or indifferent to x_2 if and only if $g(\mu_1, \sigma_1) \geq g(\mu_2, \sigma_2)$. A risk preference function is called rational, according to Neumann-Morgenstern principle if the preference relation it induces on the set of random variables x_1, x_2 can also be induced by a suitably chosen utility function $u = u(x)$. But a (μ, σ) - preference function is determined only up to some strictly increasing transformation. Hence one may restrict to that class of utility function u which induces the same preference relation as a preference function $g = g(\mu, \sigma)$ if and only if

$$g(\mu, \sigma) = U[Eu(x);\ x = x(\mu, \sigma)] \tag{2.1}$$

where E is expectation and U is some strictly increasing function. The whole class of utility functions that would be rational in the above sense can then be derived from an elegant result proved by Schneeweiss [35] and developed by others [42]. One of the most commonly used preference function is of the form:

$$g(\mu, \sigma) = \mu - \tfrac{1}{2}\lambda\sigma^2, \ \lambda > 0 \tag{2.2}$$

which induces a partial ordering among random lotteries in x. The corresponding utility function which satisfies the rationality postulate in the sense of (2.1) is of the exponential form:

$$u(x) = -\frac{1}{\lambda}\exp(-\lambda x), \ \lambda > 0 \tag{2.3}$$

where λ may be identified as the risk aversion parameter i.e.

$$\lambda = -\frac{\partial^2 u/\partial x^2}{\partial u/\partial x}$$

this parameter λ need not be constant for all levels x e.g. it may be of the form $\lambda(x)$, a nonincreasing function of income or wealth x. In this sense λ is a measure of local risk aversion when the exponential utility function (2.3) holds only approximately.

An interesting extension of Johansen [19, 20] considers a linear sum of exponential functions:

$$u(x) = -\sum_{i=1}^{n} B_i \exp(-\beta_i x_i), \ B_i > 0, \ \beta_i > 0$$

where the elements x_i of vector x are assumed to be normally distributed with mean $E(x_i)$ and variances σ_i^2. In this case one can write

$$E[u(x; \alpha)] = u[E(x); \tilde{\alpha}]$$

where $\alpha = (B_1, B_2, \ldots, B_n; \beta_1, \beta_2, \ldots, \beta_n)$,

$$\tilde{\alpha} = \prod_{i=1}^{n} \tilde{B}_i\beta_i \quad \tilde{B}_i = B_i \exp(\tfrac{1}{2}\beta_i^2\sigma_i^2)$$

It is clear that if some β_i are negative and some positive, it would represent asymmetry in preferences that have been widely applied [51].

An interesting application of the risk aversion concept is in characterizing an efficient vector point in a stochastic production process. Let x be an n-element output vector and X the set of all output vectors obtainable in a random production process such that X is closed, convex and bounded. Then one may define after Peleg and Yaari [31] a concept of efficiency that holds risk aversely. Thus, of two output vectors x, $y \varepsilon X$, y dominates x risk-aversely if

$$\sum_{i=1}^{n} p_i\, u(y_i) \geqq \sum_{i=1}^{n} p_i\, u(x_i) \tag{2.4}$$

for all utility functions $u(\cdot)$ belonging to a set $U(\cdot)$ of concave and nondecreasing utility functions and probabilities $p_i \geq 0$, $\Sigma p_i = 1$ and furthermore, there exists an utility function $u^* \varepsilon U$ such that

$$\sum_i p_i\, u^*(y_i) > \sum_i p_i\, u^*(x_i)$$

Then the output vector $x^* \varepsilon X$ is said to be "risk-aversely efficient" if there exists no other $x \varepsilon X$ that dominates x^* risk aversely. The importance of this result of Peleg and Yaari is due to its implications for a system of efficiency prices. Thus, if the output vector $x^* \varepsilon X$ is risk-aversely efficient, then they have proved that it must have a system of price vectors $\pi = (\pi_i)$ such that

$$x_i^* > x_j^* \text{ implies } \pi_j/p_j > \pi_i/p_i$$

and conversely. Hence the behavior of risk-averters can be analyzed from a set of risk aversely efficient vector points e.g. crosssection data of risk-averse decision-makers say.

To see the importance of the above result consider a deterministic case where the n-dimensional output vector x belongs to a convex set X, that specifies the resource constraints on production. Let X_{min} denote the minimal physical resources required to achieve an output level x^*, where it is assumed that X_{min} is a subset of X and is nonempty. Let x be any other vector point not belonging to X_{min}. The distance from x to the set X_{min} may then provide us with a measure of inefficiency i.e. a coefficient of resource under-utlization as has been shown by Debreu [13]. By definition, the vector point $x^* \varepsilon X_{min}$ is efficient if there exists no other $x \varepsilon X_{min}$ such that $x > x^*$. Then by the convexity of the set X_{min}, there must exist a vector of prices $\pi > 0$ such that

$$\pi' (x^* - x) \geq 0$$

ths implies that

$$\pi' x \leq \pi' x^*$$

Denote by x^o a vector collinear with x and belonging to X_{min}: $x^o = rx$, then it is clear that

$$\max_{x^* \varepsilon X_{min}} \frac{\pi' x}{\pi' x^*} = \frac{1}{r} \qquad \max_{x^* \varepsilon X_{min}} \frac{\pi' x^o}{\pi' x^*} \le \frac{1}{r}$$

$$= \rho, \ \rho = \frac{1}{r}$$

since the ratio $\pi' x^o / \pi' x^*$ equals one when $x^o = x^*$. This coefficient of resource utilization can now be given a "risk-aversely efficient" interpretation by means of concave non-decreasing utility function $u(x^*)$, $u(x)$:

$$\Sigma\, p_i\ u(x_i^*) > \Sigma\, p_i\ u(x_i) \tag{2.5}$$

where p_i are nondegenerate probabilities. Since the inequality (2.5) can be interpreted as a first order dominance relation (i.e. the average utility or profit of vector x^* is higher than that of x), one could easily define higher order dominance among such portfolios. For example, let $u(x_i) = c'(i)x(i)$ be profit associated with the i-th state of the n-dimensional vector c(i) and associated output vector x(i). A set $x^*(1)$, $x^*(2)$, .., $x^*(N)$ is dominant in the second order sense

$$\sum_{i=1}^{N} p_i[c(i)'x^*(i)]^2 > \sum_{i=1}^{N} p_i[c(i)'x(i)]^2 \tag{2.6}$$

Here it is assumed that output vectors x(i), $x^*(i)$ belong to the feasible set X for all states i = 1, 2, ..., N. Note that the second order dominance relation (2.6) along with the first order (2.5) do not necessarily imply

$$\Sigma\, p_i[c(i)'x^*(i) - \mu]^2 < \Sigma\, p_i[c'(i)x(i) - \mu]^2$$

where $\mu^* = \Sigma\, p_i c(i)'x^*(i)$, $\mu = \Sigma\, p_i c(i)'x(i)$ unless additional restriction are imposed on the utility functions $u(x^*)$, $u(x)$.

The notion of risk-aversely efficient vectors may also be applied to compare efficiency among several decision-making units e.g. N firms say, each with m inputs x_{ij}, i = 1, 2, ..., m and n outputs y_{sj}, s = 1, 2, ..., n; j = 1, 2, ..., N where efficiency is measured as the maximum of a ratio of weighted outputs to weighted inputs subject to the condition that similar ratios for every firm be less than or equal to unity. Denote the reference firm by the subscript k and assume that the observed outputs y_{sj} and inputs x_{ij} are positive and non-stochastic. Then the relative efficiency h_k of the k-th reference firm is specified by the following linear functional fractoal program in variables u_s and v_i:

$$\max h_k = \left(\sum_{s=1}^{n} u_s\, y_{sk}\right) / \left(\sum_{i=1}^{m} v_i\, x_{ik}\right)$$

subject to (2.7)

$$h_j \leq 1 \; ; \; j = 1, 2, \ldots, N$$

$$u_s \, , \, v_i \geq 0 \; ; \; s = 1, 2, \ldots, n; \; i = 1, 1, \ldots, m$$

This measure is due to Charnes, Cooper and Rhodes [45], wo have shown that it can be solved by an equivalent LP problem:

$$\min g_k = \sum_{i=1}^{m} w_i x_{ik}$$

subject to

$$\sum_{i=1}^{m} w_i x_{ij} \geq \sum_{s=1}^{n} \mu_s y_{sj} \; ; \; j = 1, 2, \ldots, N \qquad (2.8)$$

$$\sum_{s=1}^{n} \mu_s y_{sk} = 1$$

$$w_i = tv_i \geq 0 \quad \mu_s = t\, u_s \geq 0$$

where $t = \left(\sum_{s=1}^{n} \mu_s y_{sk}\right)^{-1}$ is a positive scalar. Note two very convenient implications of this measure of relative efficiency. First, it provides a scalar dimensionless measure of efficiency in terms of whch the N firms which are more or less homogeneous are to be compared and it does not specifically require the technology or the resource constraints to be specified in the model. Second, the efficiency of one member, the k-th is to be rated relative to the others in the reference set of N firms. The optimal choice of weights u_s^*, v_i^* is determined directly from observational data subject only to linear constraints of (2.7):

$$\sum_{s=1}^{n} u_s y_{sj} - \sum_{i=1}^{m} v_i x_{ij} \leq 0 \; ; \; j = 1, 2, \ldots, N$$

Under these observations and constraints no other set of common weights will give a more favorable rating to the k-th firm relative to the reference set of N firms. Hence, if the optimal value h_k^* of h_k is not equal to 1.00 under the set u_s^*, v_i^* of nonnegative weights, it will not be attained from any other set. Thus the k-th firm with $h_k^* < 1$ will be less than 100% efficient.

This method of comparing efficiency across firms would not be general however, unless the observed inputs and outputs can be treated as stochastic i.e. being subject to a probabilistic generating mechanism. It is here that the concept of risk-aversely efficient vectors due to Peleg and Yaari can be applied. For example, conider the equivalent LP problem (2.8) and assume that there exist a set of probabilities $p_i \geq 0$, $q_s \geq 0$, $\Sigma p_i = 1 = \Sigma q_s$ such that the vectors $w^* = (w_i^*)$, $\mu^* = (\mu_s^*)$ provide the optimal solution to the following LP problem

$$\min g_k = \sum_{i=1}^{m} p_i w_i x_{ik}$$

subject to

$$\sum_{i=1}^{m} p_i w_i x_{ij} \geq \sum_{s=1}^{n} q_s \mu_s y_{sj}$$

$$\sum_{s=1}^{n} q_s \mu_s y_{sk} = 1$$

$$w_i, \mu_s \geq 0; \; j = 1, 1, .., N$$

where each of the N firms is assumed to be risk averse. If the optimal value g_k^* of g_k is greater than unity for a given set of nondegenerate probabilities, then the efficient frontier of the production possibility surface has not been attained for the k-th firm at the given set of probabilities. Thus probabilistic ranking of firms according to efficiency may be attempted in this approach. An alternative way of analyzig the stochastic version of the production frontier is to consider a probabilistic version of (2.8):

$$\text{Max } \varepsilon_k = \text{Prob}[g_k \leq g_o]$$

subject to

$$\text{Prob}\,[\sum_i w_i x_{ij} \geq \sum_s \mu_s y_{sj}] = e_j \tag{2.9}$$

$$\text{Prob}\,[\sum_s \mu_s y_{sk} - 1 \geq 0]\; \tilde{e}_k$$

$$w_i, \mu_s \geq 0$$

where ε_k, e_j, $\tilde{e}_k$ are the tolerance levels and g_o is a small preassigned number.

This leads in general to nonlinear programming problems. For example if x_{ij}, y_{sj} are normally independently distributed with means $\bar{x}_{ij}$, $\bar{y}_{sj}$ and variances σ^2_{ij}, γ^2_{sj}, one version of the nonlinear program reduces to the following:

$$\text{Min } g_o = \bar{g}_k + F^{-1}(\varepsilon_k)[\sum_i w_i^2 \sigma_{ik}^2]^{1/2}$$

subject to

$$\sum_i w_i \bar{x}_{ij} - \sum_s \mu_s \bar{y}_{sj} = F^{-1}(1 - e_j)[\sum_i w_i^2 \sigma_{ij}^2 + \sum_s \mu_s^2 \gamma_{sj}^2]^{1/2}$$

$$\sum_s \mu_s \bar{y}_{sk} - 1 = F^{-1}(1 - \tilde{e}_k)[\sum_s \mu_s^2 \gamma_{sk}^2]^{1/2} \tag{2.10}$$

$$w_i, \mu_s \geq 0 \; ; \; j = 1, 2, \ldots, N$$

where $\bar{g}_k = \sum_i w_i \bar{x}_{ik}$ and $F^{-1}(r)$ denotes the inverse of the cumulative probability distribution of a unit normal variate r. Note that if the terms involving $F^{-1}(\cdot)$ can be neglected in (2.10), we would obtain an LP problem:

$$\text{Min } \bar{g}_k = \sum_i w_i \bar{x}_{ik}$$

subject to

$$\sum_i w_i \bar{x}_{ij} - \sum_s \mu_s \bar{y}_{sj} \geq 0; \; j = 1, 2, \ldots, N$$

$$\sum_s \mu_s \bar{y}_{sk} \geq 1$$

$$w_i, \mu_s \geq 0$$

This a probabilistic ranking of efficiency may be done through chance-constrained and other versions of stochastic linear programming [42].

1.2 Probability-based Criteria

Three types of probabilistic criteria hve often been used in characterizing optimal decisions under uncertainty. These may be very simply illustrated through an LP problem: max $z = c'x$, $x \varepsilon R$ where only the price vector c is subject to a stochastic mechanism but the restriction set R is convex and nonrandom unless otherwise stated.

The first criterion is the probability of ruin which is easy to apply if the probability distribution p(z) of profits z is normal or approximately so under certain conditions of the central limit theorem. Since we have

$$p(z) = p(c'x \mid x)\, p(x) = p(c'x \mid c)\, p(c) \tag{3.1}$$

it is clear that maximizing the probability p(z) is equivalent to maximizing the conditional probability $p(c'x \mid x)$, if only pure strategy solutions are chosen so that p(x) is a constant i.e.

$$p(x) = \begin{cases} 1, & \text{if } x = x^* \\ 0, & \text{otherwise} \end{cases}$$

where x^* is the optimal pure strategy vector chosen. The ruin level of the conditional probability $p(c'x \mid x)$ in the normal case is given by

$$f = c'x - 3\sqrt{x'Vx} \tag{3.2}$$

where $\bar{c}$, V are the mean and variance-covariance matrix of the random vector c and the ruin probability assumed is 0.001. The optimal decision vector x^* is then found by maximizing f with respect to x subject to $x \varepsilon R$. Note however that if mixed strategies are allowed the above procedure has to be modified [43]. Also when sequential data are available on c_t, t = 1, 2, ..., T the conditional distribution $p(c_t'x \mid x)$ can be updated with more information and then the ruin criterion (3.2) appled. Sometimes, Bayesian methods [38, 39] may be used to derive the posterior distribution $p(c'x \mid c_t)$ and then one may apply the ruin criterion on the basis of the posterior density.

A second criterion based on the concept of a statistical distance between two random points arises when we consider the problem of choosing the best treatment among a set of treatments, for each of which the response is distributed like a normal distribution say. This leads to the problem of selecting the best from a set of K normal populations say. Several types of optimal decision rules [42] are available here. As an example of one such rule, consider the stochastic LP problem and define a new decision vector $y = x - x_0$, where x_0 is preassigned and known. Assume that the event

$$y'y \geq r,\; r > 0 \tag{3.3}$$

holds with probability $\alpha > 0$. The stochastic objective function is

$$z = c'y + \varepsilon \; ; \quad \varepsilon \sim N(o, \sigma_\varepsilon^2) \tag{3.4}$$

where the conditinal expectation is $E(z|y) = \bar{c}'y$ and the stochastic component ε is independent of c. The constraint set is now $Y: \{y | Ay \geq b - Ax_0, \; y + x_0 \geq 0\}$ where A, b, x_0 are nonrandom but there is induced randomness in vector y.

Assume that the goal of the decision-maker is to attain the goal z^o fixed as $z^o = \bar{c}'y$ as closely as possible. This can be attained by minimizing the average squared distance D^2:

$$D^2(z - z^o) = E[z - z^o]^2$$

conditionally on a vector $y \varepsilon Y$ satisfying (3.3). If the constraints $Ay \leq b - Ax_0$ are not binding, either due to the choice of x_0 or to the constraint (3.3) which may be more restrictive, the optimal decision vector y^* can be solved from the eigenvalue problem:

$$[\lambda^* I - V]y^* = 0$$

$$\lambda^*(y^{*\prime}y^* - r) = 0$$

where V is the variance-covariance matrix of vector c, λ^* is the smallest eigenvalue of V with y^* as the associated eigenvector. Clearly the optimal solution $y^* = y^*(\alpha)$ depends on the probability α of the event in (3.3). Since for any other eigenvalue λ and the associated eigenvector y we would have

$$y^{*\prime}Vy^* \leq y'Vy$$

$y^*(\alpha)$ may be referred to as a risk-aversely efficient vector at the probability level α. Extensions to the case when there are K normal distributions c(1), c(2), ..., c(K) for the vector c with a homoscedastic covariance structure may be easily worked out on the basis of a multivariate distance measure known as Mahalanobis distance [27].

The third criterion for optimal decisions in a random environment is based on maximizing the probability of detection subject to a limit on the cost of search. Consider an idealized search problem in the context of stochastic LP models. Assume that the true value of vector c called the target has the probability p_1 of being in cell one i.e. c = c(1) and the probability $p_2 = 1 - p$, of being in cell two i.e. c = c(2). If c(1) is known, the optimal decision vector is to be y(1) and the reward is $z_1 = c(1)'y(1)$. Likewise for $z_2 = c(2)'y(2)$. Assume that search cost is measured in units of z_1 and z_2 and there is a limit on such costs

$$\sum_{i=1}^{2} w_i z_i = 1 \tag{3.5}$$

where w_i is a suitable nonnegative weight. How should search costs be divided between the two cells in order to maximize the probability of detecting the target? Assume the probability of detecting the target c(i)'y(i) to be exponential

$$p(z_i) = 1 - \exp(\alpha_i z_i) \ , \ z_i \geq 0$$

given that it is in cell i = 1, 2. The positive coefficient α_i may be an index of intensity of search effort. The total detection probability is therefore $\sum_{i=1}^{2} p_i(1 - \exp(\alpha_i z_i))$ and we maximize this expression with respect to x(i) subject to the limit (3.5) on search costs. In general, when there are K cells to be searched and the detection probabilities $p(z_i)$ are independent from one cell to another, the optimal search problem is a nonlinear program:

$$\text{Max} \sum_{i=1}^{K} p_i p(z_i)$$

subject to (3.5)

where p_i is the probability that the target is in cell i, i = 1, 2, ..., K.

Two comments may be made about these probability-based measures of risk-aversion. First, they assume specific probability distributions like the normal or, exponential and except for special cases these lead to nonlinear programming problems which raise computational questions. Second, the probablities may not always be empirical or objective, so that subjective probabilities or weights may also be conceived [39].

1.3 Nonparametric Measures

Measures of risk aversion which do not specifically require that we know the specific form of the sampling or population distribution are nonparametric in nature. Their uses can be characterized at three levels e.g. population level, sampling space and the latent or canonical variables.

At the population level, safety first rules [36] of different types have been applied in operational decision models under uncertainty. These rules assert that it is reasonable for an individual to seek to reduce as far as possible the chance of a disaster or ruin, when the outcome is probabilistic. However the relevant probability distribution is not known, hence the probability of ruin criterion cannot be applied. We apply therefore a distribution-free approach. For example, if the DM is concerned that profits z should not be less than z_0, then in default of minimizing the probability $P(z \leq z_0)$ we minimize its upper bound given by the Tchebychev inequality

$$P(z \leq z_0) \leq \frac{\sigma_z^2}{(z_0 - \mu_z)^2}$$

Since for stochastic LP problems with a deterministic constraint set R, profits are $z = c'x$ with mean $\mu_z = \mu_c'x$ and variance $\sigma_z^2 = x'V_cx$, this leads to the nonlinear programming problem:

$$\max_{x \varepsilon R} (z_0 - \mu_c'x)^2 (x'V_cx)^{-1} \tag{4.2}$$

This problem could be solved either by methods of nonlinear fractional functional programming or by solving the following saddle-point problem: find vectors x, $x^* \varepsilon R$ and scalars λ, $\lambda^* \varepsilon L$ where L is assumed to be a closed bounded set such that

$$F(x, \lambda^*) \leq F(x^*, \lambda^*) \leq F(x^*, \lambda) \tag{4.3}$$

where

$$F(x, \lambda) = (z_0 - \mu_c'x)^2 - \lambda x'V_cx$$

It can be shown that if an optimal solution exists for the problem (4.2), it can be identified by the optimal pair (x^*, λ^*) in (4.3), since the scalar function $F(x^*, \lambda)$ can be shown to be convex and monotonically decreasing function of $\lambda \varepsilon L$ for a fixed $x^* \varepsilon R$. If the denominator $D(x) = x'V_cx$ is assumed to be positive for all feasible $x \varepsilon R$, the convergence of $F(x^*, \lambda)$ to $F(x^*, \lambda^*)$ can be established by the computing sequence $\lambda_{k+1} = N(x_k)/D(x_k)$ where $N(x) = (z_0 - \mu_c'x)^2$ and x_k is the optimal solution vector of the concave program:

$$\text{Max } f = N(x) - \lambda_k D(x); \; x \varepsilon R, \; \lambda_k \varepsilon L$$

and as $\lambda_k \rightarrow \lambda^*$, $x_k \rightarrow x^*$.

Several extensions of the safety-first approaches have been recently made in models of risk programming [36] e.g., (i) use of bounds sharper than the Tchebychev bound, (ii) semi-variance or mean deviation around the median profit level in place of the variance term σ_z^2, (iii) use of reliability bounds from the class of distributions known as IFR (increasing failure rate) and DFR (decreasing failure rate), and (iv) use of bounds based on order statistics like extreme values.

When sample observations are available on vector $c_t = c_{jt}$, say T in number we may compute maximum profits z_t for each t and order them as $z_{(1)} \leq z_{(2)} \cdots \leq z_{(t)}$. Let F(z) be the cumulative distribution of the random variable z and $F_T(z)$ be the step function:

$$F_T(z) = 0, \; z < z_{(1)}$$

$$F_T(z) = i/T, \; z_{(i)} \leq z < z_{(i+1)}, \; 1 \leq i \leq T - 1$$

$$F_T(z) = 1, \; z_{(T)} \leq z$$

Then, the Kolmogorov-Smirnov statistic D_T:

$$D_T = \sup[F_T(z) - F(z)]$$

has a limiting distribution

$$\text{Prob}(D_T \leq r) \to 1 - \exp(-2Tr^2), \; r > 0$$

for large T, which is independent of the population distribution F(z), although it is required to be continuous. Here several choices of r implying different safety-first rules are available e.g. if $r^2 = \sigma_z^2/(z_0 - \mu_z)^2$ as in (4.1) we obtain Tchebycheff type bounds. Applications of nonparametric bounds under cost uncertainty and risk aversion include some of the following aspects: (i) cost implications of deviations from normalty [7], (ii) use of relative distance $[F_T(z) - F(z)]/F(z)$ in stochastic programming [48], (iii) reliability analysis where the probablity of a large deviation needs to be avoided and (iv) comparing distributions of optimal profits across firms foreach of which an LP model is computed [44].

The use of canonical variates as proxy scores for comparing optimal solutions of two or more mathematical programs is generally attempted at two levels, either in the beginning for stratification or screening or at the end when measuring the similarity or dissimilarity of two solution vectors. The first case aries when we have for example a large number of firms or a large number of activities. Using principal components or similar methods we here reduce the problem to a smaller dimension. composite index of resources may thus be constructed in terms of which the efficiency of firms may be evaluated through LP models [42, 45]. Secondly, the similarity or dissimilarity of two or more portfolios may be compared e.g. Farrar [16] has compared actual portfolios (x_{ij}) by means of the distance measure

$$d_{ik} = [\frac{1}{n} \sum_{j=1}^{n} (x_{ij} - x^*_{kj})^2]^{\frac{1}{2}} \tag{4.4}$$

where x_{ij} is the i-th actual portfolio's investment in security j (j = 1, 2, ..., n) where $\sum_j x_{ij} = 1$ and x^*_{kj} is the proportion of k-th optimal portfolio invested in security j where $\sum_j x^*_{kj} = 1$. Note that the distance measure is very similar to the i-th actual portfolio's standard deviation or standard error of estimate when the k-th optimal portfolio is used as the standard of comparison. Simulation data were used to cmpute d_{ik} in (4.4), where similarity is indicated by a low value and dissimilarity by a high value, when rank order correlation is computed on the basis of these values.

Another example is from the brand loyalty model used in marketing literature in various forms [50]. Assume there are three brands of a product with $y_j(t)$ denoting the proportion sold of brand j at time point t. Let p_{ij} be the transition probability for a switch from brand i to brand j, assumed to be constant. The brand switching model is of the form

$$y_j(t) = \sum_{i=1}^{3} p_{ij} y_i(t - 1) + \varepsilon_j(t) \tag{4.5}$$

where $\varepsilon_j(t)$ is the stochastic component assumed to be independently distributed with zero mean and constant variance and $\sum_j p_{ij} = 1$, $p_{ij} \geq 0$. Given the observed data on $y_j(t)$, the regression estimates $\hat{p}$ of p_{ij} may be used to test the hypothesis of brand loyalty e.g. if the inequality $\hat{p}_{11} > \hat{p}_{12} + \hat{p}_{13}$ holds with a significance level 0.95 or more, then the diagonal element $\hat{p}_{ii}$ has a row dominance; likewise we test $\hat{p}_{11} > \hat{p}_{21} + \hat{p}_{31}$ for column dominance.

Note that in (4.4) and (4.5) no specific distributional assumption is made and to that extent they provide only a measure of similarity or dissimilarity. In the transition probability model (4.5), the observed proportions $y_j(t)$ are scores which may approximate the probability of N customers choosing brand j in a random experiment. This idea can be easily applied to stochastic LP models [42]. For example, assume that the constraint set R to which the output vector x must belong has three extreme points as basic feasible solution. Denote these points by vector x_i, i = 1, 2, 3. Let the random vector c in the objective function z = c'x change over time from c(t - 1) to c(t). Due to this change, the optimal solution vector may change from x^*_i to x^*_j or remain the same. If p_{ij} is the transition probability of switch, then one can write

$$x_j^*(t) = \sum_{i=1}^{3} p_{ij} x_i^*(t - 1) + \varepsilon(t)$$

where x_j^* is an optimal vector given the observation c(t) at time t. It is clear that robustness of specific optimal vectors x_k^* may be directly estimated from the transition probability matrix p_{ij} once these are estimated either from observed time-series data on c(t) or equivalent simulation data.

1.4 Informational Measures

From an applied viewpoint three types of informational measures appear to be important e.g. (a) entropy and related concepts, (b) value of information channels, an (c) Kalman-Bucy filters in linear quadratic Gaussian models of stochastic control.

The entropy and related information theoretic measures use a function

$$H = - k \sum_{i=1}^{n} p_i \log p_i \tag{5.1}$$

(or its contnuous analogue) where k is a suitable positive constant used for normalization and p_i is the probability of state i of a scalar random variable x. If x is a continuous n-dimensional vector with a multivariate density p(x), then entropy is defined as

$$H = - \int_{-\infty}^{\infty} p(x) \log p(x)\, dx \tag{5.2}$$

If the multivariate density p(x) is normal N(μ, V) with mean vector μ and a positive definite variance-covariance matrix V, then (5.2) reduces to

$$H = \tfrac{1}{2} n(1 + \log 2\pi) + \tfrac{1}{2} \log |V|$$

where V denotes the determinant of V. Further, if we define a linear transformation from the n-element vector x to an m-element vector y by means of a constant matrix A of dimension m-by-n:

$$y = Ax$$

then the entropy H(y) of y becomes

$$H(y) = \tfrac{1}{2} m(1 + \log 2\pi) + \tfrac{1}{2} \log \left| AVA' \right|$$

An information measure $I = I(f_1, f_2)$ related to this entropy concept and known as Kullback-Leibler information (KL) number is often used in multivariate statistics:

$$I = I(f_1 , f_2) = \int \log \frac{f_1(x)}{f_2(x)} \cdot f_1(x)dx \tag{5.3}$$

to separate or discriminate between two distributions having densities $f_1(x)$, $f_2(x)$ which may have generated the random observations on vector x. If the density functions $f_i(x)$ are each n-variate normals with mean μ_i and variance-covariance matrix V_i, then (5.3) reduces to

$$I(f_1,f_2) = \tfrac{1}{2}[\delta' V_2^{-1} \delta + \log \left| V_1^{-1} V_2 \right| - n + \text{tr.} (V_2^{-1} V_1)] \tag{5.4}$$

where tr. denotes the trace and $\delta = \mu_1 - \mu_2$ is the difference of the two mean vectors. Thus, if the KL number is very small (large), the two distributions are (are not) very close.

The informational measures have been used in applied and empirical work in at least four different ways:

(i) as a criterion of choice or discrimination among probability distributions [4, 11] e.g as a design criterion in optimum feature extraction and image processing problems, as a forecasting principle in econometrics, or as statistical distance for measuring the affinity of two distributions of a particular species in two ecological environments.

(ii) as a measure of the rate of information acquisition or transmission when specific communication channels are used [12] e.g., an optimal channel capacity may be defined for a decision-maker in terms of his maximizing an objective function W:

$$W = \sum_{j=1}^{M} q_j \sum_{i=1}^{N} p_{ij} U[a_i(j)x_i - cr]$$

where the channel has a rate of transmission r, c is the cost of channel capacity per unit, M messages can be conveyed in the channel with q_j, j = 1, 2, .., M as the unconditioal probability that the j-th message is transmitted and p_{ij} is the conditional probability that the (random) state of the world is i, if the message transmitted is j; $a_i(j)$ is the action taken for state i and message j and x_i is the associated reward in state i and $U(\cdot)$ is a concave utility function, assumed to be logarithmic.

(iii) as a measure of average amount of information. Thus, Lindley [25, 26] defines the average amount of information provided by an experiment e with data x and parameters θ by

$$I(e) = H_\theta - E_x\,[H_{\theta\, x}] \tag{5.5}$$

where

$$H_\theta = -\,E_\theta[\log p(\theta)],\; H_{\theta|x} = -\,E_{\theta|x}\,[\log p(\theta|x)]$$

$p(\theta)$ = prior probability density of parameter θ

$p(\theta|x)$ = posterior density of θ

This measure I(e) evaluates the sampling experiment x as prior uncertainty (entropy) minus expected posterior undertainty. It is clear from (5.5) that if θ and x are statistically independent i.e. $p(x,\theta) = p(x)\,p(\theta)$, then I(e) is zero; otherwise I(e) is nonnegative. Hence this measure, like Shannon's concept of information channel capacity cannot allow misrepresentation through faulty experiments. Let d_t denote the terminal decision and $u(e, x, d_t, \theta)$ be the utility associated with the event (e, x, d_t, θ) such that it is decomposable into two parts: u_s: sampling utility and u_t: terminal utility as:

$$u(e,x,d_t,\theta) = u_s(e,x) + u_t(d_t,\theta)$$

Then a cost of sampling: $c_s(e,x)$ can be associated with the pair (e,x) and a value of information can be defined as follows by u^o in case of no information and by u^∞ in case of perfect information:

$$u^o = u(e_o,x_o,d_t(o),\theta) = u_t(d_t(o),\theta) - \text{zero}.$$

$$u^\infty = u(e_\infty,x_\infty,d_t(\theta),\theta) = u_t(d_t(\theta),\theta) - c_s(e_\infty,x_\infty)$$

where $d_t(o)$, $d_t(\theta)$ are defined as

$$\int u_t(d_t(o),\theta)\, p(\theta)d\theta = \max_{d_t} \int u_t(d_t,\theta)\, p(\theta)d\theta$$

and

$$u_t(d_t(\theta),\theta) = \max_{d_t} u_t(d_t,\theta)$$

thus the terminal opportunity loss of a decision $d_t(o)$ with no information is given by the nonnegative quantity: $u_t(d_t(\theta),\theta)$. This is the value $v(\theta)$ of perfect information resulting from the event $(e_\infty, x_\infty, d_t(\theta), \theta)$. The expectation of this value of perfect information, $E_\theta[v(\theta)]$ taken over the prior density $p(\theta)$ thus defines the a priori value of a message conveyed by the state of nature θ say. Thus

$$\text{EVPI} = \int v(\theta)\, p(\theta) d\theta \geq 0 \tag{5.6}$$

It is clear that the expected value of any information structure intermediate between null information and perfect information may likewise be evaluated through expressions analogous to (5.6).

(iv) as a measure of efficiency of an estimate e.g. Fisher's information matrix associated with the maximum likelihood method of estimation. Thus, if L is the likelihood function for estimating two or more parameters θ_i of a set of observations the information matrix $I = (I_{ij})$ is defined as

$$I_{ij} = \{E[\frac{1}{L}\frac{\partial L}{\partial\theta_i} \cdot \frac{1}{L}\frac{\partial L}{\partial\theta_j}]\}$$

This is widely used in the theory and applications of optimal design [10], which consider rules of allocating samples so that a scalar function of information matrix is maximized in some sense e.g. the trace or determinant of this matrix is maximized.

The applications of informational measures in Kalman filters and information channels of a team decision are extensively discussed in control theory literature [12]. The information structure for a quadratic problem arises as follows: a scalar quadratic objective function $f(u, x)$ is to be minimized by the choice of the control vector u, when the state vector x is not completely known due to incomplete information on the environment. One introduces an informational channel through the transformation H

$$y = Hx$$

where H is an m by n matrix, y is an m-element vector and x an n-element vector. Under incomplete information, the original objective function has to be modified e.g. we may minimize the expected value, $E[f(u, x)|y]$ for any given channel matrix. If the rank of H is zero, the information structure is null. But if the rank is n and m = n, then the information structure evolves over time i.e. increases or decreases, one could define sequentially optimal decisions. Also one can compare the two cases of null and complete information structures.

It is clear that risk aversion is introduced in the field of informational measures by several ways e.g., (a) through accepting estimates of parameters which are best in the sense of maximizing the information matrix as defined, (b) by decisions which maximize the average amount of information (5.5), (c) by selecting transmission of messages in a channel by maximizing a logarithmic utility function and (d) by adopting Kalman filter and other adaptive methods of sequential controls which updates successive controls using posterior data and information etc.

1.5 Measures of Diversity

Measures of diversity have been widely used in market structure analysis in economics and ecological distribution of species in natural environments. Concentration of firms with an industry or of a particular brand among several brands in a market have been analyzed as a measure of dominance and its effects on market performance e.g. price-spreads or advertising discussed. Product diversification or market segmentation by brands has been analyzed as a risk averse attitude to cope with the uncertainties of duopolistic and monopolistic competition [24, 27].

In ecology, indices of dominance in a many-species community have been analyzed in order to consider its effects on the structure and evolution of such a community. For example an index due to Simpson [32]

$$H_\alpha = (1 - \alpha)^{-1} \log \sum_{i=1}^{\infty} p_i^\alpha \quad , \quad \alpha > 0$$

where p_i is the probability that the species belongs to a particular class-size x_i, $\Sigma p_i = 1$ leads to a measure of concentration H_2 for $\alpha \to 1.0$

$$H_2 = - \log \lambda, \quad \lambda = \Sigma p_i^2 \tag{6.1}$$

where λ describes the probability that any two individuals selected at random will belong to the same species. The index of diversity is $(1 - \lambda)$ or, the function H_2 itself. For a finite collection of species, an appropriate index is

$$H = N^{-1} \log \frac{N!}{\sum_{i=1}^{n} N_i}$$

where N_i is the number of individuals of the i-th species and N is the total in the whole collection. This index is empirically analyzed if the behavior of species is in equilibrium in a distributional sense, where the term behavior means the total interaction between a species and its environment that results in a given spatial and temporal distribution. Sources of disequilibrium are traced to (a) crowding or clumping, (b) random removal of individuals, thus affecting the size and shape of the original distribution (c) partial migration and (d) truncation in the pattern of interaction between two or more species in their natural distributions [30]. The equilibrium distributions found in some natural environments evidence stability in population dynamics, where stability measures the tendency that the scale parameter e.g. variance of the species distribution remains more or less constant. Indirectly this reflects a risk averse behavior in species distributions, since migration and other natural tendencies tend to reinforce the state of the equilibrium distribution.

For two or more species distributions within a community, the diversity measure may be related to measures of distance or entropy. For example, denote by F_1, F_2 two cumulative distributions over the nonnegative integers with associated probabilities p_{ij} i.e.,

$\sum_{j=0}^{\infty} p_{ij} = 1$ for $i = 1, 2$, then the following two measures have been frequently applied in statistical ecology:

$$C_\lambda \text{ - measures: } 2 \sum_{j=0}^{\infty} p_{1j}p_{2j} / (\sum_j p_{1j}^2 + \sum p_{2j}^2) \tag{6.2}$$

$$\rho \text{ - measures: } \sum_{j=0}^{\infty} (p_{1j}\, p_{2j})^{\frac{1}{2}}$$

These measures have continuous analogues, although infrequently used in ecology. Based on the C_λ measure the quantity, $\lambda_i = \sum_{j=0}^{\infty} p_{ij}^2$, often termed by ecologists a measure of clumping has been mentioned before in (6.1), where $1 - \lambda_i$ is a measure of diversity. The ρ-measure specifies the correlation between the two species distributions.

The pattern of ecological species distributios, which evidence risk-averse behavior in maintaining equilibrium may be closely related to the index of concentration in the size distribution of firms in an industry. Denote by s_i the share of firm i in total industry sales of a product, then the index Σs_i^2, $i = 1, 2, \ldots,$

n used to measure diversity in market structure [50] is seen to be nothing other than the λ measure of concentration mentioned in (6.1).

A more interesting measure of diversity in consumer choice is provided by the existence of several brands of a product sold in a market, that is either spatially separated or monopolistically competitive [24]. In either case, it has been argued that product differentiation and the associated advertising strategies for building brand loyalties are normally expected behavior for producers who are averse to risks due to fluctuations in sales and profits. Sources of such risk-averse optimizing behavior have been traced however to different factors e.g., (a) the existence of specific distribution like Beta for brand loyalty parameter in consumer purchases, although the market share of the brand remains constant [34], (b) the profitability of the practice of price discrimination in a case where fixed costs are not negligible [47], (c) the varying price elasticities of demand for different spatial boundaries of a product market [24], (d) the need for diversification and risk spreading in the financial and market portfolio structure of firms [53].

The absence of perfectly competitive markets for contingent claims due to the nonexistence of appropriate insurance schemes for risk spreading may lead however to adverse selection and distribution of risks among individuals or firms. This may give rise to skewness in risk distribution requiring policy interventions and improved social insurance schemes [53].

1.6 Multivariate Measures

Risk-aversion measures discussed before are all univariate, because they are either scalars or may be reduced to scalars e.g. entropy or distance measures. Multivariate measures are needed when risk aversion is measured by a vector or a matrix. For instance, let R be the variance-covariance matrix, also called risk matrix [22] of the standard least squares estimate $\hat{\beta}$ of the linear regression equation $y = X\beta + e$:

$$R = E[(\hat{\beta} - \beta)(\hat{\beta} - \beta)'] \tag{6.3}$$

where $R = (X'X)^{-1}$. Suppose the observations $x(i)$, $i = 1, 2, \ldots, g$ are grouped into g strata with N_i observations in group i and $N = \sum_{i=1}^{g} N_i$, then the overall mean $\bar{x}$ which corresponds to mean response

$$\bar{y} = \bar{x}'\beta \; ; \; N\bar{y} = \Sigma y(i), \; N\bar{x} = \Sigma x(i)$$

satisfies the relation

$$\bar{x} = \sum_{i=1}^{g} \left(\frac{N_i}{N}\right) x(i)$$

where each x(i) is a k-variate column vector and there are k response parameters in vector β. The risk matrix R now becomes function $R(p_1, p_2, \ldots, p_g)$ of the allocation proportions $p_i = N_i/N$. If these proportions are decision variables how should they be chosen in some optimal sense? This question has several implications for optimizing behavior under risk e.g.,

(i) in optimal design theory [10], the allocations p_i which are the spectrum of the design are so selected that a suitable scalar function of risk matrix is minimized e.g. trace of the risk matrix.

(ii) in item selection problem, the allocation p_i may be chosen by the additional condition that only $k_1 < k$ of the total k items are to be selected by an optimizing criterion e.g. in the active approach of stochastic linear programming, the DM may have chosen to produce m out of n $(m < n)$ outputs

(iii) minimum norm quadratic unbiased estimates for β may be used [42]; other estimators known as James and Stein type minimax estimators [22] may also be considered when the response coefficients β are not all nonrandom.

A multivariate measure of risk aversion is needed very naturally in a team decision problem, when the different members of a team have different risk preference functions e.g.

$$u(i) = m(i)'x(i) - r_i\, x(i)'V(i)x(i)$$

where there are N members $i = 1, 2, \ldots, N$ in a team, each with a risk aversion parameter $r_i > 0$. The perceptions of the mean m(i) and variance-covariance V(i) of the state vector c(i) are different and hence their optimal decison vectors $x^*(i)$ will be different. Cases of complete cooperation may be compared with no cooperation in information structures, where the former may imply for example a common value r, a common mean m and a common variance-covariance matrix V. Risk pooling and risk spreading may be discussed very naturally in the context of this type of multicriteria decision problems under risk [39]. Note however that risk aversion characteristics are now indicated in terms of the closeness of r_i, V(i), m(i) to r, V, m where the latter is the risk averse behavior under complete sharing of information structures.

A very different type of characterization of multivariate risk aversion may be proposed by following the approach of James [18], which uses the variance information manifold. Let $z' = (z_1, z_2, \ldots, z_N)$ be a vector with N elements, so that $z_i = z_i(\theta)$ denotes the payoff for member $i = 1, 2, \ldots, N$ which is assumed to depend on a set of random parameters θ. Then the N dimensional vector z has a mean μ and variance V, where the variance-covariance matrix V forms a convex cone in $\frac{1}{2}N(N+1)$ dimensional Euchidean space $R^{\frac{1}{2}N(N+1)}$. Each nonsingular variance-covariance matrix V is associated with an information matrix $J = V^{-1}$. The variance information manifold is then characterized by the space in which each interior point has alternative coordinate matrices V or J^{-1}. The set of singular positive semidefinite matrices when V is singular constitutes part of the boundary of this manifold. A concept of geodesic distance is introduced in this manifold by:

$$D = [\sum_{i=1}^{N} (\log \lambda_i)^2]^{\frac{1}{2}} \tag{6.5}$$

where λ_i are the N characteristic roots of the determinantal equations

$$|V_2 - \lambda V_1| = 0 \tag{6.6}$$

where V_2, V_1 are any two positive definite symmetric matrices, representing here the variance-covariance matrices of the team. Several implications of this distance concept are useful in applied decision models under uncertainty e.g.,

(i) If V_1 represents complete information structure, whereas V_2 is for any other information structure, the above distance measure would specify the value of complete information,

(ii) If the vector z is normally distributed $N(\mu, V)$, $V = V_1$ and V_2 is the sample estimate obtained by maximum likelihood, then the statistic

$$d^2 = \tfrac{1}{2}N \sum_{i=1}^{N} (\log \lambda_i)^2 \tag{6.7}$$

is asymptotically distributed as a Chi-square variate with degrees of freedom $N(N+1)/2$. Using this statistic, one could test the similarity or dissimilarity of alternative estimates like V_2,

(iii) If the output vector $x' = (x(1), x(2), \ldots, x(N))$ of dimension k varies due to unequal risk aversion r_i, then one may compare in terms of this geodesic distance any two variance-covariance matrices $V_1(x)$, $V_2(x)$, and

(iv) a complementary set of bilinear stochastic programming problems may be set up and analyzed [41].

2. Risk Aversion in Economic Models

From an applied viewpoint, risk aversion hypotheses have played important roles in the specification and empirical estimation of economic models and the decision rules following therefrom. At the general level some of the following tendencies may be clearly identified:

A. Economic Theory

a. risk aversion in consumer and producer behavior in static and dynamic contexts and its comparison or contrast with deterministic equilibrium and its ability [1, 42].

b. adjustment costs and lags due to divergence of equilibrium and fluctuations of demand or other parameters of the environment e.g. invetory adjustments [42].

c. incomplete information and learning behavior, particularly in dynamic contexts when myopic or short run optimality may differ from long run optimality.

d. gains from policies aimed at reducing uncertainties and fluctuations in the environment e.g. commodity price stabilization policies.

e. gains from optimal diversification of risk-bearing securities through competitive allocation and distribution arrangements e.g. efficiency in Arrow-Debreu markets for contingent claims.

B. Planning Models

In economy-wide models of investment planning [44], aversion to fluctuations in demand and other conditions of uncertainty and bottlenecks in different sectors has been specifically built into the planning models through safety reserves and policies designed to stabilize the system. Thus in the context of the consumption turnpike theorem [29] on optimal growth, Morishima has suggested the need for incorporating into the objective function a strong aversion to fluctuations in sectoral output by minimizing for every sector j:

$$S_j(T) = T^{-1} \left[\sum_{t=1}^{T} \left\{ \frac{y_j(t)}{l_j(t)} - \frac{\bar{y}_j}{\bar{l}_j} \right\} \right]$$

the average of deviations of per capita output $y_j(t)/l_j(t)$ from its equilibrium or optimal value. This of course assumes that a more stabilized stream of outputs is preferred to those with fluctuations.

Sharing of the risk of fluctuations as between sectors becomes more critical, when the planning model has regional breakdowns and the framework is a mixed economy.

C. Supply Response

Recent econometric studies [23] have emphasized the importance of price and yield variabilty on farmer's production decisions and risk elements have been directly introduced through indicators such as price and yield variance. Thus Richard Just [23] has generalized the econometric form of a supply function in the framework of an adaptive expectations distributed lag model by including quadratic lag terms indicating risk aversion. Thus supply at time t, y_t is of the form

$$y_t = a_0 + \sum_i a_i x^*_{it} + \sum_{i=1}^{k} b_i w_{it} + e_t$$

where

$$x^*_t = \alpha \sum_{j=0}^{\infty} (1 - \alpha)^j$$

$$w^*_{it} = \beta \sum_{j=0}^{\infty} (1 - \beta\ j[x_{i,t-j-1} - x^*_{i,t-j-1})^2$$

Here x^*_t, w^*_t are vectors of explanatory variables, the first of which may represent the decision makers' subjective expectations about the mean price and yields on which the decisions on production or acreage allocation i.e. y_t are based, while the element w^*_{it} of w^*_t may denote his subjective evaluation of the variances of prices and yields.

Empirical applications [40] of such risk averse supply functions in agriculture show several interesting features e.g., (a) risk aversion may be partly subjective and partly objective, the latter being derived from the variance of past observed prices, (b) risk aversion parameter may vary significantly from small to large farms, and (c) corp diversification and acreage substitution reflect the risk averse behavior more strongly, when the intensity of price fluctuations is more severe.

D. Production Allocation Behavior

Linear and quadratic programming problems have been widely applied in determining optimal resource-mix and output-mix in production and allocation models [42]. Quadratic models have specified in their objective functions a quadratic component indicating risk aversion either explicitly through a parameter λ in the risk preference function (2.2) or, implicitly through adjustment costs reflecting price response under conditions of imperfect competition. For LP models however, risk aversion is implicitly observed through output-diversification e.g. change where λ_i are the N characteristic roots of the determinantal equations

$$\left| V_2 - \lambda V_1 \right| = 0 \tag{6.6}$$

where V_2, V_1 are any two positive definite symmetric matrices, representing here the variance-covariance matrices of the team. Several implications of this distance concept are useful in applied decision models under uncertainty e.g.,

(i) If V_1 represents complete information structure, whereas V_2 is for any other information structure, the above distance measure would specify the value of complete information,

(ii) If the vector z is normally distributed $N(\mu, V)$, $V = V_1$ and V_2 is the sample estimate obtained by maximum likelihood, then the statistic

$$d^2 = \tfrac{1}{2}N \sum_{i=1}^{N} (\log \lambda_i)^2 \tag{6.7}$$

is asymptotically distributed as a Chi-square variate with degrees of freedom $N(N+1)/2$. Using this statistic, one could test the similarity or dissimilarity of alternative estimates like V_2,

(iii) If the output vector $x' = (x(1), x(2), \ldots, x(N))$ of dimension k varies due to unequal risk aversion r_i, then one may compare in terms of this geodesic distance any two variance-covariance matrices $V_1(x)$, $V_2(x)$, and

(iv) a complementary set of bilinear stochastic programming problems may be set up and analyzed [41].

2. Risk Aversion in Economic Models

From an applied viewpoint, risk aversion hypotheses have played important roles in the specification and empirical estimation of economic models and the decision rules following therefrom. At the general level some of the following tendencies may be clearly identified:

A. Economic Theory

a. risk aversion in consumer and producer behavior in static and dynamic contexts and its comparison or contrast with deterministic equilibrium and its ability [1, 42].

b. adjustment costs and lags due to divergence of equilibrium and fluctuations of demand or other parameters of the environment e.g. invetory adjustments [42].

c. incomplete information and learning behavior, particularly in dynamic contexts when myopic or short run optimality may differ from long run optimality.

like water, the shadow prices have been compared wit administered prices [46]; for other resources shadow prices have been compared with market prices to imply the optimal direction of adjustment in resource planning. Quadratic risk programming has been commonly used to analyze the impact of risk aversion on optimal production decisions in farm planning. These models have used a quadratic risk preference functin

$$f(x) = \bar{c}'x - \frac{\lambda}{2}\, x'Vx, \quad \lambda > 0$$

where $x \varepsilon R$: $\{x \mid x \geq 0,\ Ax \leq b\}$ is the decision vector, e.g., production or acreage allocation for different crops and $\bar{c}$, V are means and variance-covariance matrices of net prices. It is clear that if an optimal solution x_0 exists which corresponds closely with the actual behavior of farmers, then the shadow prices y^o can be approximated by

$$A_i' \, y^o = \bar{c}_i - \lambda^o \, V_i \, x^o$$

where $\bar{c}_i$ is the i-th element of the mean price vector $\bar{c}$, V_i, A_i' are the i-th rows of matrices V and A respectively and λ^o is that level of risk aversion which corresponds to x^o. It is clear that shadow prices $y^o(k)$ of different farms may differ, yet their average $N^{-1} \sum_{k=1}^{N} y^o(k)$ would be approximately close to y^o, so long as the farms are classified into relatively homogeneous groups [37].

It is clear that the above method can be applied to estimate the risk aversion parameter λ^o from a cross-section data of N homogeneous farms, each having a quadratic programming model with approximately the same degree of risk aversion. In this case we have to assume, as Wiens [52] did that the optimal shadow prices y^o are approximately equal to the market prices (y) and then the risk aversion parameter λ^o can be estimated as an average relation from

$$\lambda^o = A_i' y / V_i x$$

thus the empirical plausibility of a particular set of shadow prices and response of the decision makers to the gap $(y - y^o)$ between the two prices may be tested against empirical cross-section data on resource allocation and production. It is here that econometric testing of LP and quadratic programming solutions become very important [42].

3. Applications in Other Models

Applications of risk-aversion hypothesis in other fields, besides economics have ranged from an explicit specification in market research studies to the need for variance reducing techniques as a basis of reliable estimation. We attempt here a selective survey.

A. Market Research

Models of brand choice and the need for reliable estimates of consumers' purchasing attitude have been heavily dependent in market research studies on optimal classification and cluster analysis techniques [42], which may be based on some of the concepts of multivariate distance we have introduced in earlier sections. For instance, suppose it has been known that people can be grouped into several types on the basis of some information regarding their attitudes and buying habits. Let the scores for an individual on the variables of interest be denoted by a vector x. Then the squared distance from an individual to a group mean u_i for group i is

$$D^2 = (x - u_i)'C^{-1} (x - u_i)$$

where C is the common covariance matrix. Under the null hypothesis that this individual is truly a member of group i, this statistic is distributed as Chi-squares if u_i, C are known. Accordingly, one can estimate the probability of an individual being this dissimilar to each group mean, given that he is truly a member of that group. By allocating individuals in proper categories we can thus maximize the response from say a direct mailing campaign.

A similar procedure is followed in optimal pattern recognition schemes and learning algorithms. For example, there are K category regions, each represented by a n-dimensional random vector x assumed to be normally distributed. An unknown vector is encountered and we have to assign it to a category region so that it has minimum probability of error, assuming equiprobable categories. In this case the optimal classification rule is to assign the unknown vector x to that category having the largest likelihood function i.e. to that category k for which $p_k(x)$

$$p_k(x) = (2\pi)^{-n/2} \left|V_k\right|^{-\frac{1}{2}} \exp[-\tfrac{1}{2}(x-\mu_k)'V_k^{-1}(x-\mu_k)]$$

is largest, where μ_k is the mean vector and V_k is the variance-covariance matrix.

B. Reliability Analysis

Risk averson enters into reliability analysis for a multicomponent series at several levels e.g., (a) concept of reliability used for the whole system,

(b) provision of standby components and its relation to component reliabilities and (c) the procedure of maintenance or inspection activities. Models of geometric programming which attempt to maximize system reliability take a stochastic character [49] when some parameters of the failure distribution of components are probabilistic and optimal standby provisions may vary depending on which k items out of n (k < n) are selected. Sampling or inspection error aspects are most common in quality control [49]. As an example consider a case where defectives in both the sample and rejected lots are repaired. Then the cost of the decision to accept a lot containing u defectives after n items are sampled and x defectives found is,

$$T_a = c_i n + c_r x + c_a u$$

where c_i is the cost of inspecting an item, c_r the cost of repairing and c_a the cost of accepting a defective item. The cost of the decision to reject a lot is given by

$$T_r = c_i S + c_r(u + x), \quad S = \text{lot size}$$

when inspection error is present, the above expressions become

$$T_a = (c_i + c_r e_1)n + (c_r \varepsilon + c_a e_2)x + c_a u$$

$$T_r = (c_i + c_r e_1)S + (c_r \varepsilon + c_a e_2)x + (c_a e_2 + c_r \varepsilon)u$$

where $\varepsilon = 1-e_1-e_2$, e_1 = error type I, e_2 type II error

Depending on the probability distributin of errors optimum inspection plan for minimizing the expected cost of the sampling plan can be determined.

C. Insurance Business

Here the criteria of probability of ruin and minimax credibility [6] are used for minimizing actuarial risks. As an example of the latter, consider a quantity x_{ij} as the performance of risk $j(j = 1, 2, \ldots, N)$ in year i $(i = 1, 2, .., n)$, which is of interest for an insurance company which can classify risks into different classes j. The probability distribution $F_\theta(x)$ of x_{ij} is not determinate but depends on an unknown parameter θ. The decision problem for the actuary is to estimate the risk performance for risk k by a linear estimator $(\gamma Y+\delta)$ where

$y_k = \frac{1}{n}\sum_{i=1}^{n} x_{ik}$ is a typical element of Y and $y_1, y_2, \ldots, y_N$ are assumed to be distributed with a common distribution function $G_\theta(x)$. Note that θ is to be chosen by nature, the second player and we denote the joint density function of λ and θ by $dP(y, \theta)$. Then the decision problem can be recast as a game of the actuary against nature with a quadratic loss function

$$r(P,A) = \int[\gamma y+\delta-\mu(\theta)]^2 dP(Y,\theta)$$

$$= \gamma^2 v+(1-\gamma)^2\ w+[(1-\gamma)m-\delta]^2$$

where

$$v = E[\sigma^2(\theta)],\ w = Var[\mu(\theta)],\ m = E[\mu(\theta)]$$

$$\mu(\theta) = \int x\ dF_\theta(x),\ \sigma^2(\theta) = \int x^2 dF_\theta(x) - [\mu(\theta)]^2$$

Nature's strategies are $P = (v, w, m)$
Actuary's strategies are $A: (\gamma, \delta)$

It can be easily shown that

$$\inf_A r(P,A) = (vw)(v + w)^{-1}$$

$$L = \sup_P \inf_A r(P,A) = \frac{v_{max}\ w_{max}}{v_{max} + w_{max}}$$

$$U = \inf \sup r(P,A) = \frac{v_{max}\ \tilde{w}}{\tilde{w} + v_{max}},\ \tilde{w} = [w_{max} + (\frac{w_{max} - w_{min}}{2})]^2$$

Since U > L, the two-person game does not have a saddle point equilibrium in pure strategies. Hence a randomized strategy $(\tilde{\gamma}, \tilde{\sigma})$ for the actuary may be recommended as follows:

$$\tilde{\gamma} = \frac{\tilde{w}}{v_{max} + \tilde{w}},\ \tilde{\delta} = (1 - \tilde{\gamma})\ (\frac{m_{max} + m_{min}}{2})$$

A minimax randomized strategy pair allows risk diversification when the opponent (i.e. nature) chooses the strategies (v, w, m) from a parametric family $G_\theta(x)$.

4. Selected Empirical Applications

Three selected applications are briefly reported here to show the empirical plausibility of the risk aversion hypothesis: (a) the role of the risk parameter in a quadratic programming model of allocation, (b) risk aversion in supply response for selected field crops in California, and (c) optimal output-mix under incomplete information.

The first example [46] maximizes a risk preference function of the form

$$f(x) = \bar{c}'x - \frac{\lambda}{2} x'Vx, \lambda > 0 \tag{7.0}$$

subject to linear constraints: $Ax \leq b$, $x \geq 0$ and the empirical data for six crops in the Oxnard Plain, Ventura County over 1960-77 are utilized to test the hypothesis: Do the quadratic programming solutions correspond more closely to the observed allocative behavior than the LP optimal solutions? Denote the distance measure between vectors x and $\bar{x}$:

$$D^2(x, \bar{x}) = (x - \bar{x})'(x - \bar{x})$$

where the reference level output vector $\bar{x}$ is the observed average behavior computed over the years 1974-77 and the other output vector x may denote the LP otpimal solutions x_L or the quadratic programming solutions x_Q. Then for a value of λ = 2.0 the distance statistic takes the value 0.1154 for x_Q but 0.4314 for the LP solution. Further in terms of total variance we observe $x_L'Vx_L > x_Q'Vx_Q$.

The second example [40] uses an optimal output response derived from (7.0) as:

$$x = (\lambda V)^{-1} [\bar{c} - A'y] = g(\bar{c}, \lambda, V, y) \tag{7.2}$$

where y is the shadow price vector which may be approximated by the average market prices for inputs. Assuming that observed variances $\tilde{V} = \lambda V$ are inclusive of the effect of risk aversion, the optimal supply relation (7.2) can be linearly approximated by

$$x_i(t) = a_{io} + a_{i1}\, x_i(t-1) + a_{i2}\, p_i(t-1) + a_{i3}\, v_i(t-1)$$

$$+ a_{i4}\, y_i(t) + e_i(t)$$

where $p_i(t)$ are prices of crop i in year t, $\sigma_i^2(t)$ are variances computed on a three year moving average basis, and $x_i(t)$ are the areas under crop i. Five major crops: cotton, rice, wheat and sugar beets and sorghum for the San Joaquin Valley in California are considered for the years 1949-60. The estimates turned out as follows:

$$x_1(t) = -198842 + 0.56\ x_1(t-1) + 31303.8\ p_1(t) + 302.50\ \sigma_1^2(t-1) - 36156.7\ z_1(t-1)$$
$$R^2 = .866$$

$$x_2 = -9317 + .76\ x_2(t-1) + 775.8\ p_2^*(t-1) - 173003\ \sigma_2^2(t-1)$$
$$R^2 = 0.631$$

$$x_3(t) = -20567 + 0.40\ x_3(t-1) + 9079.1\ p_3(t-1) + 43619\ \sigma_3^2(t-1) - 1377.2\ z_3(t-1)$$
$$R^2 = 0.491$$

$$x_4(t) = -172883 + 0.66\ x_4(t-1) + 17358.6\ p_4(t-1) - 22326.8\ \sigma_4^2(t-1)$$
$$R^2 = 0.750$$

$$x_5(t) = 161 + 0.80\ x_5(t-1) + 26319.9\ p_5(t-1) - 1004240\ \sigma_5^2(t-1)$$
$$R^2 = 0.830$$

Here $z_i(t)$ are dummy variables for the mean price to reflect higher weightage for the positive derivations of price above the man price and p_i^* is the adjusted price to reflect substantial yield effect for rice. It is clear that except for cotton and rice, the supply response estimates have negative elasticity with respect to price risk measured by variance. For cotton, there is some evidence that the mean prices have more than offset the reduction in price variances. Note that the dummy variables $z_1(t-1)$, $z_3(t-1)$ uniformly show negative coefficients, reflecting the fact that the optimistic components of variance played an important role. Using a more detailed set of weights and dummy variables to reflect acreage control programs, Richard Jut [23] found negative supply elasticity with respect to price risk measured by variance for all the crops above.

In the third example [45] we have computed LP solutions, one for each of twenty agricultural farms from the farm management data for Burdwan, India (1972-73). Twenty farms were selected by first arranging 72 farms in terms of principal component indices, so that they are relatively homogeneous. There are nine crops and six major resources for each farm. Denote by z_i^*, z_i the optimal and actual net income (objective function) for each farm i = 1, 2, ..., 20. A linear regression over these values shows the result:

$$\underset{(-1.19)}{z^* = -216.7} + \underset{(20.5)}{1.158z} \qquad R^2 = .96;\ DW = 2.18$$

where the t-values are in parentheses. It is clear that $\partial z^*/\partial z = 1.158$ i.e. optimal exceeds the actual on the average by 1.158 times. When we compute a second set of 20 LP models, on the assumption that a standard set of technologies based on all 20 farms (i.e. a new input-output matrix A*) is available to each farm, besides its own input-matrix (A_i say) the regression result is as follows:

$$z^{**} = \underset{(0.92)}{860.8} + \underset{(5.41)}{1.566}z \qquad R^2 = 0.62; \quad DW = 1.86$$

where z** is the new values of the objective function. This shows that information and availability of new technology may improve the output efficiency to a considerable extent. Further, it was found that the empirical distribution function of z*, z and z** are normal by Shapiro-Wilk test and hence the null hypotheses H_0: $\bar{z}^* = \bar{z}$, H_0: $\bar{z}^{**} = \bar{z}$, where bar denotes average values were econometrically tested by the t-test and each were rejected at 1% level. This shows that standard econometric tests may be applied in suitable cases to optimal solutions computed from a cross-section sample of LP models.

References

1. Amihud, Y: "On the Consumer Demand Theory Under Uncertainty" in R. Henn and O. Moeschlin, eds.: Mathematical Economics and Game Theory: Essays in Honor of Oskar Morgenstern. Sprinter-Verlag: Berlin, 1977.

2. Arrow, K.J.: "Value and Demand for Information," in K.J. Arrow: Essays in the Theory of Risk Bearing. North Holland: Amsterdam, 1971.

3. Batra, R.N.: The Pure Theory of International Trade Under Uncertainty. John Wiley: New York, 1975.

4. Behara, M.: "Entropy and Utility," in G. Menges, ed. Information, Inference and Decision. Reidel Publishing: Dordrecht, Holland, 1974, pp. 145-154.

5. Binswanger, H.P.: "Risk Attitudes of Rural Households in Semi-Arid Tropical India," Economic and Political Weekly, June 1978, 49-62.

6. Buhlmann, H.: "Minimax Credibility," in P.M. Kahn, ed. Credibility: Theory and Applications. Academic Press: New York, 1975, pp 1-18.

7. Bury, K.V.: "Design Optimization Under Cost Uncertainty and Risk Aversion," Infor, 14, 1976, 250258.

8. Charnes, A., W.W. Cooper and D.B. Learner: "Constrained Information Theoretic Characterizations in Consumer Purchase Behavior," Journal of Operational Research, 29, 1978, 833-842.

9. Charnes, A., W.W. Cooper and E. Rhodes: "Measuring the Efficiency of Decision-Making Units," European Journal of Operational Research, 2, 1978, 429-444.

10. Chernoff, H.: "Sequential Analysis and Optimal Design," Society for Indutrial and Applied Mathematics: Philadelphia, 1972.

11. Chernoff, H.: "Some Measures for Discriminating Between Normal Multivariate Distributions with Unequal Covariance Matrices," in P.R. Krishnaiah, ed.: Multivariate Analysis III. Academic Press: New York, 1973, 337-344.

12. Chu, K.C.: "Designing Information Structures for Quadratic Decision Problems," Journal of Optimization Theory and Applications, 25, 1978, 139-160.

13. Debreu, G.: "The Coefficient of Resource Utilization," Econometrica 19, 1951, 273-292.

14. Duncan, G.T.: "A Matrix Measure of Multivariate Local Risk Aversion," Econometrica, 45, 1977, 895-904.

15. Fama, E.F. and M.H. Miller: The Theory of Finance, Holt, Rinehart and Winston: New York, 1972.

16. Farrar, D.E.: The Investment Decision Under Uncertainty, Prentice-Hall, Englewood Cliffs, NJ, 1962.

17. Hanoch, G.: "Risk Aversion and Consumer Preferences," Econometrica 45, 1977, 413-426.

18. James, A.T.: "The Variance Information Manifold and the Functions on It," in P.R. Krishnaiah, ed., Multivariate Analysis, Vol. 3, Academic Press, New York, 1973.

19. Johansen, L.: "Targets and Instruments Under Uncertainty," in H.C. Bos, H. Linnemann and P. de Wolff, eds., Economic Structure and Development: Essays in Honor of Jan Tinbergen. North Holland, Amsterdam, 1973.

20. Johansen, L.: "Parametric Certainty Equivalence Procedures in Decision-Making Under Uncertainty," Memorandum of Institute of Economics, University of Oslo, September 1979.

21. Johnson, R.M.: "Multiple Discriminant Analysis: Marketing Research Applications," in J.N. Sheth, ed., Multivariate Methods for Market and Survey Research, American Marketing Association, Chicago, 1977.

22. Judge, G.G. and M.E. Brock: The Statistical Implications of Pre-Test and Stein-Rule Estimators, in Econometrics, North Holland, Amsterdam, 1978.

23. Just, R.E.: "An Investigation of the Importance of Risk in Farmers' Decisions," American Journal of Agricultural Economics, 56, 1974, 14-25.

24. Lancaster, K.: Variety, Equity and Efficiency, Columbia University Press, New York, 1979.

25. Levin, R.D. and M. Tribus, eds.: The Maximum Entropy Formalism, MIT Press, Cambridge, 1978.

26. Lindley, D.V.: "On a Measure of Information Provided by an Experiment," Annals of Mathematical Statistics, 27, 1956, 986-1005.

27. Mardia, K.V.: "Mahalanobis Distance and Angles," in P.R. Krishnaiah, ed., Multivariate Analysis, IV, North Holland, Amsterdam, 1977.

28. Marschak, J.: "Elements for a Theory of Teams," Management Science, 1, 1955, 127-137.

29. Morishima, M.: Theory of Economic Growth, Clarendon Press, Oxford, 1969.

30. Patil, G.P. and others: Statistical Ecology, Vol. 1: Spatial Patterns and Statistical Distributions, Pennsylvania State University Press, Pennsylvania, PA, 1971.

31. Peleg, B. and M.E. Yaari: "A Price Characterization of Efficient Random Variables," Econometrica, 43, 1975, 283-292.

32. Pielou, E.C.: Ecological Diversity, John Wiley, New York, 1975.

33. Pratt, J.: "Risk Aversion in the Small and in the Large," Econometrica, 32, 1964, 122-136.

34. Pyatt, G.: "A Model of Brand Loyalties," in M.G. Kendall, ed., Mathematical Model Building in Economics and Industry, Second Series, Charles Griffin, London, 1970.

35. Schneeweiss, H.: "On the Consistency of Classical Decision Criteria," in Inference and Decision, Toronto University Press, Toronto, 1973.

36. Sengupta, J.K.: Stochastic Programming: Methods and Applications, North Holland, Amsterdam, 1972.

37. Sengupta, J.K.: "Regression and Programming: Overview of Linkages," IIMC Working Paper No. 16, Calcutta, 1976.

38. Sengupta, J.K.: "Adaptive Decision Rules for Stochastic Linear Programming," _International Journal of Systems Science_, 9, 1978, 97-109.

39. Sengupta, J.K.: "Multiple Criteria Decisions Under Risk," Working paper in Economics #132, University of California, Santa Barbara, 1979.

40. Sengupta, J.K. and R.I. Sfeir: "Risk in Supply Resource," Economics Working paper, University of California, Santa Barbara, 1979, to be published in _Applied Economics_, London.

41. Sengupta, J.K.: "Constrained Games as Complementary Eigenvalue Problems," _Journal of Mathematical Analysis and Applications_, 73, 1980, 301-314.

42. Sengupta, J.K.: _Decision Models in Stochastic Programming_, to be published by Elsevier-North Holland, New York, ca. 1981.

43. Sengupta, J.K.: "Constrained Nonzero-Sum Games with Partially Controllable Strategies," _Journal of Optimization Theory and Applications_, 31, 1980, July.

44. Sengupta, J.K.: "Stochastic Programming: A Selective Survey of Recent Economic Applications," Chap. 30, _Stochastic Programming_, ed. by M.A.H. Dempster, Academic Press, London, 1980.

45. Sengupta, J.K. and C. Ray Subhash: "Efficiency in Activity Analysis Models: Econometric Measurements and Tests," Department of Economics, University of California, Santa Barbara, 1980.

46. Sengupta, J.K. and R.I. Sfeir: "Allocative Behavior Under Risk Aversion Through Quadratic Programming Experiments," to be published in _Applied Economics_, 12, 1980, 367-375.

47. Spence, M.: "Product Selection, Fixed Costs and Monopolistic Competition," _Review of Economic Studies_, 43, 1976, 217-236.

48. Tintner, G. and M.V.R. Sastry: "A Note on the Use of Nonparametric Statistics in Stochastic Linear Programming," _Management Science_, 19, 1972, 205-210.

49. Tsokos, C.P. and I.N. Shimi: _The Theory and Applications of Reliability_, Academic Press, New York, 1977.

50. Vernon, J.M.: _Market Structure and Industrial Performance_, Allyn and Bacon, Boston, 1972.

51. Waud, R.N.: "Assymetric Policymaker Utility Functions and Optimal Policy Under Uncertainty," _Econometrica_, 44, 1976, 53-66.

52. Weins, T.B.: "Peasant Risk Aversion and Allocative Behavior: A Quadratic Programming Experiment," _American Journal of Agricultural Economics_, 58, 1976,629-635.

53. Zeckhauser, R.: "Risk Spreading and Distribution," in R. Zeckhauser et al., eds., _Benefit Cost and Policy Analysis_, Aldine Publishing, Chicago, 1974, 206-226.

54. Ziemba, W.T. and R.G. Vickson, eds.: _Stochastic Optimization Models in Finance_, Academic Press, New York, 1976.

CHAPTER 4

LINEAR ALLOCATION RULES UNDER UNCERTAINTY

1. Introduction

Linear models have been widely used in economic and other decision-making situations due to their simplicity and perhaps flexibility. For statistical estimation problems linearity has other advantages. In practical applications to real world data, linear models have to face two basic constraints. One is that the decision variables and sometimes the state variables have to be constrained in the sense of inequalities and hence the characterization of decision regions is very important. The second concerns the generating mechanisms of the linear model, e.g., it may be generated by a quadratic objective function as in the linear decision rule (LDR) approach [4], or in the team decision approach with a quadratic pay-off function [6, 10]; it may also be generated by the expected utility function as in stochastic linear programming [12, 18].

We shall examine here the implications of selecting a linear allocation rule (LAR) under a quadratic payoff function, when there is uncertainty in the environment. Uncertainty may be present in various forms, e.g., incomplete knowledge about the response parameters, incomplete specification of the decison rule under uncertainty and incomplete learning from sample estimates of parameters from a finite set of observations. It will be assumed throughout that uncertainty is representable by probability distributions, e.g., normal or Gaussian distribution. This has, among others, two practical implications. First, any distribution of information on the parameters would induce a distribution on the decision variables; hence the decision-maker may choose either pure or mixed strategies, conditional on the knowledge about the state of information available. Second, the shape and size of the distribution of decision variables may be partly affected by the allocation rules which in effect act as conditioning variables, e.g., these rules may serve to truncate the unconditional distribution of the decision variables, or introduce subjective correction factors.

We consider here three types of allocation models under uncertainty as follows. The first case arises through the active approach of stochastic linear programming (LP), where the decision-maker (DM) has to choose between K plans x(k), k = 1, 2, ..., K. The decision vector x(k) in each plan is solved from maximizing an expected utility function u(k) wich is quadratic

$$u(k) = m'(k)\, x(k) - \frac{\alpha(k)}{2}\, x(k)'\, V(k)\, x(k) \qquad (1.0)$$

where m(k), V(k) are the means and variances of the net price vector c(k):

$$c(k) = p(k) - v \qquad (1.1)$$

where thevector v of unit costs is assumed nonrandom. Different decision vectors x(1), x(2) say, may represent different resource allocation patterns, as in stochastic LP models [12, 18], or they may denote different strategies of the DM, when the environment is one of K populations (K = 2) with different means and variances [17]. In production problems x(k) may represent output vectors as functions of resource allocation rules and mechanism. For such situations in mind, it will be ssumed that the elements m_j, v_{jj} of m and V for every k satisfy

$$m_j \geq 0,\ v_{jj} > 0,\ v_{ij} \leq 0 \text{ for } i \neq j \tag{1.2}$$

This implies that components i and j are substitutes. Also, the nonnegative variable α(k) will be interpreted as a measure of risk aversion for the DM. Several interpretations of this measure are available in theory of risk [19].

A second example is from economic planning [5, 11], where the central resource manager allocates input vectors y(i) among N firms i = 1, 2, ..., N and computes net returns z(i) from the linear model

$$z(i) = y'(i)\ \beta(i) + \varepsilon(i) \tag{2.0}$$

where the disturbance term ε(i) is assumed to be independently distributed with zero mean and unit variance and the vector β(i) is the net average contribution. Several special forms of β(i) may be applicable, e.g., the form

$$\beta(i) = \beta + \xi(i) \tag{2.1}$$

where the disturbance term ξ(i) is distributed independently of ε(i) with zero mean and fixed variance V_ξ implying that the N firms do not differ in their expected net returns. The decision variables of the resource manager are the allocation vectors y(i), y(2), ..., y(N) to the N firms. This allocation y(i) must be nonnegative for each i and the total quantity of resource allocated must not exceed a fixed upper limit. We represent the allocation constraints as:

$$\frac{1}{2} \sum_{i=1}^{N} \{[y(i) - y(0)]' \ [y(i) - y(0)]\} = 1 \tag{2.2}$$

where y(0) is a suitable positive vector used for scaling; in particular y(0) may define the minimal level of resource allocation, so that the excess y(i) - y(0) = $\tilde{y}(i)$ represents the extra allocation to firm i. Any such extra allocation is to be justified however in terms of its marginal contribution to the overall goal. If the goal is to maximize expected total net returns (or net outputs), the resource manager's decision problem is to

$$\text{Max } E(\sum_{i=1}^{N} z(i)) = E[\sum_{i=1}^{N} (y(i) - y(0))' \beta(i)] \text{ subject to (2.2)} \qquad (2.3)$$

If $\beta(i)$ is known, it is easy to determine the optimal allocation rule. However, when only an estimate $\hat{\beta}(i)$ is available, with its standard errors the decision problem becomes more complicated. This is due to two reasons. First, the standard error of the estimates will affect the allocation rules and for that matter a quadratic loss must be admitted. Second, the allocations y(i) need not be thought of as pure strategies, e.g., randomized allocations through mixed strategies may be found, which may be better sometimes.

A third example is from the theory of team decisions [6, 7, 10], where there are n enterprises each with a single output and there is a single source of some scarce resource, which is an input for each of the enterprises. Let the output of enterprise i be given by the production function:

$$f_i\ (L_i, K_i, \mu_i(s)),\ i = 1, 2, \ldots, n \qquad (3.0)$$

where the first input L_i, say, labor is determined <u>locally</u> by the enterprise manager and the second input K_i, say capital is <u>centrally</u> allocated by the resource manager and $\mu_i(s)$ is a random variable independently distributed according to some probability distribution depending on the state of nature s. The production function (3.0) is assumed to be quadratic:

$$f_i = 2\mu_{iL}(s)L_i + 2\mu_{iK}(s)K_i - L_i^2 - K_i^2 - 2qL_iK_i \text{ with } |q| < 1 \qquad (3.1)$$

and the expected payoff for the team is assumed to a linear function of output:

$$Ew(s, d) = E \sum_{i=1}^{n} w_i f_i \qquad (3.2)$$

where E is expectation over states of nature s, d is decision rule and the weights w_i may each be set equal to unity, by fixing appropriate scales. The resource manager's allocations $K_1, K_2, \ldots, K_n$ must also satisfy

$$\sum_{i=1}^{n} K_i = k(s), \text{ each s} \qquad (3.3)$$

where $K_i \geq 0$, k(s) denotes the total available amount, indexed by s. Radner and others [8, 10] have developed the implications of alternative information structures, e.g., complete or incomplete communication among team members. One such information structure arises as follows: each enterprise observes the parameter $\mu_{iL}(s)$ of his own production function f_i, while the resource manager observes the total supply, k(s) of the resource to be allocated. It is assumed that $\mu_{iL}(s)$, $\mu_{iK}(s)$, k(s) are independently distributed with fixed means and variances.

We adopt here a different framework, i.e., a two-person nonzero-sum game framework. Player I is the decision-maker comprising n enterprises and the resource manager, their control variables being L_i and K_i. Player II is nature, who chooses the parameters like means and variances of the quantities $\mu_{iL}(s)$, $\mu_{iK}(s)$, k(s). This choice may be interpreted in two ways. In a Bayesian sense, the means and variances are themselves subject to a probability distribution. Alternatively, player II may be viewed as the conscious opponent choosing the parameters affecting the technology of output response and/or the state of the market. In the latter case, the state of the market has more than one population distribution and the means and variances of each $\mu_{iL}(s)$, $\mu_{iK}(s)$, k(s) may be different according as a particular population distribution is realized or not. The implcations of alternative allocation rules in this framework will be examined in terms of cooperative and non-cooperative structures.

Thus, the three allocation models have different, though interrelated objectives and focus. The first, which may be termed decision-making under many populations basically develops a comparative analysis for alternative allocation patterns. This analysis is very useful for questions of risk spreading or risk pooling and for analyzing the impact of risk averson on optimal decisions. The second type of model, which may be called treatment allocation for optimal estimation and regulation, basically formalizes the two-step procedure of simultaneous estimation and regulation. This analysis emphasizes the need for estimation from available information and hence would be useful in improving or updating decisions that are optimal in one stage but not subsequently, when more information or better estimates are available. Whereas the first type of model assumes the parameters given, the second brings in the question of statistical estimation from sample observations and therefore the quality of alternative estimators. The third model, which may be termed collective decisions under parametric games, focuses on the alternative solution structures that are possible in a game-theoretic set-up. This type of analysis may be useful in situations of complete ignorance, where sufficient observations may be unavailable for estimating the parameters in a statistical sense, or there may be structural change.

2. Comparative Analysis of Allocation Rules

For the quadratic expected utility function (1.0) the optimal decision vector x(k) for each fixed k can be easily computed as

$$x^*(k) = (\alpha(k))^{-1}\, V^{-1}(k)\, m(k)$$

$$u^*(k) = u(x^*(k)) = \tfrac{1}{2}\,\alpha(k)\, m'(k)\, V^{-1}(k)\, m(k) \qquad (4.1)$$

A number of implications of these linear allocation rules (LAR) may be derived. First, if the elements $v_{ij}(k)$ of the covariance matrix $V(k)$ follow the condition (1.2) of substitution and have diagonal dominance in the sense

$$d_i\, v_{ii}(k) > \sum_{j \neq i} d_j\, v_{ij}(k)\ , \text{ for } i = 1, 2, \ldots, n \qquad (4.2)$$

where $d_1, d_2, \ldots, d_n$ are any positive numbers, then there exists a unique optimal vector $x^*(k)$ satisfying (4.1) for every nonnegative vector $m(k) \geq 0$ such that $x^*(k) \geq 0$. Also, since $V^{-1}(k) \geq 0$ in this case, the optimal value $u^*(k)$ of expected utility given in (4.1) cannot be zero unless $x^*(k)$ is zero. Thus, the risk sensitivity of any element x_j^* of the optimal vector $x^*(k)$ may be compared as follows:

$$\frac{\delta x_j^*(k)}{\delta\alpha(k)} \leq 0,\ \frac{\delta x_j^*(k)}{\delta m_j(k)} \geq 0,\ \frac{\delta x_j^*(k)}{\delta v_{ij}} \leq 0 \text{ for } i,j = 1, 2, \ldots, n$$

Second, if the net price vector $c(k)$ is multivariate normal with mean $m(k)$ and covariance matrix $V(k)$, then the values $u^*(k)$ in (4.1) represent multivariate statistical distance, known as Mahalanobis distance, e.g., $D_k^2 = D^2(m(k), \mu; V(k)) = (m(k) - \mu)'\, V^{-1}(k)\, (m(k) - \mu)$ represents the distance of the vector point $m(k)$ from the center at μ. In the case of (4.1) the vector point μ is the zero vector so that we get

$$u^*(k) = \tfrac{1}{2}\,\alpha(k)\, D^2(m(k), 0; V(k))$$

The DM may use this result in at least two ways, e.g., in selecting the best among K normal populations and in statistical testing of any two plans say $x^*(1)$, $x^*(2)$. Assume that the risk aversion parameter $\alpha(k)$ is such that $\tfrac{1}{2}\,\alpha(k) = 1$ for all k, i.e., a common degree of risk aversion. Then the expected utility $u^*(k)$ associated with the plan $x^*(k)$ is the multivariate distance D_k^2 from the origin to the k-th normal population and hence they may be ordered as

$$0 \leq D_{(1)}^2 \leq D_{(2)}^2 \leq \ldots D_{(K)}^2 \qquad (4.3)$$

Thus the best plan $x^*(j)$ must satisfy the property

$$D_{(j)}^2 = \max_{1 \leq k \leq K} D_{(k)}^2$$

i.e., it is the selection with the largest value of D^2. Note that these selctions are to be interpreted as alternative allocations in the active approach of stochastic LP models, conditional on which the utility function is defined, i.e., the net return or profit $c'x$, conditional on the plan $x(k)$ chosen has the conditional normal distribution with mean $m'(k)\ x(k)$ and covariance $x'(k)\ V(k)\ x(k)$. For each k fixed, we compute the optimal solutions $x^*(k)$ and the associated values of $u^*(k)$ from (4.1).

Sometimes the selection may be based on the relative rather than absolute distance, e.g., let the K normal populations be homoscedastic, i.e., have a common variance V and define the relative distance measures δ as

$$\delta_1 = D^2_{(k)} - D^2_{(1)},\ \delta_2 = D^2_{(k)} - D^2_{(2)},\ \ldots,\ \delta_{(k-1)} = D^2_{(k)} - D^2_{(k-1)}$$

where $D^2_{(j)}$ is defined in (4.3). Thus, if δ^* is the threshold value of δ for separating the indifference and preference zones, the DM may choose the k-th ordered selection $x^*(k)$, if

$$\delta_{(k-1)} = D^2_{(k)} - D^2_{(k-1)} \geq \delta^*$$

i.e., the k-th optimal selection $x^*(k)$ is better than the (k-1)th one $x^*(k-1)$ by at least degree δ^*, when the set of selections is arranged in an ascending order (4.3).

The above selection rules may also be applied by the DM to statistically test the difference between two plans $x^*(1)$, $x^*(2)$, when independent sample estimates $\hat{m}(1)$, $\hat{m}(2)$ are available. Let these estimates $\hat{m}(j)$ be generated by n-variate normal distributions $N_n(m(j),\ V(j))$ with means $m(j)$ and covariances $V(j)$ and let $M(1)$, $M(2)$ be two matrices of order N by n of independent sample observations N in number ($N > n$). Then $Q = M(1) - M(2)$ is multivariate normal with mean $(m(1) - m(2))$ and covariances $V = V(1) + V(2)$. The null hypothesis is then that the mean of Q is zero and the appropriate statistic to use is Hotelling's T^2 based on (N - 1) degrees of freedom where

$$\frac{T^2}{N-1} = \bar{Q}' \left(\frac{S}{N}\right)^{-1} \bar{Q}$$

where

$$\bar{Q} = (\bar{Q}_i),\ \bar{Q}_i = \frac{1}{N} \sum_{t=1}^{N} q_{ti}$$

$$S = (s_{ij}),\ s_{ij} = \sum_{t=1}^{N} (q_{ti} - \bar{Q}_i)(q_{tj} - \bar{Q}_j)$$

q_{ti}: observations on matrix Q

The test statistic $[(N-n)/n(N-1)]\ T^2$ has the standard F-distribution with degrees of freedom n and N-n. The critical region will be $T^2 > T^2(f, n, \alpha)$ where $T^2(f, n, \alpha)$ denotes the tabular value of T^2 with degrees of freedom $f = N-1$ and the level of sgnificance α.

If the sample sizes are infinitely large ($N = \infty$) or can be assumed to be so, it is clear from (4.1) that $u^*(1) = u^*(2)$ only if $m(1) = m(2)$ and $V(1) = V(2)$, assuming of course that $\alpha(1) = \alpha(2) = 2.0$. In case $V(1) = V(2) = V$ but $m(1) > 0$, then $u^*(1) > u^*(2)$, since

$$u^*(1) - u^*(2) = D^2(m(1) - m(2), 0; V) + 2m(2)'\ V^{-1}\ (m(1) - m(2))$$

$$> D^2\ (m(1) - m(2), 0; V) > 0$$

Also, if $m(1) = m(2) = m$ but $V(1)$ is not equal to $V(2)$, then $u^*(1) - u^*(2) = D^2(m, 0; R)$ where R is the inverse of the matrix $[V(1)^{-1} - V(2)^{-1}]$. If there exists such a matrix R and it is positive definite, then

$$u^*(1) - u^*(2) > 0$$

For example, if V(1) and V(2) differ by a scalar h say i.e., $V(1) = hV(2)$, then $R = hV(2)/(1-h)$ is positive definite if $0 < h < 1$.

So long as the two plans x(1), x(2) generated, e.g., by two resource allocation patterns are different in their conditional distributions, the DM may combine them in the sense of a mixed strategy either in the parameter space or in the decision space. In the former case he defines mixed estimates m^0, V^0 as

$$m^0 = \lambda m(1) + (1 - \lambda)\ m(2)$$

$$V^0 = \lambda^2\ V(1) + (1 - \lambda)^2\ V(2) \qquad 0 \leq \lambda \leq 1$$

and computes an optimal solution x^0 by maximizing the expected utility function

$$u(x) = m^{0'}x - x'V^0x$$

which is normalized in respect of the risk aversion parameter. The optimal solution x^0 must then satisfy the following:

$$x^0 = \frac{1}{2} V^{o-1} m^0$$

$$u(x^0)) = m^{0'} V^{o-1} m^0 = \phi(\lambda)$$

where $\phi(\lambda)$ is a continuous function of λ in the domain L: $\{\lambda\ 0 \leq \lambda \leq 1\}$. Since the set L is compact, i.e., closed convex and bounded, there must exist maximal λ^0 and minimal λ_0 elements such that

$$\phi(\lambda_0) = u(x^0, \lambda_0) \leq \phi\ (\lambda^0) = u(x^0, \lambda^0)$$

Thus, if V(1), V(2) do not differ much but m(1) is much larger than m(2), it may be optimal to choose $\lambda^0 = 1.0$. The case of equal allocations $\phi(\frac{1}{2}) = u(x^0, \frac{1}{2})$ may be compared with the polar allocations $\phi(1.0) = u(x^0, 1.0)$ and $\phi(0) = u(x^0, 0)$ where

$$\phi(\tfrac{1}{2}) = [m(1) + m(2)]' [V(1) + V(2)]^{-1} [m(1) + m(2)]$$

$$\phi(1.0) = m(1)' V(1)^{-1} m(1)$$

$$\phi(0) = m(2)' V(2)^{-1} m(2)$$

Note that λ may be interpreted in two ways. First, it denotes the proportion of times the DM chooses the two strategies. This may be in response to nature's choosing two strategies c(1), c(2) in some mixtures. Second, it allows risk diversification in the face of complete ignorance when the two distributions with (m(k), V(k)), k = 1, 2 are not estimable with any degree of reliability or precision.

Due to the game-theory framework other types of solutions may also be characterized in such cases. Denote by $X = \{x\ x'e = 1,\ x \geq 0\}$ the set of solutions obtained by optimizing the expected utility function u(x), where e is a vector with all elements unity. Then the function $\phi(\lambda)$ can be rewritten as $\phi(\lambda, x)$ where any $x \varepsilon X$ may be chosen provided the set X is not empty. A minimax type solution may then be defined by

$$\max_{\lambda \varepsilon L} \min_{x \varepsilon L} \phi(\lambda, x) = \phi(\lambda^0, x_0)$$

whereas a maximax type solution is

$$\phi(\lambda^0, x^0) = \max_{\lambda \varepsilon L} \max_{x \varepsilon X} \phi(\lambda, x)$$

Thus, a minimax type solution $\phi(\lambda^0, x_0)$, if it exists may be interpreted as follows: For any $\lambda \varepsilon L$, the DM figures the worst, i.e., x_0 that can happen and then chooses λ^0 to make the best of the worst possible.

In the second case the DM combines the two plans x(1), x(2) in terms of the mixture λ, $0 \leq \lambda \leq 1$, i.e.,

$$x = \lambda x(1) + (1 - \lambda)\, x(2)$$

the associated objective function is

$$u(x) = \lambda\mu_1 - \lambda^2\, \sigma_1^2 + (1 - \lambda)\, \mu_2 - (1 - \lambda)^2\, \sigma_2^2$$

$$\mu_k = m(k)'\, x(k);\ \sigma_k^2 = x(k)'\, V(k)\, x(k),\ k = 1, 2$$

The optimal values $x^*(k)$, λ^* must satisfy the stationarity condition:

$$\lambda^*\, x^*(k) = \tfrac{1}{2}\, V_{(k)}^{-1}\, m(k),\ k = 1, 2$$

$$\lambda^* = \tfrac{1}{2}\, (\sigma_1^2 + \sigma_2^2)^{-1}\, [\mu_1 - \mu_2) + 2.0\, \sigma_2^2]$$

It is clear that the pure strategy solution $x^*(2)$ would be chosen to be optimal, i.e., $\lambda^* = 0.0$, only if σ_2^2 is zero, i.e., V(2) is a null matrix and $\mu_1 = \mu_2$. If the two plans have identical means $\mu_1 = \mu_2$, and variances σ_k^2 are positive, the proportions λ^*, $1 - \lambda^*$ are equal only if $\sigma_1^2 = \sigma_2^2$. Otherwise, the higher the value of σ_2^2 relative to σ_1^2, the higher the optimal value of λ^*. Thus the optimal mixture λ^* reflects in a sense the relative difference in means and the relative ratio of variances. For if $\sigma_1^2 = \sigma_2^2 = \sigma^2 > 0$ then the optimal mixture is

$$\lambda^* = \tfrac{1}{2} + (\mu_1 - \mu_2)(4\sigma^2)^{-1}$$

So far we have considered the K population problems, where we have to compare in some sense the difference between two or more populations or two or more allocation plans. We may now consider the more conventional case, i.e., a single population where $c = c(\theta)$ is the true value of the parameter indexed say by θ and $\hat{c} = \hat{c}(\theta)$ is a sample estimate obtained from observations. If c is given or known, the optimal solution is denoted by x, whereas if $\hat{c}$ is taken to be an approximation of the unknown true value c, then the optimal decision vector is $\hat{x}$. The expected loss function L or risk is defined as

$$L = \tfrac{1}{2}\, E[\hat{c}'\hat{x} - c'x)'\, (\hat{c}'\hat{x} - c'x)] \tag{5.1}$$

where the expectation is over the sampling distribution of vector $\hat{c}$. If the estimate $\hat{c}$ is unbiased, i.e., $E\hat{c} = c$, it may be natural to impose the condition

$$(E\hat{c})'\hat{x} = c'\hat{x} \gtreqless c'x = z_0 \qquad (5.2)$$

where may be interpreted as the desired target. Denoting the Lagrange multiplier for (5.2) by r and $\hat{G} = E\hat{c}\hat{c}$, $G = cc'$, the optimal decision vector $\hat{x}^*$ which minimizes the risk L in (5.1) subject to (5.2) is

$$\hat{G}\hat{x}^* = Gx + rc$$

$$L^* = L(\hat{x}^*) = \hat{x}^{*\prime}\ (\hat{G} - G)\ x = \hat{x}^{*\prime}Vx > 0$$

where V is the variance-covariance matrix of $\hat{c}$. If the optimal value of r is zero, i.e., the inequality $c'\hat{x}^* > c'x$ holds at the optimal, then

$$\hat{G}\hat{x}^* = Gx,\ L^* = L(\hat{x}^*) = x'Gx - \hat{x}^{*\prime}\hat{G}\hat{x}^* \geq 0$$

Note that if the estimate $\hat{G}$ is such that $\hat{G} - G/N$, where N is the sample size, then

$$\hat{x}^*/N = x + rG^{-1}c \qquad (5.3)$$

This shows that the average decision vector $\hat{x}^*/N$ equals the goal, x if r is zero. This may be seen more clearly by writing (5.3) as

$$\frac{E\hat{c}'\hat{x}^*}{N} = c'x + rc'G^{-1}c = c'x,\ \text{if } r = 0$$

Note however that $\hat{c}$ may not equal to c with probability one and so are the quantities $\hat{G}$ and G. The implications of the difference of $\hat{c}$ from c and of $\hat{G}$ from G may be evaluated in terms of the decision vector $\hat{x}^*$. If the true value c were known, the optimal choice is x, so the term c'x may be termed as the desired goal. The loss function (5.1) may then be interpreted as minimizing a quadratic cost of deviations from this goal. It is clear from (5.3) that short of knowledge of true c and the associated x, the DM's choice of $\hat{x}^*$ depends on this goal and $\hat{G}$, G and the Lagrange multiplier r, of which the optimal value is

$$r^* = (c'\hat{x}^*)^{-1}\ [\hat{x}^{*\prime}(\hat{G}(\hat{x}^* - x) + (\hat{G} - G)\ x]$$

It is clear that $r^* = 0$, if $\hat{G} = G$ and $\hat{x}^* = x$. Thus the deviation $(\hat{x}^* - x)$ of policy depends essentially on three factors: to what extent $\hat{c}$ differs from c, whether $\hat{G}$ equals G and the penalty price r, the Lagrange multiplier for (5.2) for example. In particular the unbiasedness condition (5.2) may not hold when the sample size N is very small. Let $\hat{c}_N$ be the mean estimate based on N samples for the unknown parameter c, such that $\hat{c}_N$ is not equal to c for sample sizes N. We then replace the condition (5.2) by

$$(\hat{c}_N - c)' (\hat{x}_N - x) \geq \varepsilon, \ \varepsilon > 0 \tag{5.4}$$

where $\hat{x}_N$ is the decision vector implicitly based on $\hat{c}_N$. The optimal decision rule is then

$$\hat{x}^*_N = \hat{G}_N^{-1} Gx + r\hat{G}_N^{-1} (\hat{c}_N - c) \tag{5.5}$$

$$r^* = [(\hat{G}_N \hat{x}^*_N - Gx)' (\hat{x}^*_N - x)]/\varepsilon$$

where it is assumed that at the optimal solution, equality holds in (5.2). It is now apparent that if $\hat{c}_N$ tends to c in the limit when $N \to \infty$ such that $\hat{G}_N$ tends to G, then $\hat{x}^*_N$ would asymptotically converge to the ideal policy or goal x. Otherwise the two decision vectors, $\hat{x}^*_N$ and x would differ, e.g., due to the gaps $(\hat{G}_N - G)$, $(\hat{c}_N - c)$ and r which depends on ε. The higher the value of $\varepsilon \to 0$, the greater the freedom of variation of $\hat{x}_N$ from the goal x and this increases the expected loss. Thus the decision vector $\hat{x}^*_N$ may be said to be ε-optimal.

The use of these LAR (5.5) is for updating and evaluating the risk cost of using small sample estimates, when the underlying sampling distribution is not known. For instance, the updated values $\hat{c}_{N+1}$, G_{N+1} may be easily derived as

$$\hat{c}_{N+1} = (N + 1)^{-1} [N\hat{c}_N + c_{N+1}]$$

$$\hat{G}_{N+1} = (N + 1)^{-1} [N\hat{G}_N + N\hat{c}_N \hat{c}'_N + c_{N+1} c'_{N+1}]$$

$$- (N + 1)^{-2} [(N\hat{c}_N + c_{N+1})(N\hat{c}_N + c_{N+1})']$$

$$G_N = 0, \text{ if } N = 1$$

where c_{N+1} is the sample observation from (N + 1)-st sample and $\hat{c}_{N+1}$ denotes the mean estimate. Using these updated estimates $\hat{c}_{N+1}$, $\hat{G}_{N+1}$ an optimal decision vector $\hat{x}^*_{N+1}$ can be determined in principle. Further, two optimal decision vectors $\hat{x}^*_N$ and $\hat{x}^*_{N+h}$, h > 0 can be statistically tested for their difference if any, by following some approximate tests. For instance, if $\hat{x}^*_N$ and $\hat{x}^*_{N+h}$ are asymptotically homoscedastic, i.e., have the same variance-covariance matrix, then the appropriate test statistic to use is Hotelling's T^2 for which numerical tables are available [14].

3. Estimation and Regulation by Allocation

In this case we have the allocation problem (2.0) through (2.2) and the resource manager has a vector of inputs, $\tilde{y}(i)$ in some normalized scale to allocate to ith firm, $i = 1, 2, \ldots, N$. The true response coefficients $\beta(i)$ are unknown and he can make only estimates of it from past observations T in number. Hence the decision problem is

$$\max J_1 = E \sum_{i=1}^{N} \tilde{y}(i)'\beta(i) \tag{2.3}$$

$$\text{subject to } \tfrac{1}{2} \sum_{i=1}^{N} \tilde{y}'(i)\, \tilde{y}(i) = 1$$

where the constraint of (2.3) implies that total input budget is limited and that each firm must be allocated a minimal positive amount. Assume that from past observations on $(z(i), y(i))_t$, $t = 1, 2, \ldots, T$ the resource manager forms a least squares (LS) estimate $\hat{\beta}(i)$ of $\beta(i)$, when $\beta(i)$ is an unknown constant and not random. The optimal solution is then $\tilde{y}^*(i)$ where

$$\tilde{y}^*(i) = \frac{\hat{\beta}(i)}{\lambda_0^*}, \quad i = 1, 2, \ldots, N$$

$$\lambda_0^* = \tfrac{1}{2} \sum_{i=1}^{N} \tilde{y}^*(i)'\hat{\beta}(i) \tag{2.4}$$

$$J_1^* = J_1(\tilde{y}^*(i)) = \sqrt{2}\, [\sum_i \hat{\beta}'(i)\, \hat{\beta}(i)]^{\frac{1}{2}}$$

and λ_0^* is the optimal value of the Lagrange multiplier associated with the constraint of (2.3). It is clear for any pair of allocations $\tilde{y}^*(1)$, $\tilde{y}^*(2)$ that

$$\tilde{y}^*(1) \geq \tilde{y}^*(2), \text{ as } \hat{\beta}(1) \geq \hat{\beta}(2)$$

Hence $\tilde{y}^*(1) > \tilde{y}^*(2)$ if $\hat{\beta}_j(1) > \hat{\beta}_j(2)$, i.e., the higher the estimated response for any activity, the higher the optimal allocation. However the allocation rules defined by (2.4) fail to capture the unequal standard errors of the estimates and to that extend they are not optimal. To see this, let us specify the response function for the i-th firm:

$$z_t(i) = \tilde{y}'_t(i)\ \beta(i) + \varepsilon_t(i);\ t = 1, 2, \ldots, T$$

and the least squares estimates $\hat{\beta}(i)$ satisfy the normal equations

$$M(i)\ \hat{\beta}(i) = q(i)$$

where

$$M(i) = \sum_{t=1}^{T} \tilde{y}_t\ (i)\ \tilde{y}'_t\ (i),\ q(i) = \sum_{t=1}^{T} z_t(i)\ \tilde{y}_t\ (i)$$

and the variance-covariance matrix $V(\hat{\beta}(i))$ of $\hat{\beta}(i)$ is

$$V(\hat{\beta}(i)) = M(i)^{-1},\ i = 1, 2, \ldots, N$$

Since $M(i)$ depends on the allocation vectors $y_{-t}(i)$, it is clear that the covariances of $\beta(i)$ could be affected by such allocation. Let p_t denote the probability of the event $\{\ \tilde{y}_t(i)\ \tilde{y}_t(i)'\}$, where

$p_t > 0,\ \sum_{t=1}^{T} p_t = 1.$ It is clear that each allocation matrix $M(i)$ may be

expressed as a convex linear combination:

$$M(i) = \sum_{t=1}^{T} p_t\ \tilde{y}_t\ (i)\ \tilde{y}'_t(i) \tag{2.5}$$

i.e., each $M(i)$ can be written as $M(\tilde{y}(i),\ p(i))$ where $p(i)$ denotes the probabilities appropriate to the i-th allocation. Since the estimate $\hat{\beta}(i)$ with highest precision has to be utilized, one may at first choose $p(i)$ such that $V(\hat{\beta}(i))$ is in some sense reduced and then use the estimates of $\beta(i)$ in deciding the allocations. But since $V(\hat{\beta}(i)) = M(i)^{-1} = M^{-1}(\tilde{y}(i),\ p(i))$ is a matrix, the concept of minimum is not unique. To give it uniqueness one may choose the generalized variance which is nothing but the determinant of $V(\hat{\beta}(i))$, or the trace of this matrix and minimize it by the choice of $p(i)$. In statistical theory, the optimal choice of probabilities $p(i)$ which minimizes the generalized variance, i.e., $V(\hat{\beta}(i))$ is called D-optimal designs [1, 15]. Using this approach, one may combine the two interrelated problems of efficient estimation and optimal allocation, the former in backward time T, T-1, ... and the latter in forward time T+1, T+2, ... Thus the two-stage problem is

$$\max J_2 = \sum_{i=1}^{N} \tilde{y}(i)' \hat{\beta}_T(i) - \tfrac{1}{2} \sum_{i=1}^{N} \tilde{y}(i)' M_T^{-1}(i) \tilde{y}(i) \tag{2.6}$$

$$\text{subject to } \tfrac{1}{2} \sum_{i=1}^{N} \tilde{y}(i)' \tilde{y}(i) = 1$$

where $\hat{\beta}_T(i)$, $M_T^{-1}(i)$ are estimates based on past T samples and the optimal solutions $\{\tilde{y}^*(i),\ 1 \leq i \leq N\}$ of the model (2.6) are to be applied in forward time. The optimal solutions are now

$$\tilde{y}^*(i) = [M_T^{-1}(i) + \lambda_0^* I]^{-1} \hat{\beta}_T(i)$$

$$\lambda_0^* = \tfrac{1}{2} [\sum_{i=1}^{N} \{\tilde{y}^*(i)' \hat{\beta}_T(i) - \tilde{y}^*(i)' M_T^{-1}(i) \tilde{y}^*(i)\}] \tag{2.7}$$

$$J_2^* = \tfrac{1}{2} \alpha + \lambda_0^*$$

where $\alpha = \sum_{i=1}^{N} \tilde{y}^{*\prime}(i) \hat{\beta}_T(i)$ is solved from the quadratic equation

$$\alpha^2 - \alpha \sum_{i=1}^{N} \tilde{y}'(i) M_T^{-1}(i) \tilde{y}(i)$$

$$- 2 \sum_{i=1}^{N} \hat{\beta}_T(i)' [M_T^{-1}(i) + \lambda_0^* I]^{-1} \hat{\beta}_T(i) = 0$$

Several implications follow from a comparison of the two optimal solutions (2.4) and (2.7), where the latter incorporates variance of the estimates $\hat{\beta}(i)$. First, an increase in the diagonal elements of the covariance matrix $V(\hat{\beta}(i))$ implies through (2.7) a decrease in the optimal value of $\tilde{y}^*(i)$ for firm $i = 1, 2, \ldots, N$. Thus, any two allocations $\tilde{y}^*(1)$, $\tilde{y}^*(2)$ would differ even if $\hat{\beta}_T(1) = \hat{\beta}_T(2)$, provided $M_T^{-1}(1)$ does not equal $M_T^{-1}(2)$. If $M_T(1) = M_T(2) = M_T(0)$, but $\hat{\beta}_T(1) \neq \hat{\beta}_T(2)$, then

$$\tilde{y}^*(1) - \tilde{y}^*(2) = [M_T^{-1}(0) + \lambda_0^* I]^{-1} [\hat{\beta}_T(1) - \hat{\beta}_T(2)]$$

This implies

$$(\hat{\beta}_T(1) - \hat{\beta}_T(2))' (\tilde{y}^*(1) - \tilde{y}^*(2)) = [\hat{\beta}_T(1) - \hat{\beta}_T(2)]' [M_T^{-1}(0) + \lambda_0^* I]^{-1} [\hat{\beta}_T(1) - \hat{\beta}_T(2)]$$

The right hand side may be expressed as the multivariate distance function $D(\cdot)$, known as Mahalanobis distance [16] as follows:

$$2D^2 (\delta_{12}, 0; V^a) = \delta_{12}'(V^a)^{-1} \delta_{12}$$

where

$$\delta_{12} = \hat{\beta}_T(1) - \hat{\beta}_T(2), \; V^a = 2M_t^{-1}(0) + 2\lambda_0^* I$$

Here V^a is total adjusted variance, adjustment being the term $2\lambda_0^* I$. If λ_0^* is zero (e.g., the constraint of (2.6) was not there), then one gets

$$2D^2 (\delta_{12}, 0, V^a) = \delta_{12}' (2M_T^{-1}(0))^{-1} \delta_{12}$$

where $2M_T^{-1}(0)$ is the sum of variances of $\hat{\beta}_T(1)$ and $\hat{\beta}_T(2)$.

Second, consider the constraint of (2.6) in inequality form, i.e.,

$$\tfrac{1}{2} \Sigma \, \tilde{y}(i)' \, \tilde{y}(i) \leq 1$$

and assume that it is not binding at the optimum in the sense that $\lambda_0^* = 0$, then the optimal solution (2.7) becomes:

$$J_2^* = \tfrac{1}{2} \sum_{i=1}^{N} \tilde{y}^{*\prime}(i) \, V(\hat{\beta}_T(i)) \, \tilde{y}^*(i) = \tfrac{1}{2} \sum_{i} \hat{\beta}_T(i)' \, V^{-1}(\hat{\beta}_T(i)) \, \hat{\beta}_T(i)$$

$$= \tfrac{1}{2} \sum_{i=1}^{N} D_i^2, \; D_i^2 = D^2(\hat{\beta}_T(i), 0; V(\hat{\beta}_T(i))) \qquad (2.8)$$

$$\tilde{y}^*(i) = V^{-1} (\hat{\beta}_T(i)) \, \hat{\beta}_T(i)$$

In the analogous case for (2.3), when variances are ignored but $\lambda_0^* = 0$ is assumed, the optimal solution is $\tilde{y}^*(k)$:

$$\tilde{y}^{*\prime}(k)\,\hat{\beta}_T(k) = \max_{1 \le i \le N} \tilde{y}'(i)\,\hat{\beta}_T(i) \tag{2.9}$$

$$\tilde{y}^*(i) = 0 \text{ for all other } i \ne k,\ i = 1, 2, \ldots, N.$$

provided the maximum is unique. However, since the optimal solution $\tilde{y}^*(i)$, $1 \le i \le N$ in (2.8) incorporates variances of $\hat{\beta}_T(i)$ in its optimization, it is more risk diversifying than the polar solution specified in (2.9).

Third, if one defines the convex linear combination (2.5) slightly differently, so that the variance of $\tilde{y}(i)'\,\hat{\beta}_T(i)$ is given a nonnegative weight w_i, $w_i \ge 0$, $\Sigma w_i = 1$, then another two-stage decision problem can be set up by the resource manager as follows:

$$\max J_3 = \sum_{i=1}^{N} \tilde{y}(i)'\,\hat{\beta}_T(i) - \tfrac{1}{2} \sum_i w_i \tilde{y}'(i)\,M_T^{-1}(i)\,y(i) \tag{3.1}$$

subject to

$$\tfrac{1}{2} \sum_i \tilde{y}\,(i)'\,\tilde{y}(i) = 1, \quad \Sigma\, w_i = 1,\ w_i \ge 0$$

where $M_T(i) = \sum_{t=1}^{T} \tilde{y}_t\,(i)\,\tilde{y}_t'(i)$ and the weights w_i may be inversely proportional to the variance of $\tilde{y}(i)'\,\hat{\beta}_T(i)$ estimated. It is clear from the linearity of w_i that the optimal values of w_i are

$$w_r^* = 1, \text{ all other } w_i^* = 0 \tag{3.2}$$

$$\text{if } \tilde{y}'(r)\,M_T^{-1}(r)\,\tilde{y}(r) = \min_{1 \le i \le N} \tilde{y}'(i)\,M_T^{-1}(i)\,\tilde{y}(i)$$

provided the minimum is unique. Like (2.9), this defines a polar solution: choose $\tilde{y}^*(r)$ as the optimal allocation since it has the estimated response $\tilde{y}^*(r)'\,\hat{\beta}_T(r)$ with a minimum variance. For any fixed choice of w_i's, the optimal solutions of (3.1) are:

$$\tilde{y}^*(i) = [w_i M_T^{-1}(i) + \lambda_0^* I]^{-1}\,\hat{\beta}_T(i)$$

$$\lambda^* = \tfrac{1}{2} \sum_{i=1}^{N} [\tilde{y}^{*\prime}(i)\,\hat{\beta}_T(i) - w_i \tilde{y}'(i)\,M_T^{-1}(i)\,\tilde{y}(i)]$$

Thus, the implications of equal weights $w_i = 1/N$, polar weights $w_r = 1$, $w_i = 0$ for $i \neq r$ and other stratifications may be directly introduced in the optimal allocation rule.

There is another use of the two-stage decision problem (3.1), i.e., in the form of a minimum variance strategy. This is specified for any fixed choice of w_i's as follows:

$$\min J_4 = \tfrac{1}{2} \sum_{i=1}^{N} w_i \tilde{y}'(i)\, V(i)\, \tilde{y}(i) \tag{3.2}$$

where $V(i)$ denotes $V(\hat{\beta}_T(i)) = M_T^{-1}(i)$. This may be compared with the optimal unbiasedness strategy in (2.3) and the mixed case in (3.1). The optimal solutions in (3.2) are:

$$[w_i V(i) - \lambda_0^* I]\, \tilde{y}^*(i) = 0, \quad i = 1, 2, \ldots, N \tag{3.3}$$

where $\lambda_0^* = \lambda_{0i}^*$ is the minimum eigenvalue of the matrix $w_i V(i)$, assuming $w_i > 0$. The minimal value of the objective function J_4 is

$$J_4^* = \sum_{i=1}^{N} \lambda_{0i}^* > 0$$

where each λ_{0i}^* is positive, if $w_i > 0$ and $V(i)$ is positive definite for each $i = 1, 2, \ldots, N$. Thus, according to this minimum variance strategy, two allocations $\tilde{y}^*(1)$, $\tilde{y}^*(2)$ will be identical, only if the minimum eigenvalues λ_{01}^*, λ_{02}^* of $w_1 V(1)$ and $w_2 V(2)$ are identical. Otherwise, the two will be different and in particular if $\lambda_{01}^* < \lambda_{02}^*$, the first allocation $\tilde{y}^*(1)$ would be more dominating than the second $\tilde{y}^*(2)$. The contrast with the unbiasedness strategy in (2.9) is apparent.

Two general comments may be added on these allocation rules under estimation. First, the programming framework may be more generalized, e.g., the active approach of stochastic linear programming [12] have considered additional constraints like $y(i) \geq 0$ and other decision regions including sampling distributions of $\hat{\beta}(i)$ which are not normal. Second, the N firms are here assumed to be passive to the resource manager's allocation problem; othereise if they develop cooperative or non-cooperative behavior, other game-theoretical solutions [16] would be found appropriate.

4. Team Decisions as Games

The team decision model (3.1) through (3.3) may be specified in a compact notation as follows: Player I maximizes

$$J = E \sum_{i=1}^{n} 2\, \underline{c}_i' \, \underline{x}_i - \sum_{i=1}^{n} \underline{x}_i \, V_0 \, \underline{x}_i \tag{3.4}$$

subject to

$$\sum_{i-1}^{n} N \, \underline{x}_i - \underline{b} = 0 \tag{3.5}$$

where $\underline{c}_i' = (\mu_{iL}(s), \mu_{iK}(s))$, $\underline{x}_i = \binom{L_i}{K_i}$, $V_0 = \begin{bmatrix} 1 & q \\ q & 1 \end{bmatrix}$

$$N = \begin{bmatrix} 1 & 0 \\ 0 & 0 \end{bmatrix}, \quad \underline{b} = \begin{pmatrix} k(s) \\ 0 \end{pmatrix}$$

E: expectation over the states s

V_0, N: matrices with known constant elements.

He assumes that the state of nature s follows a fixed distribution in the sense that $\underline{c}_i$ and b have fixed means and variances and thereby determines his allocation rules as follows:

$$\bar{c}_i - V_0 \, \underline{x}_i^* - \tfrac{1}{2} N' \bar{\lambda}^* = 0$$

$$\bar{\lambda}^{*\prime} (\bar{b} - \sum_{i=1}^{n} N \, \underline{x}_i^*) = 0 \tag{3.6}$$

with expected pay-off

$$J(\underline{x}_i^*) = 2 \sum_{i=1}^{n} \bar{c}_i' \, \underline{x}_i^* - \sum_{i=1}^{n} \underline{x}_i^{*\prime} \, V_0 \, \underline{x}_i^* \tag{3.7}$$

where $\bar{c}_i$ is the mean vector when s follows a particular distribution and λ is the vector of Lagrange multipliers associated with (3.5) with its expected value denoted by $\bar{\lambda}$ when s follows a given distribution.

For Player II however, the mean vectors $\bar{c}_i$, $\bar{\lambda}$ are not fixed once for all but subject to a choice mechanism, e.g., there may be more than one set of values of these parameters and both pure and mixed strategies may be chosen. Following the Bayesian approach, this choice set may be described by informative or noninformative prior distributions of parameters [8]. We prefer to adopt a slightly different approach, e.g., the characterization of the strategy by a distance function

$$\sum_{i=1}^{n} D^2(\bar{c}_i, \gamma; \Sigma) = \sum_{i=1}^{n} (\bar{c}_i - \underline{\gamma})' \Sigma^{-1} (\bar{c}_i - \gamma) = r_0 \tag{3.8}$$

where

$$\bar{c}_i = \underline{\gamma} + \underline{\varepsilon}_i \tag{3.9}$$

$$\underline{\varepsilon} \sim G(\underline{0}, \Sigma)$$

that is, each $\bar{c}_i$ is distributed around the industry mean γ, independently of each other and the errors $\underline{\varepsilon}_i$ have zero means and fixed variance matrix for all i. In Radner's example [10], this assumption (3.9) has been interpreted to mean that the enterprises are similar. However in our case the covariance matrix Σ need not be diagonal; also the constant r_0 may be increased or decreased depending on the perceived distance D^2. Setting r_0 equal to 1 we would take (3.8) in a more flexible form:

$$\text{either } \sum_{i=1}^{n} (\bar{c}_i - \underline{\gamma})' \; \Sigma^{-1}(\bar{c}_i - \underline{\gamma}) \leq 1 \tag{3.8a}$$

or

$$\sum_{i=1}^{n} (\bar{c}_i - \underline{\gamma})' \; \Sigma^{-1} (\bar{c}_i - \underline{\gamma}) \geq 1 \tag{3.8b}$$

Note that the multivariate distributin $G(\underline{0}, \Sigma)$ of $\underline{\varepsilon}_i$ need not be normal, although if it is normal, i.e., $G = N(\underline{0}, \Sigma)$ then the D^2-statistic (3.8) defines the well-known Mahalanobis distance commonly used in multivariate statistics. The distance function in (3.8) defined for arbitrary distribution $G(\underline{0}, \Sigma)$ satisfies the following properties

$$D^2(\underline{x}, \underline{y}; \Sigma) \geq 0 \text{ and if } \underline{x} \neq y,\; D^2(\cdot) > 0$$

$$D^2(\underline{x}, \underline{y}; \Sigma) = D^2(\underline{y}, \underline{x}; \Sigma) = 0, \text{ if } \underline{x} = \underline{y}$$

$$D^2(\underline{x}, \underline{y}; \Sigma) \leq D^2(\underline{x}, \underline{z}; \Sigma) + D^2(\underline{z}, \underline{y}; \Sigma)$$

For any two vector points $\underline{x}$, $\underline{y}$ in the space of the distribution $D^2(\underline{x}, \Sigma)$.

The decision problem for Player II is thus to choose the parameters $\bar{c}_i$ so that the expected payoff (3.7) is maximized (or, minimized) object to (3.8a) (or, (3.8b)). Let the optimal solution be $\bar{c}_i^*$ in the former case and $\bar{c}_{i*}$ in the latter case. The pairs $(\bar{c}_{i*}, \underline{x}_i^*)$ and $\bar{c}_i^*, \underline{x}_i^*)$ for $1 \leq i \leq n$ may be called minimix and maximax solutions of the game problem.

Clearly the minimax solution $\bar{c}_{i*}$ satisfies the Kuhn-Tucker conditions:

$$\tau\, \Sigma^{-1}\, \bar{c}_{i*} - \underline{x}_i^* = \tau\, \Sigma^{-1}\, \gamma$$

$$\tau(1 - D^2\, (\bar{c}_{i*}, \gamma; \Sigma)) = 0 \qquad (3.9)$$

$$\tau \geq 0$$

where τ is the Lagrange multiplier. But, for a given $\bar{c}_{i*}$, the optimal solution $\underline{x}_i^*$ of player I must satisfy the stationarity condition

$$\bar{c}_{i*} - V_0\, \underline{x}_i^* = 0 \qquad (3.10)$$

Hence, by combining (3.9), (3.10) one gets the saddle point condition:

$$V_0^{-1}\, \bar{c}_{i*} - \tau\, \Sigma^{-1}\, (\bar{c}_{i*} - \gamma) = 0 \qquad (3.11)$$

If we adopt the convention that $\underline{\gamma}$ is a zero vector, then the system (3.11) defines an eigenvalue problem:

$$\left| V_0^{-1} - \tau\, \Sigma^{-1} \right| = 0 \qquad (3.12)$$

where, from symmetry and positive definiteness of V_0, Σ all the eigenvalues are real and positive. Clearly the smallest eigenvalue, τ_* has to be chosen and $\bar{c}_{i*}$ must therefore be the eigenvector associated with this smallest eigenvalue.

In the analogous case for the maximax solution we have to choose the highest eigenvalue, τ^* and the associated eigenvector $\bar{c}_i^*$ satisfying

$$[V_0^{-1} - \tau^*\, \Sigma^{-1}]\, \bar{c}_i^* = 0 \qquad (3.13)$$

Clearly, the cooperative solution $(\bar{c}_i^*, \underline{x}_{i*}; 1 \leq i \leq n)$ differs from the noncooperative one, $(\bar{c}_{i*}, \underline{x}_i^*)$ if the eigenvalues are distinct, i.e., $\tau^* > \tau_*$ and hence the two solutions $\bar{c}_i^*$, $\bar{c}_{i*}$ cannot be identical. Several implications follow from (3.11) through (3.13). First, the noncooperative solution has for player I the interpretation of playing safe, e.g., he first considers the worst (i.e., $\bar{c}_{i*}$) that can happen and its probability is given by (3.8a) or (3.8b) and then assuming $\bar{c}_{i*}$ given, by arranging the eigenvalues $0 < \tau_1 < \tau_2 < \ldots < \tau_n$ and assuming them to be distinct, one could generate other solutions [13, 17]. Second, it follows from the saddle point condition (3.11) that any two firms can be compared in terms of their distances from $\gamma = 0$, since $D^2(\bar{c}_{1*}, 0, V_0) > D^2(\bar{c}_{2*}, 0, V_0)$ implies that $D^2(\bar{c}_{1*}, 0, \Sigma) > D^2(\bar{c}_{2*}, 0, \Sigma)$. Thus, V_0 which is assumed to be nonrandom in Radner's example may be compared with the covariance matrix. Rewriting (3.12) as

$$\left| V_0^{-1} \Sigma - \tau I \right| = 0$$

it becomes clear that τ must be an eigenvalue of Σ, if V_0 is an identity matrix, i.e., the element q is zero in (31). A zero value of q implies a lack of complementarity in the choice of decision variables $\underline{x}_i$ by members of the team designated as player I. Thus, if q were a statistical quantity, V_0 would have been an estimate of covariance matrix Σ; thus a statistical test of complementarity could be devised to see if at the minimax solution the null hypothesis

$$H_0 : \mathrm{ch}(V_0^{-1} \Sigma)_* = 1$$

is rejected, where $\mathrm{ch}(M)_*$ denotes the smallest eigenvalue of matrix M.

Let the equilibrium solution of the two players be $\bar{c}_i^0$, $\underline{x}_i^0$ for $1 \leq i \leq n$. If they exist, they must satisfy their optimal reaction functions

$$\tau \Sigma^{-1} \bar{c}_i^0 - \underline{x}_i^0 = 0$$

$$\bar{c}_i^0 - V_0 \underline{x}_i^0 = 0$$

Hence $\underline{x}_i^0$ must satisfy the complementary eigenvalue problem

$$(V_0 - (\tfrac{1}{\tau}) \Sigma) \underline{x}_i^0 = 0 = (V_0^{-1} - \tau \Sigma^1) \bar{c}_i^0 \; ; \; 1 \leq i \leq n$$

Thus, if τ_* is the minimum eigenvalue of $V_0^{-1} \Sigma$ from (3.12), then $1/\tau_*$ is the maximum eigenvalue of $V_0 \Sigma^{-1}$. Note that the minimax pair $(\bar{c}_{i*}, \underline{x}_i^*)$ defines a pure strategy solution at which the value of the game is attained. This is so because

$$\underline{\min}_{c_i} \max_{\underline{x}_i} g(\bar{c}_i, \underline{x}_i) = \max_{\underline{x}_i} \underline{\min}_{c_i} g(\bar{c}_i, \underline{x}_i)$$

where

$$g(\bar{c}_i, \underline{x}_i) = 2 \sum_{i=1}^{n} \bar{c}_i' \underline{x}_i - \sum_{i=1}^{n} x_i' V_0 \underline{x}_i + \tau(1 - \sum_{i=1}^{n} D^2(\bar{c}_i, 0, \Sigma))$$

However, in many cases if the restrictions like (3.5) and (3.8) on the strategy sets are not imposed, pure strategy solutions may not exist. For instance, if (3.8a), rather than (3.8b) is used as a constraint, solution $\bar{c}_{i*} = 0$ may emerge. However if the strategy sets C and X where $\bar{c}_i \in C$, $\underline{x}_i \in X$ are compact and non-empty, there would always exist a minimax pair in mixed strategies.

This leads to the consideration of mixed strategies by player I, when it is known that player II follows them. Two cases will be considered following the team decision framework (3.4) except for two differences. We would ignore the constraint (3.5), assume n = 2 and replace V_0 by V_i, where V_i is the variance-covariance matrix of vector $\underline{c}_i$ which has mean $\bar{c}_i$ for i = 1, 2. It is assumed that $\underline{c}_i$'s are statistically independent so that the covariance of $\underline{c}_1$ and $\underline{c}_2$ is zero. The first case arises when the decision maker (player I) defines average estimates

$$\bar{c} = p\bar{c}_1 + (1 - p)\,\bar{c}_2;\ \bar{V} = p^2\, V_1 + (1 - p)^2\, V_2$$

$$0 \leq p \leq 1$$

and use them to maximize the payoff function

$$g(\bar{c}, \bar{V}) = 2\bar{c}'x - x'\bar{V}x$$

The optimal value x* of vector x is then

$$x^* = \bar{V}^{-1}\,\bar{c};\ g(x^*) = x^{*\prime}\bar{V}x^*$$

where g(x*) is the corresponding optimal payoff. However player II chooses p optimally subject to $0 \leq p \leq 1$. Hence for a minimax case p will be chosen to minimize g(x*). This determines the optimal value of p as p_* where

$$p_* = \frac{x^{*\prime}V_2x^*}{x^{*\prime}(V_1 + V_2)x^*}$$

Hence p_* is zero if V_2 is null and $p_* = 1.0$ if $x^{*\prime}V_1x^* > x^{*\prime}V_2x^*$.

A second case arises as follows: the state of the world is characterized by two parameter sets: either $(\bar{c}_1, V_1)$ or, $(\bar{c}_2, V_2)$. If $(\bar{c}_i, V_i)$ occurs, player I chooses action $\underline{x}_i$ i = 1, 2 either as pure strategies or, as mixed strategies. In the latter case he defines a probability mixture of pure strategies as follows:

$$\bar{x} = \lambda\underline{x}_1 + (1 - \lambda)\,\underline{x}_2;\ 0 \leq \lambda \leq 1$$

If the true state were known, e.g., the event $(\bar{c}_i, V_i)$ occurs, then $\underline{x}_i$ would be optimally chosen by maximizing

$$g_i = 2\bar{c}_i' \underline{x}_i - \underline{x}_i' V_i \underline{x}_i$$

hence

$$\underline{x}_i^* = V_i^{-1} \bar{c}_i, \; i = 1,2$$

$$\underline{x}_i^* = \underline{x}_2^* \text{ if } V_1^{-1} \bar{c}_1 = V_2^{-1} \bar{c}_2$$

Let λ be the probability of detecting the event $(\bar{c}_1, V_1)$ when it occurs and choosing action $\underline{x}_1$ and $(1 - \lambda)$ is the corresponding probability for $(\bar{c}_2, V_2)$ and choosing action $\underline{x}_2$. Total rewards from such a plan are

$$g_0 = 2(\lambda\bar{c}_1' \underline{x}_1 + (1 - \lambda)\, \bar{c}_2' \underline{x}_2) - (\lambda^2 x_1' V_1 \underline{x}_1 + (1 - \lambda \;\; \underline{x}_2' V_2 \underline{x}_2)$$

The optimal solutions λ^0, $\underline{x}_1^0$, $\underline{x}_2^0$ are:

$$\lambda^0 = (\sigma_1^2 + \sigma_2^2)^{-1} [m_1 - m_2 + \sigma_2^2]$$

$$\underline{x}_1^0 = (1/\lambda^0)\, V_1^{-1} \bar{c}_1 \qquad (3.14)$$

$$\underline{x}_2^0 = (1 - \lambda^0)^{-1} \;\; V_2^{-1} \bar{c}_2$$

$$g_0(\lambda^0, \underline{x}_1^0, \underline{x}_2^0) = \sum_{i=1}^{2} \bar{c}_i V_i^{-1} \bar{c}_i$$

where $m_i = \bar{c}_i' \underline{x}_i^0$, $\sigma_i^2 = \underline{x}_i^{0'} V_i \underline{x}_i^0$, $i = 1,2$. It is clear that the random environment appears here in a discrete manner characterized by two parameter sets $(\bar{c}_1, V_1)$ and $(\bar{c}_2, V_2)$. Hence it is apparent from (3.14) that mixing the two pure strategies $x^0(1)$, $\underline{x}(2)$ is preferable if for example $m_1 > m_2$ but $\sigma_1^2 > \sigma_2^2$. It is clear that the pure strategy $\underline{x}_2^0$ is preferable when $m_1 = m_2$ and σ_2^2 is zero for example. If the parameter sets $(\bar{c}_i, V_i)$ are generated by a normally distributed random environment, then $\underline{x}_1^0$ contributes more to the optimal payoff $g_0(\lambda^0, \underline{x}_1^0, \underline{x}_2^0)$ than $\underline{x}_2^0$, if

$$D^2 (\bar{c}_1, 0; V_1) > D^2 (\bar{c}_2, 0; V_2)$$

i.e., the Mahalanobis distance from the origin to the first population is greater. Thus $\underline{x}_1^0 = \underline{x}_2^0$ only if the two distances are equal.

One may show further the consequences of not choosing λ optimally as in (3.14). For instance, let w be any value $0 < w < 1$ used for mixing or averaging and let the means $\bar{c}_1$, $\bar{c}_2$ be equal to $\bar{c}$. However V_1 is assumed to be different from V_2. Define the action plans x^0, $\tilde{x}^0$ as:

$$x^0 = [wV_1 + (1 - w)\, V_2]^{-1}\, \bar{c}$$

$$\tilde{x}^0 = w\, \tilde{\underline{x}}_1^0 + (1 - w)\, \underline{x}_2^0; \tag{3.15}$$

$$\tilde{\underline{x}}_1^0 = V_1^{-1}\, \bar{c},\ \tilde{x}_2^0 = V_2^{-1}\, \bar{c}$$

It is clear we have $x^0 < \tilde{x}^0$, so long as w is not equal to zero or one, i.e., $0 < w < 1$. This follows due to the inequality

$$[wV_1 + (1 - w)\, V_2]^{-1} \leq [wV_1^{-1} + (1 - w)\, V_2^{-1}],\ 0 < w < 1$$

which is strict so long as V_1 is not equal to V_2. Thus combining the action plans $\tilde{\underline{x}}_1^0$, $\tilde{\underline{x}}_2^0$ into a mixed strategy $\tilde{x}^0$ may be less preferable to x^0, a plan based on an average of the two variances, provided the means are equal.

5. Allocation Under Imperfect Competition

An allocation problem closely related to the team decision problem under uncertainty considers the question of efficiency in risk allocation in markets with many traders, e.g., contingency claims markets, pure exchange markets [3]. We consider in this section a simple example, where the market for a given good has m producers (or traders), each with output y_i, $i = 1, 2, \ldots, m$ and a profit function $\pi_i(s)$ where s belongs to a finite set Ω of states of nature:

$$\pi_i(s) = (a(s) - c_i(s))\, y_i - b(s)\, (y_i \sum_{j=1}^{m} y_j) \tag{6.1}$$

$$p(s) = a(s) - b(s) \sum_{j=1}^{m} y_j$$

and p(s) is the price in state s. There is an overall allocation restriction:

$$\Sigma y_i \leq 1 \tag{6.2}$$

which may be interpreted either as a budget condition or as an upper limit of demand, which is assumed to equal one. We consider y_i here to be scalars and the vector $\underline{y}' = (y_1, y_2, \ldots, y_m)$ is called feasible if it satisfies (6.2) and nonnegativity of each y_i. We consider only pure strategies for each trader so that $y_i = y_i(s)$ for all s. It is assumed that the random variables a(s), $c_i(s)$, b(s) are statistically independent with finite means a, c_i, b and variances σ_a^2, σ_i^2, σ_b^2. If state s is for future time points, then the decisions y_i are contingent on suitable forecases of the random quantities. It is assumed that each trader i maximizes expected profit g_i over $s\varepsilon\Omega$

$$g_i = E\pi_i(s) = (a - c_i)\, y_i - b(y_i \sum_{j=1}^{m} y_j) \tag{6.3}$$

subject to

$$\sum_{i=1}^{m} y_i \leq 1, \; y_i \geq 0$$

Using λ as the Lagrange multiplier, the optimal solutions are:

$$y_i^* = \frac{1}{m+1}\,\frac{a - \lambda^*}{b} - \frac{1}{b}\,(c_i - \frac{m}{m+1}\,\bar{c})$$

$$\sum_{i=1}^{m} y_i^* = \frac{1}{m+1}\,\frac{a - \lambda^*}{b} - \frac{m}{m+1}\,\bar{c} \tag{6.4}$$

$$\lambda^*(1 - \sum_{i=1}^{m} y_i^*) = 0$$

where $\bar{c} = \Sigma c_i/m$ denotes average marginal cost in the industry and λ^* is assumed exogenously determined. If we assume firms to be "similar" in marginal costs in the sense

$$c_i(s) = \bar{c} + \varepsilon_i(s) \tag{6.5}$$

where the error component $\varepsilon_i(s)$ has zero mean and constant variance σ_ε^2 over firms in the industry, then

$$\sigma_\varepsilon^2 = \sigma_i^2 + (c_i - \bar{c})^2$$

this means that if all firms are alike, then $\sigma_\varepsilon^2 = \sigma_i^2$, since $c_i = \bar{c}$ for each i = 1, 2, ..., m.

It is clear from (6.4) that if m is very large (i.e., the perfectly competitive case), we would get

$$y_i^* = \frac{1}{m+1}\,\frac{a-\bar{c}-\lambda^*}{b}$$

$$\Sigma y_i^* = \frac{m}{m+1}\,\frac{a-\bar{c}-\lambda^*}{b}$$

$$p = \lambda^* + \bar{c}$$

This implies for large m,

$$y_i^* = \bar{y}_0^* \;, \; \Sigma y_i^* = (a - \bar{c} - \lambda^*)/b$$

$$\bar{y}_0^* = \Sigma y_i^*/m = \text{average industry output}$$

$$\text{var } (\Sigma y_i^*) = \Sigma\sigma_i^2/m^2b^2 = \sigma_0^2/mb^2, \text{ if } \sigma_i^2 = \sigma_0^2, \text{ all } i$$

$$\text{var } p = \Sigma\sigma_i^2/m^2 = \sigma_0^2/m \text{ if } \sigma_i^2 = \sigma_0^2, \text{ all } i$$

$$\text{var } y_i^* = \Sigma\sigma_i^2/(b^2m^4) = \sigma_0^2/b^2m^3, \text{ if } \sigma_i^2 = \sigma_0^2$$

Hence individual optimal outputs would tend to be distributed around the industry average $\bar{y}_0^*$ with a variance tending to zero for $m \to \infty$. Thus

$$\text{Prob } [\; y_i^* - \bar{y}_0^* \;>\; k] \leq \frac{\sigma_0^2}{k^2b^2m^3} \to 0$$

showing that as $m \to \infty$, y_i^* converges in probability to the industry average. If the errors are Gaussian, then the probability distribution function of y_i^* converges to a Gaussian distribution.

In the monopoly case m = 1 and the situation is different, e.g.,

$$y_1^* = (a-\bar{c}-\lambda^*)/(2b); \; \bar{c} = c_1$$

$$p = \tfrac{1}{2}\,(a + \bar{c} + \lambda^*)$$

$$\text{var } y_1^* = \sigma_0^2/4b^2$$

$$\text{var } p = \sigma_0^2/4$$

Clearly for m > 4, variance of price and total industry output is lower in competitive case than in monopoly. For m = 2, the results are:

$$\Sigma y_i^* = \frac{2}{3} \cdot \frac{a - \bar{c} - \lambda^*}{b}$$

$$p = \frac{1}{3}\,(a + 2\lambda] + 2\bar{c})$$

$$\text{var}\,(\Sigma y_i^*) = 4\sigma_0^2/9mb^2$$

$$\text{var}\ p = 4\sigma_0^2/9$$

In these formulations λ^* could be set to zero, since the price equation describes the equilibrium behavior. However, if we consider joint profit maximization, i.e.,

$$\max \Sigma g_i$$

under the cost similarity condition (5.6), the allocation restriction

$$\Sigma y_i \leq 1,\ y_i \geq,\ 0$$

may be appropriate. In this case, if the common marginal cost $\bar{c}$ is known, the optimal value y_T^* of total output $y_T = \Sigma y_i$ can be derived as follows:

$$y_T^* = (a - \bar{c} - \lambda^*)/2b;\ p_T = \tfrac{1}{2}\,(a - \bar{c} + \lambda^*)$$

$$y_T^* = (a - \bar{c} - \lambda^*)/b;\ p_T = \bar{c} + \lambda^*$$

where the first is for monopoly and the second for competition. It is easy to check that these results are similar to those derived before. However since the industry parameter $\bar{c}$ is not completely known, the aggregation defined by y_T would have errors and hence the optimal outputs y_T^* would have variability. But under perfect competition, the risk of output variance would be shared among m firms, whereas under monopoly only one firm has to bear it [9]. Hence output and price variance under competitive conditions would be lower than those under monopoly if the number m of firms exceeds four.

Also, both in the aggregative (y_T) and disaggregative case (y_i), the reaction of a price taker to risk associated with the random environment would be different. Under monopoly or imperfect competition, a given increase in the variance of costs, var $(c_i(s)\ y_i)$ would tend to reduce equilibrium output more than under perfect competition, since the latter tends to allocate risks for large m in such a way that an individual share could become very small.

Thus it is clear that policy instruments or incentive systems which can reduce the gap in variances of optimal outputs and prices in the two cases need to be analyzed. Tax subsidy schemes or suitable pricing rules whch would facilitate such analysis would be very helpful for optimal decision-making under uncertainty.

6. Concluding Remarks

Our discussion of the allocation rules under uncertainty has focussed on three major aspects of decision-making through decision models, e.g., resource allocation in stochastic programming, allocation under estimated response coefficients and team decisions under a random environment.

Two related aspects which are equally important have not been mentioned here. The first is the problem of multicriteria objective functions [15, 17] and the second the problem of informational designs associated with any allocation schemes. The first arises very naturally in team decisions, where different members may have different objective functions that are only partly compatible. The second arises due to the fact that outputs may not be directly observable, so that the observable state vectors are the only means through which output response has to be estimated. Designing information systems [2, 6, 7] in such situations lead to interesting allocation rules with several optimality properties.

References

1. Chernoff, H., Sequential Analysis and Optimal Design, Society for Industrial and Applied Mathematics, Philadelphia, 1972.

2. Chu, K.C., "Designing Information Structures for Quadratic Decision Problems," Journal of Optimization Theory and Applications, 25, 1978, 139-160.

3. Guesnerie, R. and T. de Montbrial, "Allocation Under Uncertainty: A Survey," in J.H. Dreze, ed., Allocation Under Uncertainty: Equilibrium and Optimality, John Wiley, New York, 1974, 53-70.

4. Hay, G.A. and C.C. Holt, "A General Solution for Linear Decision Rules: An Optimal Dynamic Strategy Under Uncertainty," Econometrica, 43, 1975, 231-260.

5. Lange, O., Optimal Decisions: Principles of Programming, Pergamon Press, Oxford, 1971.

6. Marschak, J., "Elements for a Theory of Teams," Management Science, 1, 1955, 127-137.

7. Marschak, J., "The Payoff-Relevant Description of States and Acts," Econometrica 31, 1963, 719-725.

8. Miyasawa, K., "A Bayesian Approach to Team Decision Problems," in M. Shubik, ed., Essays in Mathematical Economics, Princeton University Press, Princeton, 1967.

9. Nikaido, H., "Economic Adjustments Under Noncompetitive Pricing," in R.H. Day and T. Groves, eds., Adaptive Economic Models, Academic Press, New York, 1975, 453-477.

10. Radner, R., "Allocation of a Scarce Resource Under Uncertainty: An Example of a Team," in C.B. McGuire and R. Radner, eds., Decision and Organization: A Volume in Honor of Jacob Marschak, North Holland, Amsterdam, 1972, 217-236.

11. Sandee, J., "Optimum Policy Alternatives," in Modeling for Government and Business, Martinus Nijhoff Social Sciences Division, Leiden, 1977, 149-164.

12. Sengupta, J.K., Stochastic Programming: Methods and Applications, North Holland, Amsterdam, 1972.

13. Sengupta, J.K., "Adaptive Decision Rules for Stochastic Linear Programming," International Journal of Systems Science, 9, 1978, 97-109.

14. Sengupta, J.K., "Testing and Validation Problems in Stochastic Linear Programming," Journal of Cybernetics, 9, 1979, 17-42.

15. Sengupta, J.K., "Multiple Criteria Decisions Under Risk," Working paper in Economics #132, University of California, Santa Barbara, 1979.

16. Sengupta, J.K., "Constrained Nonzero-sum Games with Partially Controllable Strategies," Journal of Optimization Theory and Applications, 31, 1980.

17. Sengupta, J.K., "Selecting an Optimal Solution in Stochastic Linear Programming," International Journal of Systems Science, 11, 1980, 33-47.

18. Sengupta, J.K., Decision Models in Stochastic Programming, to be published by Elsevier-North Holland, New York, ca. 1981.

19. Ziemba, W.T. and R.G. Vickson, eds., _Stochastic Optimization Models in Finance_, Academic Press, New York, 1975.

CHAPTER 5
ECONOMIC PLANNING UNDER UNCERTAINTY

1. Introduction

Models of economic planning in less developed countries (LDC) have increasingly used mathematical programming techniques to analyze optimal pattern of investment allocation between sectors. Usually, some version of the open static or open-dynamic Leontief input-output model is used in such formulations along with an econometric framework for estimating final demand and production coefficients for final inputs like labor and capital. Since this formulation can be viewed as a large-scale linear programming (LP) or nonlinear programming model, it is interesting to note that any uncertainty in estimates of the parameters affect the optimal decisions calculated from such models. From a practical standpoint an analysis of such uncertainty is most important for several reasons. First, the planner's objective function must retain some flexibility in the plan in the sense of appropriate responses for likely shortages or oversupply of goods in some sectors. Second, the behaviorial response of private producers in a sector under conditions of uncertainty may be far from perfectly competitive in nature, in which case the cost of uncertainty, reflected in market prices and resource allocation processes would lead to inoptimal production and distribution relations. The model must recognze it. Third, for specific sectors like agriculture with a major export crop, fluctuations in agricultural income may build up political pressures for stabilization policies. The latter may not always be stabilizing in a world of uncertainty, unless polcies are designed, monitored and implemented properly, since in an imperfectly competitive world, information lags and risk aversion may be very unequally spread between large and small producers.

In some countries, a few of the above types of uncertainty have been explicitly recognized and its effects on the overall plan evaluated. Thus Kornai [10] has noted for Hungary that the effects of divergences from the plans caused by uncertainty are influenced by three main factors: adaptability of the plan, the intersectoral structure and the supply of stocks and reserves and he proposed a method of safety programming by building appropriate safety levels in different sectors of the overall plan. Lange [11] has introduced the notion of penalty price to be imposed for meeting average shortages in sectors, where supply falls short of demand. In a project evaluation study for Kenya's agricultural settlement programs [20], where shadow prices were used for computing social profits for various selections, it was found that 57% or more of the variation in social profits is accounted for by fluctuations in input and output prices; further, under such market price uncertainty it was found optimal for feedlot projects to carry substantial feed and grain inventories thus reducing the fluctuations in export of grain and stabilizing farm incomes.

In the programming model for Mexican agriculture, Duloy and Norton [5] distinguished between two forms of market equilibrium for agriculture e.g. the competitive case with producers as price takers and the monopolistic case where the sector is assumed to maximize its net income by equating marginal revenue with marginal cost. The latter leads to a quadratic programming formulation, since prices respond linearly to demand. However no distinction in response to uncertainty between a competitive and monopolistic producer is admitted into the model, although there is some empirical evidence that agricultural supply shows risk aversion in international cross-section data [2, 8, 26, 33].

The response of supply to price or market uncertainty has been explicitly recognized in commodity models and the related stabilization policies [13, 23]. The expected gains from price stabilization policies [13] have been explicitly estimated, when errors or noises are linearly additive to the demand and supply functions and market equilibrium is known. However if the market is not fully competitive e.g. world coffee market or the suppliers are more risk averse to price fluctuations than demanders, the stabilization policies which assume linearly additive independent errors may have destabilizing impacts.

Our objective here is to show how some specific concepts of risk aversion in the sense of aversion to fluctuations may be utilized in the various methods of economic planning mentioned before. The optimal decision rules derived here admit risk sensitivity and hence the economic problems of risk sharing and risk spreading can be directly introduced into the conventional planning model. For the planner or the policymaker such risk sharing may involve both economic and political costs and these may be viewed as adjustment costs.

2. Input-Output Model Under Risk Aversion

Economic planning applications of open-static input-output (IO) model have used in the short run [3, 6, 12] an LP version of minimizing total costs $C = C(L) + C(K) + C(M_n)$ of labor (L), capital (L) and noncompetitive imports (M_n) subject to a demand constraint i.e.,

$$\begin{aligned} \min_x \; & C = (wa_o + rb_o + sc_o)'x \\ & \text{subject to} \\ & (I - A)\,x \geq \hat{d} \\ & x \leq x^u \\ & x \geq 0 \end{aligned} \tag{1.1}$$

Here a_o, b_o, c_o are column vectors (prime denotes transpose) of sectoral labor-output, capital-output and intermediate noncompetitive import-output ratios, w, r, s are prices of labor (wage), capital (user cost) and noncompetitive imports (foreign exchange costs). $\hat{d}$ is the vector of final demands net of competitive imports (M_c), which is usually estimated from past time series data e.g., by linear expenditure methods, using the proportions of net national income spent on sectoral demand. Finally, x^u is an upper limit of output i.e., output ceiling permitted by full capacity utilization. For policy purposes it may be convenient to introduce a lower limit x^L also, so that

$$x^L \leq x \leq x^u \;;\; x^u > x^L > 0 \tag{1.2}$$

One may interpret $x = x^L$ as the pessimistic variant and $x = x^u$ as the optimistic variant of the output plan, whereas the optimal plan is most likely to be $x > x^L$ and $x < x^u$. Denoting $(wa_o + rb_o + sc_o)$ by v and assuming $x^L < x < x^u$, the above LP model may be written as

$$\begin{aligned} &\min_x C = v'x \\ &\text{subject to } Bx \geq \hat{d};\ B = (I - A) \\ &\qquad\qquad\qquad x \geq 0 \end{aligned} \tag{1.3}$$

The dual to this LP maximizes national income (Y) as:

$$\begin{aligned} &\max_p Y = p'\hat{d} \\ &\quad \text{subject to } p'B \leq v' \\ &\qquad\qquad p \geq 0 \end{aligned} \tag{1.4}$$

Noise or uncertainty components may enter into the above LP models in at least three ways that are important. First, the final demand forecasts $\hat{d}$ may contain errors thus necesstating plan revisions whenever appropriate. At the sectoral level such revisions imply shortages or oversupply which get reflected in the optimal shadow prices p if the market process is competitive. Denote inventories by h_t, which represents excess of supply over demand

$$h_t = Bx_t - d_t \tag{1.5}$$

where t is the time subscript and let $\hat{h}_t$ be the vector of estmated inventories when final demand forecast is $\hat{d}_t$. Any deviation of forecasts from actual demand results in inventories, that may be positive or negative and the planner can associate a cost, $C(h_t)$ with such inventories.

A second source of error is the assumption that the prices implicit in the vector v of the objective function of (1.3) are constant for all output levels. Such an assumption eliminates substitution possibilities between labor and capital and any disequilibrium behavior in the factor markets. Again, at the short run aggregate level, a cost of adjustment function e.g., of the quadratic form

$$C(x_t, x_t^D) = \bar{v}'\, x_t + \tfrac{1}{2}\,(x_t - x^D)'\, W(x_t - x^D)$$

may represent inconsistency due to such errors, where x^D is desired output and W is a matrix of weights, assumed positive definite. If the desired output levels x^D are proportional to lagged output (x_{t-1})

$$x^D = k\, x_{t-1}$$

then the adjustment cost function would be

$$C(x_t, x_{t-1}) = \bar{v}'x_t + \tfrac{1}{2}\,(x_t - kx_{t-1})'\, W(x_t - kx_{t-1}) \qquad (1.6)$$

which incorporates in the quadratic term the cost of changes in output levels at different time points. Such adjustment functions have been used very successfully in micromodels of output inventory behavior [24].

A third source of uncertainty is associated with the shadow prices p in the dual LP model (1.4). If the demand process $\hat{d}_t$ is successively revised in forward time t+1, t+2, ..., the optimal shadow prices $p_t, p_{t+1}, p_{t+2}, \ldots$ solved from (1.4) successively would be generated thereby. The cost associated with this error-correcting process may be directly incorporated by letting the shadow prices vary in response to demand variability. For instance, if the demand d_t follows a normal stochastic process with a mean vector m and a variance-covariance matrix D, for which best statistical estimates from past data are $\hat{m}$ and $\hat{D}$, then the linear objective function of the LP model (1.4) may be transformed as a quadratic:

$$\max_p \; Y_\alpha = \hat{m}'p - \frac{\alpha}{2}\, p'\hat{D}p$$

$$\text{subject to} \qquad (1.7)$$

$$p'B \leq v', \; p \geq 0$$

where α is a positive (or, nonnegative) constant denoting the intensity of risk averson. Note that the objective function of (1.7) may be derived from the expected value of an exponential utility of income function

$$u(Y) = 1 - \exp(-\alpha Y),\; \alpha > 0$$

where Y is normally distributed with mean $\hat{m}'p$ and variance $p'\hat{D}p$. When $\hat{d} = \hat{m}$ equals m with probability one, variance of demand is zero and we get back the LP model

(1.4). Note further that the error-correcting process related to demand fluctuations is partly reflected in the adjustment costs or inventories $C(h_t)$ and partly in the risk-adjustment component of the objective function of (1.7). Whereas the former is a quantity adjustment, the latter one of price adjustment. Hence the former is an appropriate strategy for the central planner, the latter for the sectoral producers. The two models (1.3) and (1.7) may then be viewed as a two-person nonzero sum game: player I (the planner) choosing an x by (1.3) with his own forecast $\hat{d}$ of demand, player II (the sectoral producers) chooses an optimal p by model (1.7) with his own estimates $\hat{m}$, $\hat{D}$ and the sum of the two payoff functions is not zero.

By the special property or the input-output coefficient matrix A, we know that the inverse matrix B^{-1} has all positive elements and hence the optimal price vector p^* must satisfy the linear decision rule (LDR):

$$p^* = \hat{m}\,(Bx^* + \alpha\hat{D})^{-1} \tag{1.8}$$

This risk-adjusted LDR has a number of implications for planning. First, the higher the value of α, the lower the optimal price p^*. The sectoral producers interpret this as a signal for lower production. In contrast, player I, the central planner computes an optimal shadow price $\hat{p}^*$ from his risk-less LP model (1.3) which is higher than p^*. The planner's shadow price $\hat{p}^*$ is a signal for higher outputs. The divergence between the two prices, p^* and $\hat{p}^*$ thus generates a disequilibrium system. Second, the optimal risk-adjusted income $Y_\alpha = p^{*\prime}Bx^* + \tfrac{1}{2}\alpha p^{*\prime}\hat{D}p^*$ is always positive and higher than the otpimal value $Y = \hat{p}^{*\prime}\hat{d} = \hat{p}^{*\prime}\hat{m}$ of the planner's objective function in (1.4). Hence the net income $(Y_\alpha - p^{*\prime}Bx^*)$ which equals $\tfrac{1}{2}\alpha p^{*\prime}\hat{D}\hat{p}$ is strictly positive for player II, the sectoral producers. This net income is like monopoly profits when the producers' perceived demand functions do not agree with those of the planner. This interpretation corresponds with the approach of Negishi [16], Nikaido [17], and Arrow and Hahn [1].

Third, the LDR approach (1.8) may be applied by the second player for updating p^* whenever the mean estimate $\hat{m}$ is revised with additonal information about the planner's achievement in realizing output targets. For instance, if the reliability of the estimate $\hat{m}$ can be improved by appropriate stabilization policies, the second player's anticipation of optimal price will improve and given the capacity available it will induce output increase. The sequence of successive revisions of $\hat{m}$ leading to those of p^* may thus reduce the divergence or inconsistency between the two prices in the planning period.

It is clear that for the central planner, the introduction of a quadratic adjustment cost function e.g. equation (1.6) leads to an optimal LDR as follows:

$$\hat{h}^*_t = \frac{1}{\gamma_o} (\lambda^*_t - \lambda^*_{t+1}) + \tilde{\beta} (Ax^*_t + \hat{d}_t)$$

$$x^*_t = [W + \gamma_o A'\tilde{\beta}\tilde{\beta}A]^{-1} [kWx^*_{t-1} + kWx^*_{t+1} - B'\lambda^*_t - \gamma_o A'\tilde{\beta} (\tilde{\beta}\hat{d}_t - \hat{h}^*_t) - \bar{v}] \quad (1.9)$$

for $t = 0, 1, \ldots, T$, where T is the short run planning horizon. Here it is assumed that inventory costs $C(\hat{h}_t)$ are quadratic:

$$C(\hat{h}_t) = \frac{1}{2} \gamma_o [\hat{h}_t - \tilde{\beta} (Ax_t + \hat{d}_t)]$$

$\tilde{\beta}$: a diagonal matrix with positive elements in the diagonal

$\tilde{\beta}(Ax_t + \hat{d}_t)$: normal or desired inventories

and the palnner's objective function is

$$\sum_{t=0}^{T} Q_t, \text{ where } Q_t = C(x_t, x_{t-1}) + C(\hat{h}_t) \quad (1.10)$$

where λ_t being the vector of Lagrange multipliers associated with the inventory equation

$$\hat{h}_t = \hat{h}_{t-1} + x_{t-1} - \hat{d}_t$$

It follows from these optimal LDR (1.9) that if $\lambda^*_t = \lambda^*_{t+1}$, then the expected inventories $\hat{h}^*_t$ are at their desired level and the optimal outputs evolve according to the difference equation

$$x^*_t = k(x^*_{t-1} + x^*_{t+1}) - W^{-1} (B'\lambda^*_t + \bar{v}) \quad (1.11)$$

If the coefficient k is a scalar, the characteristic roots of the system (1.11) would be complex if $k^2 > 0.25$. This implies that the optimal output path would be oscillatory even when λ^*_t's are constant over time. If k is a matrix, then the characteristic equation is

$$\theta^2 k - \theta I + k = 0$$

where the roots θ evidently occur in pairs, so that if θ_i is a root, θ_i^{-1} is also a root. Taking the stable roots only, the steady-state solution x^* can be derived as follows:

$$x^* = -(I - 2k)^{-1} W^{-1} (B'\lambda^* + \bar{v})$$

this is quite different from the conventional form of the steady-state equation of the Leontief model, as it includes the policy parameters k, λ^*, W and $\bar{v}$, besides the input-output matrix $B = I - A$. Risk aversion is built into this LDR through policy parameters. For instance, a rise in the penalty price λ^*, or in the diagoal elements of the inverse weight matrix W^{-1} induces in the steady state a reduction in equilibrium output. A strong aversion to fluctuations in the sense of oscillations may also be secured through damping via the elements of the matrix k e.g. in the scalar case a value of $k < 0.25$ would ensure real roots and hence a non-oscillatory behavior.

It is clear therefore that in the nonsteady state, the planner has to follow the optimal LDR given in (1.9), which involves forecasting λ^*_{t+1} i.e., forecasting shortages or over supply in the next period and plan current output accordingly. Likewise, current optimal outputs x^*_t depend on the forecast of future shortages or oversupply in sectors. An estimation of this error-correcting process should thus form an essential component of models of planning based on static input-output models.

A similar error-correcting process could be defined in terms of the second player's strategy vector p in (1.7). Introducing the adjustment cost function $C(q_t, q_t^D)$ and $C(\Delta p_t)$ where $q_t' = v' - p'_tB$, $\Delta p_t = p_t - p_{t-1}$ and q_t^D denotes the desired level of q_t we may rewrite the objective function of (1.7) as

$$Y_\alpha = \hat{m}'p - \frac{\alpha}{2} p'\hat{D}p - C(\hat{q}_t, q_t^D) - C(p_t - p_{t-1})$$

where expected adjustment cost and price variation costs are deducted before calculating net income.

For an extenson of this approach to the case of dynamic I-O models, consider the dynamic formulation [3] where total demand $\hat{d}_t$ is decomposed into consumption $\hat{c}(t) = \xi c_T(t) + \bar{c}(t)$ and investment $\hat{j}(t) = k(t + 1) - k(t)$ demand vectors, where $c_T(t)$ is total national consumption, ξ is the vector of consumption shares by sectors, $\bar{c}(t)$ is the autonomous component:

$$\max c_T(t)$$
subject to
$$(I - A)\, x(t) \geq \hat{c}(t) + \hat{j}(t)$$
$$\tilde{a}_0\, x(t) \leq \bar{\ell}(t)$$
$$\tilde{g}\, Hx(t) \leq \bar{k}(t)$$

Here $\bar{\ell}(t)$, $\bar{k}(t)$ are sectoral availability limits of labor and capital and $\tilde{a}_0$ is a diagonal matrix of labor requirements and $\tilde{g}$ is a diagonal matrix with diagonal elements g_i indicating the expected growth rate of capital stock $k_i(t)$ in sector i as perceived by the planner; the matrix H denotes the pattern of utilization of the capital stock vector k(t), so that if there is full capacity utilization of capital in the lan period we would have

$$\tilde{g}\, Hx(t) = \bar{k}(t)$$

since total consumption $c_T(t)$ is positive, the vector of prices p(t) of consumption goods must satisfy the numeraire condition

$$p'(t)\xi = 1$$

and by the duality principle f LP models we must have

$$p'(t)\,(I - A) = r'(t)\,\tilde{g}H + w'(t)\,a_0$$

where p(t), r(t), w(t) are the shadow price vectors associated with the constraints of (2.1) and it is assumed that equality signs hold at the optimal so that the shadow prices are positive.

It is clear that in this dynamic formulation, three sources of error i.e. overestimate or underestimate of net sectoral demand are present e.g. unintended inventories of goods, unemployed volume of labor and underutilized level of sectoral capital stocks created. Again, costs of adjustment due to these errors may be built into the design of the planning model by taking a quadratic form and deriving an optimal set LDR. The two shortcomings of the quadratic form of the adjustment costs e.g. symmetry around the average and insensitivity to nonnegativity may be remedied by e.g., by first requiring nonnegativity of the solution as a condition of its acceptability and allowing a quadratic component to the LDR (1.9). The latter has been empirically substantiated by Just [8] in his studies of the importance of risk aversion in farmers' decisions.

3. Output Planning Under Imperfect Competition

Application of the I-O model for planning implicitly assumes a competitive market structure for outputs and inputs. Thus for the LP model (1.3) if demand d is known with certainty, the optimal shadow prices p* of output must satisfy the marginal cost rule

$$p^* = wa_0 + rb_0 \qquad 2.1)$$

if noncompetitive imports are ignored. For many LDC such a competitive assumption may not be valid for several sectors. On the cost side, labor is more organized in manufacturing than in agricultural sectors and on the demand side food producing consumer goods industries are less price elastic than non-food durable goods. Two issues therefore appear to be important to the planner. First, he may misspecify the market framework to be competitive, although it is not and thereby overestimate the equilibrium output. Second, the price distortions in monopolistic competition may imply welfare losses [9] for the economy.

Elements of monopolistic competition in the I-O framework have been introduced by Negishi, Arrow and Hahn and Nikaido through the assumption that each ector, behaving as a single decision-making unit uses its price strategy monopolistically to maximize his own profits on the basis of a perceived demand function. This may lead to Cournot-Nash noncooperative equilibrium. Morishima [15] has considered the situation where sectoral profit rates may be neither equal nor zero.

We consider here two types of Cournot-Nash equilibrium solutions, in one the payoff matrix has stochastic components not completely known to each player and in the other each player has to make conjectural estimates of his opponent's strategies. The framework is one of two-person nonzero sum games, where player I is the aggregate of sectors following a monopolistic strategy and the second player is the planner who assumes a competitive market structure and determines his output strategies accordingly.

Player I maximizes total profit π by choosing output strategies (x) when the price response of excess demand in each sector is taken into account:

$$\max_x \pi = p'Bx - (wa_0 + rb_0)'x \qquad (2.2)$$

where $B'p = \tilde{\alpha}(d - Bx) = \alpha - Cx; \ \alpha = \tilde{\alpha}d$

$C = \tilde{\alpha}B$

where $\tilde{\alpha}$ is a diagonal matrix with positive coefficients indicating the intensity of price reaction to excess demand. The optimal solution in terms of output and price vectors is then

$$x_M = \frac{1}{2} C^{-1} (\alpha - v)$$

$$P_M = \frac{1}{2} B'^{-1} (\alpha + v) \qquad (2.3)$$

$$\pi_M = x_M' C x_M, \text{ where } v = wa_o + rb_o$$

Player II's competitive solution, under the assumption that the demand function $p = \alpha - Cx$ is correctly forecast is of course

$$x_c = C^{-1} (\alpha - (wa_o + rb_o))$$

$$p_c = B'^{-1} (wa_o + rb_o) \qquad (2.4)$$

$$\pi_c = 0$$

If the demand function is not correctly foreseen but unintended excess demands develop, player II may consider the target supply x_o such that

$$x_o = B^{-1} d$$

$$p_o = B'^{-1} (wa_o + rb_o) \qquad (2.5)$$

$$\pi_o = 0$$

Since $\alpha > (wa_o + rb_o)$, it is clear that $x_o > x_c > x_M$ and $p_M > p_o = p_c > 0$ since B'^{-1} is a matrix with positive elements. Also $\pi_M > \pi_c = \pi_o$. Thus the consequence of monopolistic competiton is to generate lower output, higher price and higher profits compared to competitive situations. It is interesting to note that in some LDC such price and output distortions due to monopolistic competition have been directly estimated [18] and found to be quite substantial.

It is clear from (2.3) and (2.4) that taxing monopoly profits by a proportional tax τ_i on each output x_i so that player I's profits become

$$\pi = (p - \tau)' Bx - v'x, \; v = wa_o + rb_o$$

would not induce player I to produce at the competitive level; rather it would have the reverse effect, i.e., it would contract monopoly outputs x_M further thus accentuating the excess demand problem. Since the central planner's objective is to attain his target price p_c on the assumption that the demand function is

$$B\hat{x} = a - Gp \tag{2.6}$$

his optimizing model is to maximize

$$\pi(p) = p'B\hat{x} - v'\hat{x} \tag{2.7}$$

subject to $p \geq 0$ and (2.6)

The first player's objective is to maximize

$$\pi(x) = \hat{p}'Bx - v'x = \alpha'x - x'C'x - v'x$$
$$\text{subject to } x \geq 0 \tag{2.8}$$

Note that $a \neq BC^{-1}\alpha$, $G \neq BC^{-1}B'$, since the two perceived demand functions, one by each player are not identical.

The first player's optimal solutions are given by (2.3) as before, whereas the second player, who guesses $\hat{x}$ according to (2.6) chooses the optimal strategies as

$$p = \frac{1}{2} G^{-1} [a + G'B'^{-1}v]$$

this price would be consistent with first player's expected price $\hat{p}$ only if

$$a = BC^{-1}\alpha, \; G = BC^{-1}B' \tag{2.9}$$

thus the condition (2.9) may be viewed as the rationality postulate of the private market. If this holds, player I leads and player II follows. On the other hand, if player II intends player I to follow his target price p_c, he may offer a subsidy x(s) proportional to x so that the effective demand function perceived by player I becomes

$$B'\hat{p} = \alpha - Cx + s(x), \text{ where } s(x) = \tfrac{1}{2} Cx$$

Subsidy may also be viewed in terms of reducing the effective cost v of inputs, so that player I is induced to produce at the level determined by price equalling marginal cost.

Two other features of the trial and error process in this two-person nonzero sum game must be noted. First, the perceived demand functions may include adjustment costs and risk aversion. In particular if player I is risk averse, i.e., he thinks that equilibrium targets planned by player II cannot be realized by the market, he would react by producing less equilibrium output, whereas player II by his optimism may be much less risk averse. Thus, the gap between two optimal outputs widens. Second, the cost of noncooperative behavior may be reduced considerably by the two parties agreeing on the plan targets and coordinating their decisions accordingly. It is clear that in this cooperative framework the main concern of the two players would be to forecast the demand function as accurately as possible and then adopt a cooperative payoff function. This is the rationality behind the mixed company framework of national planning e.g., one such plan may be to let player I (the producers) maximize

$$\pi(x) = \alpha'x - x'Cx - v'x \qquad (2.10)$$
$$\text{subject to } \pi(x) \leq \pi_0$$

where π_0 is the minimum level of profits determined by the second player (the planner). Note that π_0 must be positive although it may be small; for otherwise there would be no basis of cooperation. It is of course assumed that in (2.10) the forecast of demand, agreed to by both players satisfies the rule

$$B'p = \alpha - Cx$$

given in (2.2). It is clear from (2.10) that optimal output, price and profit (x^*, p^*, π^*) would satisfy

$$x_M \leq x^* \leq x_C;\ p_C \leq p^* \leq p_M;\ \pi_C \leq \pi^* < \pi_M$$

and generally speaking, these inequalities would be strict implying that the welfare loss measured by

$$W = \sum_{i=1}^{n} W_i = \frac{1}{2} \sum_{i=1}^{n} (p_{iM} - p_{ic})(x_{ic} - x_{iM})$$

would be less in the cooperative plan. if the degree of cooperation is denoted by δ and the welfare loss is viewed as a function $W = W(\delta)$ with a negative slope, an optimal degree of cooperation δ^* may be defined by

$$\partial W/\partial\delta = 0, \quad \partial^2 W/\partial\delta^2 > 0$$

if the welfare loss function is convex around δ^*.

Thus, a planning model based on I-O analysis may necessarily generate welfare losses due to market imperfections, unless the optimal degree of cooperation δ^* is built into the plan. As an empirical illustration, we may refer to a study of investment planning strategy for Columbia [22, 30] which showed that planning by itself would accentuate the degree of inequality of income distribution measured by the share of profits in national income and also the Lorenz coefficient. Similar evidence exists for other countries [14, 18].

Next we consider a second type of Cournot-Nash noncooperative framework, where player I (the sectoral producers) use the optimization model (1.3) except that he allows for the demand fluctuations (i.e. variance of elements d_i of vector d) e.g.

$$\text{player I:} \qquad \max_{x} \; f_1 = -v'x$$

$$\text{subject to}$$

$$Bx \geq d^e; \; d^e = (d_i^e); \; d_i^e = \bar{d}_i - q_i\sigma_i \tag{3.1}$$

$$x \geq 0$$

Here d^e is the vector of estimated demands d_i^e in sector i which equals mean demand $\bar{d}_i$ less a factor proportional to the standard deviation σ_i of demand. The central planner's model has a payoff function $f_2 = f_2(p)$;

$$\text{player II:} \qquad \max_{p} \; f_2 = p'\bar{d} - \frac{1}{2}\lambda p'\sigma p$$

$$\text{subject to}$$

$$p'B \leq v' \; ; \; p \geq 0$$

Here σ is the variance-covariance matrix of demand d and $\bar{d}$ is the mean in terms of the subjective probability distribution of the planner; λ is a constant weight on the variance term. It is clear from (3.1) and (3.2) that if λ and q_i are each zero so that $d^e = \bar{d}$, then for any optimal solution x^* of LP (3.1) there exists an optimal solution p^* of (3.2) such that (x^*, p^*) constitutes a saddle point equilibrium for the two-person game which is zero sum, since $p^{*\prime}\bar{d} = v'x^*$. However, for positive values of λ and q_i, the two-person game is nonzero sum. Hence the shadow prices, p^e say computed from (3.1), for a give estimate d^e may not be consistent with the optimal strategies p^* computed from (3.2) assuming a nonzero λ. This leads to the problem of price inconsistency in the planning model which has been recognized in several applications [4, 14, 29]. However the method of solution proposed for resolving such inconsistency e.g., through market adjustment in response to two sets of prices p^e and p^* has not been very satisfactory. This is due to two basic reasons. First, adjustments through excess demand functions introduced exogenously appear to be very artificial, unrelated to the game theory considerations. Second, the usual Kuhn-Tucker theory fails to hold in its sufficiency conditions. This is because, the factor λ may be negative in which case $f_2 = f_2(p)$ may be strictly convex rather than concave. However, in a game theory framework, concavity is not a necessary condition for a Cournot-Nash equilibrium solution.

Since the central planner is likely to be more optimistic about meeting demand targets, it is natural to assume that he would expect an average demand level $\bar{d}$ higher than d^e, which is player I's estimate. Denoting the optimal shadow price of the linear constraints of (3.2) by $x^*(2)$ and those of (3.1)by p^e we may easily derive at the Cournot-Nash equilibrium solutions:

$$p^* = \frac{1}{\lambda} \sigma^{-1} (\bar{d} - Bx^*(2)) = \frac{1}{\lambda} \sigma^{-1} (\bar{d} - d^e) \tag{3.3}$$

where it is assumed that $x^*(2)$ equals x^*, the optimal solution for (3.1). It is clear that the inconsistency of the two sets of prices and hence of the two sets of output can be resolved, if the discrepancy between $\bar{d}$ and d^e may be reduced or eliminated. This calls for two types of coordination at the policy level. First, information about sectoral demand-supply discrepancies must be made available monthly or quarterly in a competitive fashion and the overall five or six year plan should be flexible in terms of quarterly variations. In this sense, flexibility and forecasting of short-term developments of sectoral imbalances must form a basic component of the design of a development planning model. Second, due to the elements of risk aversion, which may in part be due to expectations about the future performance of the economy and of central planning, any policy which reduce environmental uncertainty would be most helpful in reducing the price inconsistency. Hence the need for developing an appropriate stabilization policy, especially for strategic sectors like agriculture, power and transport which affect the basic elements of the production distribution process in the economy.

4. Stabilization Policy Under Constraints

The framework of stabilization policy in a national planning model has three interrelated components: (a) commodity price stabilization in sectors which are sensitive to price fluctuations e.g., buffer stock policies, (b) monetary and financial policies [23, 31] aimed at consumption, production and investment decisions, and (c) trade and fiscal policies aimed at stimulating capacity utiliztion and long-run resource transfer to sectors which contribute most to long-run output growth [21, 28, 30]. The targets in the three cases are: commodity price stability, monetary and financial stability and steady economic growth. Whereas the instruments for (b) and (c) are generally macro-economic e.g., money supply, interest rate and government investment and tax policies, those in case of (a) have emphasized several micro-economic factors, besides the macro ones e.g., (i) expectations that sectoral balances may not be realized, (ii) government's price policy may not be very effective and, (iii) there may be considerable lags in adjustment of demand and supply [6].

In the short-run, commodity stabilization policies are most important for most LDC, since the macroeconomic factors are taken care of in the design of the planning model through I-O and other macro-econometric relations like consumption and investment functions. A second major reason is that in key sectors like agriculture which is sensitive to weather fluctuations and other forms of market uncertainty, such policies if properly designed and implemented may imply substantial welfare gains for the whole economy. For instance, risk aversion may be a major reason why small farmers may fail to produce cash crops that are exportable; they may fail to adopt improved production methods, because of a lack of subsidy in buying new inputs like chemical fertilizers. Lastly, due to lack of appropriate storage and warehouse facilities and the lack of accessible loan markets, the short-run price fluctuations may be far wider than if futures markets prevail.

We consider now two types of commodity stabilization policies, where prices are affected by government policies in the sense that mean prices are stabilized by buffer fund or other operations at a cost which may be assumed to be zero. Such models [13] have been considered before in price stabilization analysis except that we consider here two types of constraints i.e., one on the control budget and the other on the total market uncertainty. We consider first a scalar case, where quantities of supply and demand are q_s, q_d and the price p are characterized by its mean $\bar{p}$ and variance σ_p^2. The demand supply relations of the market are

$$q_s = a + b\bar{p} - c\,\sigma_p^2 \tag{4.1}$$

$$q_d = \alpha - \beta\bar{p} - \gamma\,\sigma_p^2 \tag{4.2}$$

$$q_s = q_d = q \tag{4.3}$$

Positivity of the parameters c, γ implies that suppliers and demanders are risk averse in the sense that they react negatively to price fluctuations. Rationale for such risk aversion in agricultural supply may be found in both empirical and applied work e.g., empirically such risk aversion has been observed in both developed and LDC [26, 27]. Theoretically, (4.1) can be derived by maximizing the expected value of an exponential utility of income function

$$u(y) = 1 - \exp(-\alpha\, y),\ \alpha > 0$$

where income y equals $(p - c_0)\, q_s$ with p being randomly distributed like a normal distribution with mean $\bar{p}$ and variance σ_p^2 and c_0 being a positive constant denoting marginal cost per unit of output. On general grounds it may be expected that $c > \gamma$

≥ 0 i.e. suppliers are likely to be more risk averse than demanders. One may also adjoin to each of the two equations (41.), (4.2) a linear additive noise term, which is independent of $\bar{p}$ and σ_p^2. But since this does not affect the basic elements of the model, it will be ignored. The stabilization policy will be indicated by

$$p = p_o + ku + \varepsilon \tag{4.4}$$

where u is the control variable to be used by the planning authority and k denotes its intensity, ε is an independent random variable with mean $\bar{\varepsilon}$ and variance σ_ε^2 and p_o is market price which will obtain if there were no control u = 0. In particular, p_o may equal the equilibrium price $\bar{p}$ solved from (4.1) through (4.3) as:

$$\bar{p} = \frac{\alpha - a}{b + \beta} + \frac{c - \gamma}{b + \beta}\sigma_p^2$$
$$\bar{q} = \frac{b\alpha + a\beta}{b + \beta} - \frac{b\gamma + \beta c}{b + \beta}\sigma^2{}_p \tag{4.5}$$

It is clear that equilibrium prices $\bar{p}$ and quantities $\bar{q}$ are not free from market fluctuations represented by σ_p^2. If $c = \gamma = 0$ i.e., both demanders and suppliers are risk-neutral, only then prices and quantities reach their constant steady states except for additive noise components which are purely random or white noise e.g.

$$\bar{p} = (b + \beta)^{-1}(\alpha - a); \quad \bar{q} = (b + \beta)^{-1}(b\alpha + a\beta) \tag{4.6}$$

On the other hand, if the demanders are risk-neutral, i.e., $\gamma = 0$ but the suppliers are not i.e., $c > 0$, we would have lower equilibrium output and higher price compared to (4.6); this is so because along (4.5) we have:

$$\partial\bar{p}/\partial c > 0, \quad \partial\bar{q}/\partial c < 0 \tag{4.7}$$

In this case, for a fixed $q = \bar{q}$ the supplier's gain $q_s(\bar{q})$, in terms of expected utility of income may be obtained on integration of (4.5) as follows:

$$g_s(\bar{q}) = (a + b\bar{p})\,\bar{q} - \frac{1}{2}\,\bar{q}\,(\bar{q} + 2c\sigma_p^2) \tag{4.7}$$

Here net gain is $g_s(\bar{q}) - a\bar{q}$, expected return is $b\bar{p}\bar{g}$ and adjutment cost is $A_s(\bar{q}) = \frac{1}{2}\,\bar{q}\,(\bar{q} + 2c\sigma_p^2)$; similarly, for the demanders, net gain can be derived as:

$$g_d(\bar{q}) - \alpha\bar{q} = -\beta\bar{p}\bar{q} - \frac{1}{2}\bar{q}(\bar{q} + 2\gamma\sigma_p^2) \tag{4.8}$$

where the consumers' adjustment cost is $A_d(\bar{q}) = \frac{1}{2}\bar{q}(\bar{q} + 2\gamma\sigma_p^2)$. Total gain is then

$$g = g_s(\bar{q}) + g_d(\bar{q}) = (a + \alpha)\bar{q} + (b - \beta)\bar{p}\bar{q} - A(\bar{q}) \tag{4.9}$$

$$A(\bar{q}) = A_s(\bar{q}) + A_d(\bar{q}) = \bar{q}^2 + (c + \gamma)\bar{q}\sigma_p^2 \tag{4.10}$$

several implications of these formulations are important for policy and planning. First, the central planner may stabilize prices in the sense of raising $\bar{p}/\sigma_p^2$ i.e. raising $\bar{p}$ and reducing σ_p^2. If the consumers and producers are risk-averse with $c > \gamma \geq 0$ and the market is competitive, this will increase the total gain $g = g_s(\bar{q}) + g_d(\bar{q})$. In the limit, if the term σ_p^2 can be reduced to zero, by the planner having sufficient buffer stocks or sufficient imports, the gain is maximum possible i.e.

$$g_{max} = (a + \alpha)\bar{q} + (b - \beta)\bar{p}\bar{q} - \bar{q}^2 > g.$$

In the situation (4.4) where the control variable u may be used to stabilize prices, σ_p^2 need not be a constant. Let p* be the level desired by the planner, which is different from $\bar{p}$, then

$$\bar{p} - p^* = k(\bar{u} - u^*) + (\bar{\varepsilon} - \varepsilon^*)$$

$$E(\bar{p} - p^*)^2 = k^2(\bar{u} - u^*)^2 + E(\bar{\varepsilon} - \varepsilon^*)^2$$

where E is expectation over the distribution of equilibrium price $\bar{p}$ around their desired levels. Replacing σ_p^2 by $E(\bar{p} - p^*)^2 = \sigma_{p*}^2$ in the total gain equation (4.10), where the latter may be called the adjusted variance, total gain per unit of $\bar{q}$ becomes

$$f = \frac{g}{\bar{q}} = (a + \alpha) + (b - \beta\ (p_o + k\bar{u} + \bar{\varepsilon}) - \bar{q} - (c + \gamma)\sigma_{p*}^2 \tag{4.11}$$

Since f is a function $f(k, \bar{u})$ of the control variable $\bar{u}$ and its feedback element k, it can be maximized by the choice of $\bar{u}$ and k. The first order conditions lead to the optimal values k, $\bar{u}^o$ as follows:

$$k^o = \frac{(b^2 - \beta^2)}{2(b+\beta)(c+\gamma)} \cdot \frac{\bar{u}^o}{(\bar{u}^o - u^*)^2} \tag{4.12}$$

$$\bar{u}^o = u^* + \frac{b - \beta}{2(c + \gamma)k^o}$$

were it is assumed that $\bar{u}^o$ is not equal to its desired level, thus necessitating the choice of the feedback element k. The second relation of (4.12) implies the need for a higher $\bar{u}^o$, wherever the desired goal u^* is higher, or the supply reaction is greater than demand i.e., $b > \beta$. The first relation suggests that higher k^o will lead to a lower gap measured by $(u - u^*)^2$ for any given $\bar{u}^o$; also it implies that the higher the supply reaction over that of demand i.e., $b > \beta$ the greater the need for a higher feedback; otherwise suppliers will be affected.

Second, the estimation of net gain in (4.7) and (4.8) is symmetrical with respect to price fluctuations measured by σ_p^2. However this need not be the case e.g. if $\sigma_p^2 = w\sigma^2(1) + (1 - w)\sigma^2(2)$, where $\sigma^2(1)$ is the lower variance computed on the assumption that market prices are lower than the average and $\sigma^2(2)$ is the upper variance, then $w = 0.5$ denotes symmetry; otherwise we have asymmetry in risk aversion [32]. Suppliers are more likely to be risk-averse in the sense of lower variance $\sigma^2(1)$, so that the term σ_p^2 in (4.7) needs to be replaced by $w\sigma^2(1)$, where w is a positive weight different from 0.5. Demanders on the other hand are likely to be risk averse in the sense of upper variance $\sigma^2(2)$ so that the term σ_p^2 in (4.8) should be replaced by $(1 - w)\sigma^2(2)$. However since upper variance is favorable to suppliers and lower variance to consumers, the gain equations (4.7), (4.8) would be modified as follows:

$$g_s = (a + b\bar{p})\bar{q} - \frac{1}{2}\bar{q}\,(\bar{q} + 2cw\sigma^2(1) - 2c(1 - w)\sigma^2(2))$$

$$g_d = (\alpha - \beta\bar{p})\,\bar{q} - \frac{1}{2}\bar{q}\,(\bar{q} + 2\gamma(1 - w)\sigma^2(2) - 2\gamma w\sigma^2(1))$$

The weights w reflect evaluation of market uncertainty by the suppliers and demanders and are therefore affected by their expectation about the planner's strategy as it influences the market.

Third, the stabilization policy in (4.4) is oriented to price fluctuations alone, a quantity orientation can be easily built into it. The latter may in particular be very important when the adjustment process is through time lags.

The above analysis for stabilization policy can be easily generalized to many goods and the adjustment process can be viewed over time. Let x_t, y_t denote the vectors of supply and demand in time t and p_t be the market prices. The pricing process in the market is described by the state equation

$$p_{t+1} = p_t - Ay_t - B(x_t - y_t);\ p_t \text{ at } t = 0 \text{ given} \tag{5.1}$$

where A and B are suitable matrices. Since $(x_t - y_t)$ is the excess supply, it would normally have a depressing effect on price change i.e. $\partial(p_{t+1} - p_t)/\partial s_t < 0$ where $s_t = x_t - y_t$ but the effect of a change in y_t for given x_t may be positive or negative. The supplier's risk adjusted objective function may be written as a profit functional

$$J(x) = \sum_{t=0}^{n} [p_t' x_t - A_1(x_t, x_{t-1}, V_p)] \tag{5.2}$$

where $A_1(\cdot)$ is the adjustment cost function, assumed to depend on x_t, x_{t-1} and the variance-covariance matrix of prices V_p. For the demanders, the objective functional may be similarly viewed as

$$J(y) = \sum_{t=0}^{T} [p_t' y_t - A_2(y_t, y_{t-1}, V_p)] \tag{5.3}$$

the market process may now be viewed as a nonzero sum difference game between player I, the suppliers who choose x_t subject to the state equation (5.1) and player II, the consumers who choose y_t subject to (5.1). The two adjustment cost functions may be approximated by suitable quadratic functions e.g.,

$$A_1(x_t, x_{t-1}, V_p) = \frac{1}{2}(x_t - x_{t-1})' W_1 (x_t - x_{t-1}) + \frac{1}{2}\lambda x_t' V_p x_t$$

$$A_2\ (y_t, y_{t-1}\ V_p) = \frac{1}{2}(y_t - y_t)' W_2 (y_t - y_{t-1}) + \frac{1}{2}\mu y_t' V_p y_t$$

Here W_1, W_2 and V_p are time-independent constant matrices and the first component indicates the cost of varying supply or demand at two consecutive time points and the second component denotes adjustment due to price fluctuations. The risk aversion parameters λ , μ indicate whether player I is more risk averse $\lambda > \mu$ or less. In this framework of nonzero sum two person game, the central planner's role is to reduce the variances V_p or the risk aversion parameters λ, μ so that the total value $J = J(x) + J(y)$ can be increased. Further, using Pontryagin's maximum principle, it can be shown [25] that if there exist steady state strategies $\bar{x}$, $\bar{y}$ such that for some λ, μ it holds $\bar{x} = \bar{y}$ and these lie on the Nash-equilibrium trajectory, then λ must be an eigenvalue of $V_p^{-1}(A + B')$ and μ that of $V_p^{-1}(A + A' - B')$ i.e.

$$[\lambda I - V_p^{-1}(A + B')\bar{x} = 0 = [\mu I - V_p^{-1}(A + A' - B')]\bar{y}$$

the two sets of n eignevalues $(\lambda_1, \lambda_2, \ldots, \lambda_n)$ and $(\mu_1, \mu_2, \ldots, \mu_n)$ characterize the whole spectrum of risk aversion as the price fluctuations V_p are filtered through the terms $V_p^{-1}(A + B')$ and $V_p^{-1}(A + B' - B')$. If these eigenvalues are all real and positive (which will be the case if the matrices $A + B'$, $A = A' - B'$ are positive definite and symmetric), then these can be ordered as $0 < \lambda_1 \leq \lambda_2 \leq \cdots \leq \lambda_n$ and $0 < \mu_1 \leq \mu_2 \leq \cdots \leq \mu_n$. The pair (λ_n, μ_n) may represent risk aversion to the highest degree, whereas (λ_1, μ_1) may represent the lowest. The central planner's coordination problem would be to design a policy so that (λ_n, μ_n) can be successively lowered to (λ_1, μ_1).

The above analysis of stabilization policy is however restricted to specific sectors like agriculture, where buffer stock and other optimal inventory policies can be appropriately applied. At a more general macroeconomic level monetary and fiscal instruments would be necessary. These aspects are not discussed here. Note however that even in long run models of growth planning, the need for fluctuation aversion has been emphasized very strongly [15, 29, 30].

5. Concluding Remarks

Applications of input-output and LP models to national economic planning in LDC generally assume a competitive market framework for the outputs and inputs, reliable forecast of demand by sectors and no errors of adjustment by private sector producers. In the real life situations however, each of these assumptions may fail to hold e.g. imperfect or monopolistic market power may lead to lower output and higher prices, inaccurate forecast by the planner may lead to substantial gaps or fluctuations around the targets and the planner's failure to forecast the private sector's supply behavior under conditions of market uncertainty may lead to substantial cost of adjustment. These costs must then be counted as the necessary cost of the planning design itself. Three types of methods are suggested above for handling these problems and thereby making the process of planning in a mixed economy more effective and realistic.

It must be pointed out that there remain several other sources of uncertainty that affect the formulation and implementation of economic planning, particularly in a mixed economy framework. Some of the important ones are: (a) planning as a team decision approach, where decentralized decisions and allocations under uncertainty are to be optimized; problems of inconsistency of goals of different members due to different perceptions, of multicriteria objective functions [28] and the need for coordination and for developing realistic incentive systems appear to be important here; (b) planning as a method of coordination between short and long run models where the former may have monetary variables and instruments and the latter real variables affecting capacity investment and growth; problems of reconciling short and long run objectives, through linkages between short and long run models, of developing suitable compromises among policy alternatives [19, 20] and of applying a satisficing rather than maximizing criterion are some of the most important issues in this framework and (c) use of shadow prices in project evaluation and benefit cost analysis, when the overall socio-economic framework is not perfectly competitive either due to conditions of market failure in domestic markets of LDC or to tax-subsidy rules by government which may impede competitive forces and thereby lead to second best results; problems of choosing an open-loop policy by committing once for all furture decisions determined now or, a discretionary policy with options to revise the plan as the future evolves appear to be most important in this set up.

References

1. Arrow, K.J. and F.H. Hahn: General Competitive Anlysis, Holden-Day, San Francisco, 1971.
2. Behrman, J.R.: Supply Response in Underdeveloped Agriculture, North Holland, Amsterdam, 1968.
3. Blitzer, C.R., P.B. Clark and L. Taylor: Economy-Wide Models and Development Planning, Oxford University Press, London, 1975.
4. Cornelisse, P.A.: Price Consistency in Development Planning, Rotterdam University Press, Rotterdam, 1973.
5. Duloy, J.H. and R.D. Norton: Chac: A Programming Model of Mexican Agriculture, in Goreux, L.M. and A.S. Manne eds.: Multilevel Planning: Case Studies in Mexico, pp. 291-337, North Holland, Amsterdam, 1973.
6. Fox, K.A., J.K. Sengupta and E. Thorbecke: The Theory of Quantitative Economic Policy with Applications to Economic Growth, Stabilization and Planning, Second edition, North Holland, Amsterdam, 1972.
7. Johansen, L: Lectures on Macroeconomic Planning, Vol. 1-2, North Holland, Amsterdam, 1977, 1978.
8. Just, R.E.: An Investigation of the Importance of Risk in Farmers' Decisions," American Journal of Agricultural Economics, 56, 1974, 14-25.
9. Kawamata, K.: Price Distortion and Potential Welfare, Econometrica, 42, 1974, 435-460.
10. Kornai, J.: Mathematical Planning of Structural Decisions, North Holland, Amsterdam, 1967.
11. Lange, O.: Optimal Decisions, Principles of Programming, Pergamon Press, Oxford, 1971.
12. Manne, A.S.: Multi-sector Models for Development Planning: A Survey, in Intriligator, M.D. and D.A. Kendrick, eds., Frontiers of Quantitative Economics, vol. 2, North Holland, Amsterdam, 1974.
13. Massell, B.F.: Price Stabilization and Welfare, Quarterly Journal of Economics, 83, 1969, 284-298.
14. Meade, J.E.: The Theory of Indicative Planning, Manchester University Press, Manchester, 1970.
15. Morishima, M.: Theory of Economic Growth, Clarendon Press, Oxford, 1969.
16. Negishi, T.: General Equilibrium Theory and International Trade, North Holland, Amsterdam, 1972.
17. Nikaido, H.: Monopolistic Competition and Effective Demand, Princeton University Press, Princeton, NJ, 1975.
18. Nugent, J.B.: Linear Programming Models for National Planning: Demonstration of a Testing Procedure, Econometrica, 38, 1970, 831-855.

19. Sandee, J.: Optimum Policy Alternatives in Modeling for Government and Businss, Martinus Nijhoff Social Sciences Division, Leiden, 1977, 149-164.

20. Scott, M.F., J.D. MacArthur and D.M.G. Newberry: Project Appraisal in Practice, Heinemann Educational Books, London, 1976.

21. Sengupta, J.K.: Economic Policy Simulatin in Dynamic Control Models Under Econometric Estimation, in W. Sellekaerts ed., Econometrics and Economic Theory, MacMillan, London, 1974, Ch. 5, 115-138.

22. Sengupta, J.K.: A Consistent Planning Method for Income Growth and Distribution with an Application, Working Paper No. 18, Indian Institute of Management, Calcutta, June 1977.

23. Sengupta, J.K. and R.I. Sfeir: The Adjustment of Output-Inventory Process Under Linear Decision Rules, Journal of Economic Dynamics and Control, 1, 1979, 361-381.

25. Sengupta, J.K.: Optimal Resource Allocation Under Stochastic Prices and Yields," Journal of Economics, 39, 1979, 83-104.

26. Sengupta, J.K. and R.I. Sfeir: "Risk in Supply Response," working paper No. 124, Dept. of Economics, University of California, Santa Barbara, 1979, to be published in Applied Economics, London.

27. Sengupta, J.K.: Decision Models in Stochastic Programming, to be published by American Elsevier and North Holland, ca. 1981.

28. Sfeir-Younis, A. and D.W. Bromley: Decision Making in Developing Countries: Multiobjective Formulation and Evaluation Methods, Praeger Publishers, New York, 1977.

29. Taylor, L.: Theoretical Foundations and Technical Implications, Ch. 3 in Blitzer, C.R., Clark, P.B. and L. Taylor, eds., Economy-Wide Models and Development Planning, Oxford University Press, London, 1975.

30. Thorbecke, E. and J.K. Sengupta: "A Consistency Framework for Employment, Output and Income Distribution Projections Applied to Columbia," Mimeographed Report, Development Research Center, World Bank, Washington, DC, 1972.

31. Turnovsky, S.J.: Macroeconomic Analysis and Stabilization Policies, Cambridge University Press, Cambridge, 1977.

32. Waud, R.N.: "Asymmetric Policymaker Utility Functions and Optimal Policy under Uncertainty," Econometrica, 44, 1976, 53-66.

33. Wiens, T.B.: "Peasant Risk Aversion and Allocative Behavior: A Quadratic Programming Experiment," American Journal of Agricultural Economics, 58, 1976, 629-635.

CHAPTER 6

STOCHASTIC PROGRAMS AS NONZERO SUM GAMES

1. Introduction

A linear programming (LP) model for determining an optimal decision vector x, which satisfies the following system

$$\max z = c'x \tag{1.1}$$

$$\text{subject to } x \varepsilon R,\ R: \{x\ Ax \leq b,\ x \geq 0\} \tag{1.2}$$

may be related to a two-person game-theoretic formulation in two ways. In the first case, which is based on the saddle point property of the optimal solution of the LP problem, the two players have an identical strategy space, say $p' = (\bar{x}', \bar{y}', \bar{v}) = q'$ and the payoff matrix is B:

$$B: \begin{bmatrix} 0 & -A' & c \\ A & 0 & -b \\ -c' & b' & 0 \end{bmatrix} \tag{2.1}$$

Here y is an m-element vector of dual variables associated with the vector b in (1.2), x is an n-element vector of primal variables and $\bar{v}$ is a positive scalar used for normalization of the strategies i.e.

$$\bar{x} = rx,\ \bar{y} = ry,\ \bar{v} = rv$$

and

$$r = \left(\sum_{j=1}^{n} x_j + \sum_{i=1}^{m} y_i + v\right)^{-1} > 0 \tag{2.2}$$

since we require p and q to be probability vectors:

$$\begin{aligned} &\Sigma p_s = \Sigma q_k = 1,\ p_s,\ q_k \geq 0 \\ &\quad s,\ k = 1, 2, \ldots, (n + m + 1) \end{aligned} \tag{2.3}$$

For a deterministic LP model with a fixed parameter set S: (A, b, c), it is known [3, 11] that a two-person zero-sum game in normal form G = (P, Q; B) can be associated with any saddle point solution (x, y) of the LP formulation given by (1.1) and (1.2). Here $p \varepsilon Q$ where P and Q are subsets of the (n + m + 1)-dimensional nonnegative Euclidean space E^+. The LP problem (1) is stochastic, if the parameter set S is generated by a probabilistic mechanism, i.e., $S = \{S(w),\ w \varepsilon \Omega\}$ where w characterizes the state of the world. We have then the two-person nonzero sum formulation:

Player I: $\max_{p \varepsilon P} p'B_1(w)q$ (3.1)

subject to (2.3)

Player II: $\max_{q \varepsilon Q} p'B_2(w)q$ (3.2)

subject to (2.3)

where $B_1(w)$, $B_2(w)$ are the payoff matrices for the two players respectively. These may be interpreted in different ways, e.g., different payoffs may be due to different perceptions of the state of the world, or different channels of information on the state of nature. In case $B_1(w) = -B_2(w)$, we have a zero sum game, otherwise it is nonzero sum.

A second type of game theoretic formulation arises when player I, the decision maker who controls strategies $x \geq 0$, $x \varepsilon M$, with M being the subset of E^+ plays against nature, player II who has strategies $(A(w), b(w), c(w), w \varepsilon \Omega)$, where the set Ω now defines the set of points in the Euclidean space of dimensions $(mn + m + n)$ corresponding to the feasible domain of change of the elements $(a_{ij}(w), b_i(w), c_j(w);\ i = q, w, \ldots, m;\ j = 1, 2, \ldots, n)$. Denote the strategy set of player II by N and let the payoff function be $g = g(x; A(w), b(w), c(w))$

$$g = \sum_{j=1}^{n} c_j(w)x_j + \sum_{i=1}^{m} h_i \left(\sum_{j=1}^{n} a_{ij}(w)x_j - b_i(w) \right) \qquad (4.1)$$

were $h_i(z)$, $i = 1, 2, \ldots, m$ are continuous nondecreasing functions satisfying $h_i(z) = 0$ if $z \leq 0$. The game is zero sum in the sense that player I maximizes the payoff g in (4.1), whereas player II minimizes it. The game in normal form is $G = (M, N: g)$. Denote the set of probability distributions F_x of vector x of player I by $\underset{\sim}{F}$ and the set of probability distributions F_{Abc} of (A, b, c) of the player II by F. Kolbin [4] has reported such zero-sum formulations, which show that if the strategy sets M and N are compact, then there always exist a pair of mixed strategies (F_x^*, F_{Abc}^*) where $F_x^* \varepsilon F$ and $F_{Abc}^* \varepsilon \tilde{F}$ are optimal choices in the sense of minimax, i.e.

$$\max_{F_x \varepsilon F} \min_{F_{Abc} \varepsilon \tilde{F}} \int_{MxN} g(\xi, \alpha, \beta, \gamma) dF_x(\xi)\, dF_{Abc}(\alpha, \beta, \gamma)$$

$$= \min_{\tilde{F}_{Abc} \varepsilon F} \max_{F_x \varepsilon F} \int_{MxN} g(\xi, \alpha, \beta, \gamma)\, dF(\xi)\, dF_{Abc}(\alpha, \beta, \gamma) \tag{4.2}$$

$$= \int_{MxN} g(\xi, \alpha, \beta, \gamma)\, dF^*_x(\xi)\, dF^*_{Abc}(\alpha, \beta, \gamma)$$

where the value of the game is attained. This two-person zero sum formulation appears to be very restrictive however in applied work, because of two reasons. First, the strategies of the two players are rarely unconstrained in reality i.e., they are in some sense always restricted by the environment e.g., the decision maker gains the experience of previous moves of his opponent and this he may profitably combine with his own subjective estimates to decide on the actual strategy. Ths leads to the concept of partially controllable strategies, which have been applied in nonzero sum games associated with chance-constrained linear programming [1, 8]. In this game, for example, the actual strategy $(\tilde{x})$ used by player I is taken to be a linear combination of a preassigned strategy (x_0) and a chosen strategy (x) so that $\tilde{x} = kx + (1 - k)\, x_0$, where k is fixed positive scalar weight; likewise for player II. Second, there is almost always some learning or adaptive behavior by player I, the decision maker who anticipates possible reactions of his opponent and attempts to incorporate them in his own choice of strategies. For instance, if the state of nature is the product market, a particular supplier (player I) may incorporate into his output or price policy some form of advertisement policy. Thus, if x_0 is the initial probability estimates of player I according to his subjective distribution, the decision problem before him is how much to perturb his initial estimates to obtain his maximum expected payoff such that it is consistent with the optimal strategies of the other player. These considerations lead to a nonzero sum framework where the two players' strategies are interactive. Sengupta [7, 9] has shown the conditions under which such game models have Cournot-Nash equilibria defined by complementary eigenvalue problems.

Our objective here is to develop further these two-person nonzero sum formulations for some special cases of the above stochastic LP models, which are mostly applicable in market games and competitive systems, where information may be unequally shared. Two aspects are emphasized in particular: the role of information and the cost of search or learning about the strategy interactions.

2. Games with Unknown Parameters

Consider first the two-person nonzero sum formulation (3.1), (3.2) where the true state of the world is B(w), but the players have incomplete information so that $B_k(w)$ does not equal B(w) for k = 1, 2. Two interpretations of B(w) may be suggested. One is that it is the long-run payoff available to the players asymptotically (i.e., infinite sample size), after a very large number of moves are observed by them. Rosenfeld [6] has developed this interpretation and analyzed the conditions under which the zero-sum property of the competitive game would be retained. A second interpretation, which is adopted here is that the quantity $B_k(w)$ for player k = 1, 2 is based on information I_k available to him. This information may take several forms, of which only two will be analyzed here. The first assumes that two separate estimates, one by each player is made of the parameters contained in B(w) and optimal strategies developed. The second allows linear combination of the separate estimates through information sharing, before optimal strategies are developed.

For reasons of simplicity, we restrict to the case when only the vector c = c(w) in B(w) is subject to a probabilistic mechanism. Denote the true values of the parameter associated with c(w) by μ and V say, where for example μ may be the mean and V the variance-covariance matrix (i.e., dispersion), if the distribution of c is multivariate normal. The sample estimates of μ and V are denoted by $\bar{c}(k)$, V(k) for the two players k = 1, 2 respectively. The information structure is denoted by $I = (I_1, I_2)$ where I_1, I_2 may vary in different situations or different channels. In the simplest case, the players may have identical information e.g., public information so that $\bar{c}(1)$ and $\bar{c}(2) = \bar{c}$ say and V is known. In this case, player I solves the LP model

$$\text{player I:} \quad \max_{x \varepsilon R_1} \; \bar{c}'x; \quad R_1: \{x \,|\, Ax \leq b, \; x \geq 0\} \tag{5.1}$$

whereas the second player solves his model

$$\text{player II:} \quad \min_{y \varepsilon R_2} \; b'y; \; R_2: \{y \,|\, y'A \geq \bar{c}', \; y \geq 0\} \tag{5.2}$$

It is assumed that the sets R_1, R_2 are nonempty. By the saddle point property, it follows that if x^o is the optimal strategy of player I in terms of (5.1) then there exists an optimal strategy y^o of player II in terms of (5.2). Hence, if $\bar{c}(1)$ is not equal to $\bar{c}(2)$, due to incomplete information e.g., some information is not <u>public</u>, the game would not be zero sum since $\bar{c}(1)'x^o(1)$ would not equal $b'y^o(2)$, where $x^o(1)$, $y^o(2)$ are the respective optimal strategies of the two players. The estimates $\bar{c}(k)$ are defined to be unbiased if $E\bar{c}(k) = \mu$, where E is expectation over each player's subjective probability distribution and let $S(k) = E[(c(k) - \mu)(\bar{c}(k) - \mu)']$ denote the variance-covariance matrix fo each player k = 1, 2. Several results may now be derived as follows:

<u>Theorem 1</u>

Assume there is an utility function U(1) for player I with its expected value given by (6.1) and he derives an optimal strategy vector $x_o(1)$ by maximizing it:

$$EU(1) = \bar{c}(1)'x(1) - \lambda\, x(1)'S(1)x(1),\ \lambda > 0 \tag{6.1}$$

$$\max_{x(1)\varepsilon R_1} \quad EU(1) \text{ leads to } x_0(1)$$

Then there exists an optimal zero sum strategy $y_0 = y_0(x_0(1)) = y_0(1)$ say for player II. However this need not equal the nonzero sum optimal strategy $y_0(2)$ of player II, if the estimates $\bar{c}(k)$, $S(k)$ are not equal for $k = 1, 2$.

Proof

Since $x_0(1)$ exists by assumption, the following LP problem derived by linearizing the quadratic objective function EU(1) around $x_0(1)$:

$$\max_{x(1)\varepsilon R_1} \quad f(x) = [\bar{c}(1) - 2\lambda S(1)\ x_0(1)]'\ x(1) \tag{6.2}$$

must have an optimal solution at $x(1)= x^o(1)$. The equivalent LP problem (6.2) has a dual solution vector y which must satisfy

$$\min_y\ b'y,\ y\varepsilon R_2$$

$$\text{where } R_2\text{: } \{y | y \geq 0,\ y'A \geq (\bar{c}(1) - 2\lambda S(1)\ x_0(1))\} \tag{6.3}$$

By LP duality it follows that

$$\bar{c}(1)'x(1) \leq c'(1)\ x^o(1) = b'y_0 \leq b'y$$

Hence $y_0 = y_0(1)$ is a zero sum optimal strategy, given that player II follows the extimate $\hat{c}$ of μ from player I and $\hat{c} = \bar{c}(1) - 2\lambda S(1)\ x_0(1)$. However, his own estimate, $\hat{c}(2)$ say may differ from $\hat{c}$ and therefore his own optimal strategy $y_0(2)$ may differ from $y_0(1)$ which is a zero sum strategy.

Remark 1.1

A nonzero sum optimal strategy $y_0(2)$ of player II, using his own estimates $\bar{c}(2)$, $S(2)$ denoted by $\hat{c}$ may be solved from the bilinear model:

$$\min_y\ g(y) = b'y$$

subject to (6.4)

$$y'Ax(1) \geq \hat{c}'\ x(1)$$

$$y \geq 0,\ x(1) \geq 0$$

This becomes an LP problem provided x(1) is either known or taken as a given parameter by the second player. It is clear from (6.4) that if the individual estimates $\bar{c}(k)$, S(k) are equivalent in the following sense

$$\hat{c} = \bar{c}(2) - \tilde{\lambda}S(2)\, x_0(1) = \bar{c}(1) - \lambda S(1)\, x_0(1) \qquad (6.5)$$
$$\tilde{\lambda} = \lambda > 0$$

then the nonzero sum optimal strategy $y_0(2)$ equals the zero sum optimal strategy $y_0 = y_0(1)$ corresponding to $x_0(1)$. Note that the equivalence in the sense of (6.5) implies any of the following:

(a) $\bar{c}(1) = \bar{c}(2) = c_0,\ S(1) = S(2) = S_0$

(b) $\bar{c}(1) > \bar{c}(2)$ and $x_0'(1)\,[S(1) - S(2)]\, x_0(1) = x_0'(1)\,[\bar{c}(1) - \bar{c}(2)]$

(c) $S(1) - S(2) > 0$ and $x_0'(1)\,[S(1) - S(2)]\, x_0(1) = x_0'(1)\,[\bar{c}(1) - \bar{c}(2)]$

Remarks 1.2

The weight coefficients λ, $\tilde{\lambda}$ in (6.5) are usually interpreted as parameters of risk aversion i.e., a higher positive value implies that a greater weight is given to losses due to variance. If λ is not equal to $\tilde{\lambda}$ for the two players, then even the condition $\bar{c}(1) = \bar{c}(2)$, $S(1) = S(2)$ is not sufficient for the nonzero sum optimal strategy $y_0(2)$ to equal $y_0(1)$, the zero sum optimal one. It implies that even for an identical information structure available to the two players, nonzero sum optimal strategies are more likely than the zero sum ones.

Remark 1.3

Let the price vector c(w) be normally distributed N(μ, V) with mean μ and a dispersion matrix V and the expected utility function (6.1) be of the form:

$$EU(1) = \bar{c}(1)'x(1) - t_1\,[x'(1)S(1)x(1)]^{\frac{1}{2}}\,(N_1 - 1)^{-\frac{1}{2}} \qquad (6.6)$$

where N_1 is the sample size of information I_1 available to player I and t_1 is $\alpha/2$ value of the standard t-statistic

$$t = t_{\alpha/2,N\ -\ 1} = \frac{[\bar{c}(1)'x(1) - \mu'x(1)]}{(x((1)'S(1)x(1))^{\frac{1}{2}}} \cdot (N_1 - 1)$$

having $(N_1 - 1)$ degrees of freedom. Then, as information N_1 increases indefinitely i.e. $N_1 \to \infty$, the sample mean $\bar{c}(1)$ converges to the population mean μ and the precision of this estimate $\bar{c}(1)$ increases till in the limit

$$EU(1) = \bar{c}(1)'x_0(1, N_1) \leq \bar{c}_\infty(1)'x_0(1, \infty)$$

where $\bar{c}_N(1)$, $x_0(1, N)$ denote the mean estimate and optimal strategy of player I depending on sample size N. Furthermore, it is clear that if N_2 is the information structure available to player II with $N_2 > N_1$, we would have

$$b'y_0(2, N_2) \leq b'y_0(2, \infty)$$

$$b'y_0(2, N_2) \geq b'y_0(2, N_1)$$

provided the method used in (6.2) and (6.3) for deriving zero sum optimal strategies are followed and an identical probability level α in the t-statistic is used. Note that for both N_1, N_2 tending to infinity, the game with the payoff function (6.6) tends to a zero sum form with a common value $v = \bar{c}_\infty'(1)\ x_0(1, \infty) = b'y_0(2, \infty)$, this common value v may be interpreted as the long-run payoff of the game.

Since the common value v may be interpreted as a function of true values of the unknown parameters of c(w), a short run policy for the two players, each with information N_k may be stated in terms of the deviations $v - \bar{c}'(1)\ x_0(1, N_1)$ or, $v - b'y_0(2, N_2)$. This is closely related to Rosenfeld's approach mentioned before, where the game process is assumed to continue for N steps and then terminate for $N < \infty$; here the optimal strategy for the first player is one that maximizes total expected return over N steps of the play and the other player's objective is to minimize it. Since our framework is not necessarily zero sum, we adopt a different approach. We now denote the strategy vectors of two players by x(1) and x(2) and these are interpreted as transformed or partially controllable strategies

$$x(k) = \tilde{x}(k) - x(\infty);\ k = 1, 2 \tag{7.1}$$

where $\tilde{x}(k)$ is the short-run strategy of player k, based on an estimate derived from N_k observations, while $x(\infty)$ is the long run goal. Since $\bar{c}_N(k)$ differs from $\bar{c}_\infty(k)$, the short run optimal $\tilde{x}(k)$ differs from $x(\infty)$. The difference of short-run policy from the long-run goal, measured in terms of expected profits or losses may thus be interpreted as adjustment costs for each player. It is clear that as deviations, x(k) need not always be nonnegative; hence it belongs to the Euclidean space of dimension n. As before $\bar{c}(k)$ denotes the sample mean estimate and we assume it is normally distributed with mean μ and variance-covariance matrix $V_k = V/N_k$, where N_k is the sample size of information available to player k, V is the population variance-covariance matrix; the constraints on the strategy space are now assumed to be of the form

$$x(k)'x(k) \leq a_0, \; a_0 > 0 \tag{7.2}$$

These constraints on the strategy space replace those of (2.3) or, (5.1) since we are now dealing with partially controllable or transformed strategies. The positive quantity a_0 indicates the cost of perturbation of the transformed strategies. When this cost is binding on each player, we may set it in the form

$$x(k)'x(k) = 1, \; k = 1, 2. \tag{7.3}$$

The short run decision problem for each player k now is to choose an optimal vector $x_0(k)$ which minimizes the payoff function f(k)

$$f(k) = (\mu - \bar{c}(k))'x(k) + \lambda_k x(k)'Vx(k) \tag{7.4}$$

subject to either (7.2) or (7.3). Here $\lambda_k = \alpha/N_k$, where α is the risk aversion parameter common to the two players. This is equivalent to the nonlinear programming problem (NLP) as follows

$$\max g(x) = (\bar{c}(k) - \mu)' \, x(k) - \lambda_k \, x(k'Vx(k)) \quad \text{subject to (7.2)} \tag{7.5}$$

Denote the optimal solution of the NLP (7.5) by $x_0(k)$ and let $D_k^2 = D^2(\bar{c}(k), \mu; V_k)$ be the multivariate distance between vectors $\bar{c}(k)$ and μ, where

$$D_k^2 = (\bar{c}(k) - \mu)' \; V_k^{-1} \; (c(k) - \mu) \tag{7.6}$$

Theorem 2

Any nontrivial solution $x_0(k)$ of the NLP (7.5) is a Nash equilibrium solution and if the constraint (7.2) is not binding, the expected loss to each player is proportional to D_k^2, the distance between $\bar{c}(k)$ and the true value μ. The player with lower expected loss has higher N_k for a fixed size of error $\delta(k) = (\bar{c}(k) - \mu)$. If the constraint (7.2) is binding, the optimal solution $x_0(k)$ satisfies the property

$$\delta(k)'x_0(k) = \frac{1}{2} \, \delta(k)'(rI + \lambda_k V)^{-1} \, \delta(k) = \frac{1}{2} \, \tilde{D}_k^2$$

where $\tilde{D}_k^2$ is D_k^2 with V_k replaced by $(rI + \lambda_k V)$.

Proof

Since N_k is finite and trivial solutions are excluded, x(k) cannot be zero. Moreover, the function g(x) in (7.5) is strictly concave for $\lambda_k > 0$. Hence there exists an optimal vector $x_0(k)$ for each k, which is also a Nash equilibrium. By applying the necessary condition, one obtains

$$x_0(k) = \tfrac{1}{2} (\lambda V + rI)^{-1} \delta(k) \tag{7.7}$$

where r is the Lagrange multiplier with the constraint (7.2). If the constraint is not binding, then, r is zero and we obtain

$$g_0 = g(x_0(k)) = \frac{N_k}{4\alpha} D_k^2 = \frac{N_k}{4\alpha} D_k^2 (\bar{c}(k), \mu; V) > 0 \tag{7.8}$$

It is clear that so long as $\bar{c}(k)$ is not equal to μ i.e., there is some uncertainty in the subjective estimates, the optimal loss which is the negative of $g(x_0(k))$ in (7.7) is not zero; also a higher value of g implies a lower value of loss. But a higher value of g, under the assumptions of the model may be only due to a higher sample size for a fixed size of the error $\delta(k) = \bar{c}(k) - \mu$ on the average. Hence $g(x_0(1)) > g(x_0(2))$ if $N_1 > N_2$.

If the constraint (7.2) is binding, then r may be positive. Hence (7.7) will imply that $\delta(k)'\underset{0}{x}(k) - \tfrac{1}{2} \tilde{D}_k^2$ i.e., the linear part of the expcted loss for each player will be proportional to the weighted distance term $\tilde{D}_k^2$.

Remark 2.1

In case $\bar{c}(1)$ is not equal to $\bar{c}(2)$ and the expected losses are proportional to D_k^2, then the difference of $\bar{c}(1)$ and $\bar{c}(2)$ leading to different optimal solutions $x_0(1)$ and $x_0(2)$ may be statistically tested through the statistic

$$D_1^2 - D_2^2 = (\bar{c}(1) - \bar{c}(2))'V^{-1} (\bar{c}(1) - \bar{c}(2))$$
$$+ 2(\bar{c}(1) - \bar{c}(2))'V^{-1} (\bar{c}(2) - \mu)$$

If $\bar{c}(2)$ is very close to μ, i.e., N_2 is very large, this statistic becomes approximately equal to Hotelling's T^2 statistic, which is commonly used to test the significance of difference of two sample means from a normal population.

Remark 2.2

So long as sample information N_k is not infinitely large, $\bar{c}(k)$ does not equal μ with probability one. Hence player I will have lower expected losses even if $\bar{c}(1) = \bar{c}(2)$, if his mean estimate $\bar{c}(1)$ is more efficient than $\bar{c}(2)$ in the sense $D_1^2 > D_2^2 > 0$.

Remark 2.3

The larger the risk aversion parameter α in (7.8) for any player, the greater the expected loss. Hence for unequal risk aversion i.e., $\alpha_1 \neq \alpha_2$ say, the total expected losses could be lower by pooling of risk.

Two implications of theorem 2 are useful for practical applications. First, the efficiency of alternative estimates $\bar{c}(k)$ of the parameter μ may be directly related to the optimal expected loses of the two players. Thus, the value of improving the estimates through additional information may be compared with the cost of information, where the latter may in part depend on the sample size. Further, if the sample size is fixed and identical, this leads naturally to the choice of a sufficient statistic if it exists. Second, the Nash equilibrium character of the solution indicates that cooperative estimates may be developed either through pooling of samples N_1, N_2 or, through defining weighted estimates. The latter approach is comparable to the so-called two-armed bandit problems [2] in statistics, where the problem is how to efficiently estimate the common parameter μ, when two instruments of unknown procesion V_1^{-1}, V_2^{-1} are available for measurement. Let us consider a simple example of cooperative estimates in our framework, when we assume $N_1 + N_2 = N$ with N fixed and N_1 does not necessarily equal N_2. Denote the proportions $N_k/(N_1 + N_2)$ by p_k and assume that the constraint (7.2) is not binding. The information available to each player is also assumed to be statistically independent. Then define the cooperative or weighted estimates by $\bar{c}$ and its variance-covariance matrix $V(\bar{c})$:

$$\bar{c} = p_1\, \bar{c}(1) + p_2\, \bar{c}(2),\ p_1 + p_2 = 1,\ p_k \geq 0 \tag{8.1}$$

$$\text{Var}\ \bar{c} = V(\bar{c}) = V(1) + V(2)$$

$$\text{where } V(k) = p_k V/N$$

The decision problem now is how to optimally choose N_1, N_2 for a fixed total N and the vector x? The problem now can be stated as a two-stage decision problem. In the first stage, N_1, N_2 are determined, thus determining p_1, p_2 and in the second stage we solve the NLP model:

$$\max_x g(\bar{x}\ ,\ \bar{N}_1, \bar{N}_2) = (\bar{c} - \mu)'\ x - \alpha x' V(\bar{c}) x \tag{8.2}$$

were $\bar{N}_1$, $\bar{N}_2$, are the fixed values determined in the first stage.

Note that (8.1) is not the only way to characterize cooperative estimates e.g., there may be cooperation through methods other than pooling of sample observations. For example, if there is other extraneous information, then the two players may cooperate in the mean in the sense $\bar{c}(1) = \bar{c}(2)$ but not in variance, i.e., $V_1 \neq V_2$; alternatively they may cooperate in precision or reliability $V_1^{-1} = V_2^{-1}$ but not in the means i.e., $\bar{c}(1) \neq \bar{c}(2)$ due to unequal weights p_1, p_2.

<u>Theorem 3</u>

Let N_k^o and N_k^* be two optimal choices of (N_1, N_2) for a fixed $N = N_1 + N_2$, where

$$\max_{N_k} g(x, N_1, N_2) \rightarrow N_k^o,\ N_1^o + N_2^o = N$$
$$\min_{N_k} g(x, N_1, N_2) \rightarrow N_k^*,\ N_1^* + N_2^* = N \tag{8.3}$$

and $g(x, N_1, N_2)$ is given in (8.2). These two optimal choices N_k^o, N_k^* lead to an identical optimal solution $x^o = x^*$ if and only if $N_k^o = N/2 = N_k^*$. The maximax solution $g^o = g(x^o, N_1^o, N_2^o)$ is otherwise different from the maximin solution $g^* = g((x^*, N_1^*, N_2^*)$ i.e.

$$g^o \geq g^* \tag{8.4}$$

where

$$g^o = \max_x \max_{N_k} g(x, N_1, N_2)$$

$$g^* = \max_x \min_{N_k} g(x, N_1, N_2)$$

<u>Proof</u>

For any feasible x, the function $g = g(x, N_1, N_2)$ given by (8.2) is a linear function of p_1 and p_2 where $p_1 + p_2 = 1$ and $p_k \geq 0$. This defines an LP problem in variables p_1, p_2. Clearly, both solutions (p_1^o, p_2^o), (p_1^*, p_2^*) exist. For the maximax case

$$p_1^o = 1,\ p_2^o = 2,\ \text{if } \bar{c}(1)'x > \bar{c}'(2)x$$
and
$$p_1^o = \tfrac{1}{2} = p^o{}_2,\ \text{if } \bar{c}(1)'x = \bar{c}(2)'x \tag{8.5}$$

Likewise for the maximin case:

$$p_1^* = 1,\ p_2^* = 0,\ \text{if } \bar{c}(1)'x < \bar{c}'(2)x$$

$$p_1^* = 0,\ p_2^* = 1,\ \text{if } \bar{c}(1)'x > \bar{c}(2)'x \tag{8.6}$$

$$p_1^* = \tfrac{1}{2} = p_2^*,\ \text{if } \bar{c}(1)' = \bar{c}(2)'x$$

The only case common to (8.5) and (8.6) is when $p_1^* = \frac{1}{2} = p_1^o = 1 - p_2^o$. Using this common value we thus obtain $g^o = g^*$. Otherwise $g^o \geq g^*$.

Remark 3.1

In terms of the loss function, which is the negative of $g(x, N_1, N_2)$ the maximin solution is the minimax loss solution.

Remark 3.2

Note that the variance term $x'V(\bar{c})$ has no role in determining the optimal p_k's in the first stage. This is because the risk aversion parameter α is the same and a common V can be used for both players. Consider a case when the players agree to use the same $\bar{c}$ defined by (8.1) but different variances $\bar{V}_1$, $\bar{V}_2$ say. Then player k's optimal solution $x = x_o(k)$ maximizes

$$\max_x\ g(k) = (\bar{c} - \mu)'x - \alpha_k\ x'\bar{V}_k x \tag{8.7}$$

so that at the optimum we have

$$g_o(1) = \frac{1}{4\alpha_k} D^2(\bar{c},\ \mu,\ \bar{V}_k);\ k = 1,\ 2 \tag{8.8}$$

It may be natural to define $g_o(1)$ as the more efficient, for $\alpha_1 = \alpha_2 > 0$ if the difference $(g_o(1) - g_o(2))$ is positive e.g., if the difference of the variance-covariance matrices, $(\bar{V}_1 - \bar{V}_2)$ is positive definite, then $g_o(1) > g_o(2)$ necessarily.

Remark 3.3

If the source of information for the mean estimates $\bar{c}(k)$ is different from that for the variances $\bar{V}_k$, then pooling in terms of cooperative estimates may be defined separately for the mean and the variances.

Theorem 4

Suppose the players cooperate in the mean but not in the variances, due to differentiated information structures. Let the optimal solutions in this case, obtainable from (8.7) be denoted as $x_o(1)$, $x_o(2)$ respectively with corresponding payoffs $g_o(1)$ and $g_o(2)$. Denote the first type of cooperative decision by $x_o^o = wx_o(1) + (-w)x_o(2)$ where w is a nonnegative number $o < w < 1$, which has a combined payoff $g_0^o = wg_0(1) + 1 - w)g_0(2)$. Denote a second type of cooperation where $\bar{V}_k$ in (8.7) is replaced for each player by $V^* = w\bar{V}_1 + (1 - w)\bar{V}_2$ where the optimal solution is x^* with a payoff g^* as:

$$g^* = \frac{1}{4\alpha} D^2(\bar{c}, \mu; V^*) \tag{8.9}$$

We then have $g_0^o \geq g^*$, with equality holding if $\bar{V}_1 = \bar{V}_2$. In other words, if $\bar{V}_1 \neq \bar{V}_2$ aggregating variances is less efficient than aggregating separate optimal solutions.

Proof

Since the variance-covariance matrices $\bar{V}_1$, $\bar{V}_2$ are symmetric positive definite, we have for any w $(0 < w < 1)$,

$$[w\bar{V}_1 + (1 - w) \bar{V}_2]^{-1} \leq w\bar{V}_1^{-1} + (1 - w) \bar{V}_2^{-1} \tag{8.10}$$

with equality holding if $\bar{V}_1 = \bar{V}_2$. Premultiplying and postmultiplying both sides by $(\bar{c} - \mu) = \delta$ we get

$$\delta'(w\bar{V}_1^{-1} + (1 - w)\bar{V}_2^{-1}) \delta \geq \delta'[w\bar{V}_1 + (1 - w)\bar{V}_2]^{-1} \delta$$

from which the inequality $g_0^o \geq g^*$ fllows.

Remark 4.1

The weight w may be termed an index of dominance, since each player will attempt to have it as close to one as possible, before agreeing to the collective decison. However so long as $\bar{V}_1$ is not equal to $\bar{V}_2$ it may not be optimal to use equal weights $w = 0.5 = 1 - w$.

Remark 4.2

Since the objective function g(k) in (8.7) is linear in w when V^* replaces $\bar{V}_k$, the optimal choices of w, for a fixed estimate $\bar{c}$ are given as follows:

$w = 1$, if $x'\bar{V}_1x < x'\bar{V}_2x$

$w = 0.5$, if $x'\bar{V}_1x = x'\bar{V}_2x$

$w = 0$, if $x'\bar{V}_1 x > x'\bar{V}_2x$

assuming an indentical risk aversion $\alpha_k = \alpha$ for two players.

3. Constrained Statistical Games

We consider now a special case of the game G = (M, N; g) where g is defined in (4.1). This is a statistical game where the second player called nature plays a game atainst the statistician, who represents the first player, the decision maker. We consider however a nonzero sum framework, where a special form is used of the payoff function(4.1), where only the vector $c = c(i)$, $i = 1, 2, \ldots, I$ of dimension n is the strategy of player II and the vector $x = x(j)$, $j = 1, 2, \ldots, J$ of dimension m is the strategy of player I.

The strategies of the two players are assumed constrained in the sense of partially controllable strategies [8] as follows:

$$
\begin{aligned}
&R_2\text{: } \{c(i) = \tilde{c}(i) - c_0,\ c(i)'c(i) \leq 1 \text{ for all } i = 1, 2, \ldots, I < \infty\} \\
&R_1\text{: } \{x(j) = \tilde{x}(j) - x_0,\ x(j)'x(j) \leq 1 \text{ for all } j = 1, 2, \ldots, J < \infty\}
\end{aligned}
\tag{9.1}
$$

where the actual strategies chosen are taken as deviations from a reference point (c_0, x_0). This reference point may be variously interpreted depending on the structure where is applied. It may be a threat point in the sense of Nash equilibrium, so that it is the worst that can happen to each player. Alternatively, it may be a preassigned goal or desired level, each player is seeking to attain. Here the actual strategies are viewed as differential perturbations around the reference point. The objective functions of the two players are taken to be of the form:

$$
\begin{aligned}
&\text{player I: } g_1(x) = \sum_j s_j[\sum_i \pi_i c(i)'M(ij)x(j)] \\
&\text{Player II: } g_2(c) = \sum_i \pi_i[\sum_j c(i)'N(ij)s_j x(j)]
\end{aligned}
\tag{9.2}
$$

where M and N are matrices of order n by m for each $i = 1, 2, \ldots, I$ and $j = 1, 2, \ldots, J$ and π_i and s_j are probabilities associated with the events $c(i)'M(ij)$ and $N(ij)x(j)$ respectively with $\Sigma\pi_i = \Sigma s_j = 1$ and $\pi_i, s_j \geq 0$. The objective functions (9.2) may be interpreted as follows. Player I the decision maker has to guess the state of nature c(i) which occurs with probability π_i and depending on the guess has an average payoff indicated by $g_1(x)$ in (9.2). Likewise for player II, except that the matrix N(ij) may be different from M(ij). It will be assumed that if his guess is correct, his payoff or return is highest i.e.

$$u_{ii} > u_{ij},\ i \neq j;\ \text{player I} \tag{9.3}$$

$$v_{jj} > v_{ji},\ j \neq i;\ \text{player II}$$

where $u_{ij} = c(i)'M(ij)x(j)$, $v_{ji} = c(i)'N(ij)x(j)$. It is clear that in this bilinear game, each player has to guess which of the states the other player's strategy does occupy. Hence the strategies of the two players are interdependent. One important class of interdependent strategies [10] is the Stackelberg strategies, where one player is the leader and the other a follower. It may therefore be of interest to investigate conditions under which Stackelberg strategies exist under this model. Furthermore, two special cases of the payoff function (9.2) would be relevant in practical applications. First, $x(j)$ may be viewed as a search for the unknown target which has a distribution over $c(1), c(2), \ldots, c(I)$: the search (time or effort) may be related only to the cell for which it is directed. Hence $g_1(x)$ will appear as:

$$g_1(x) = \sum_i \pi_i c(i)'M(i)x(i) \tag{9.5}$$

where π_i is now the probability of detecting the target. Likewise for $g_2(c)$. The problem of optimal search is to find a set of $x(i)$ which will maximize the average return from search effort subject to the cost restriction (9.1). A second special case arises when the reward matrices $M(i) = M_0$, $N(j) = N_0$ are constant independent of i and j and the payoffs are as follows:

$$g_1(\bar{x}) = \bar{c}'M_0\bar{x};\ g_2(c) = \bar{c}'N_0\bar{x} \tag{9.6}$$

where

$$\bar{c} = \sum_i \pi_i c(i),\ \bar{x} = \sum_j s_j x(j)$$

In this case the constraints on the strategies appear as

$$\begin{aligned} &\bar{c}'\bar{c} < 1,\ \bar{c} = \sum_i \pi_i(\tilde{c}(i) - c_0) \\ &\bar{x}'\bar{x} \leq 1,\ \bar{x} = \sum_j s_j(\tilde{x}(j) - x_0) \end{aligned} \tag{9.7}$$

Several results may now be stated on the LP-related statistical games.

Theorem 5

If the constraints (9.3), (9.4) hold for the payoffs $g_i(x)$, $g_2(c)$ defined in (9.2), then there exists no pair (c(i), x(j)) of pure strategies satisfying the saddle point or minimax property

$$\min_i \min_j u_{ij} = \max_j \min_i u_{ij}$$

$$\min_j \max_i v_{ij} = \max_i \min_j v_{ij}$$

However, saddle point strategies exist in mixed strategies.

Proof

With pure strategies, the payoffs are

$$g_1 = c(i)'M(ij)x(j) \text{ and } g_2 = c(i)'N(ij)x(j)$$

but if (9.3) holds then

$$u_{ii} = \max_j u_{ij} \text{ and } \min_i u_{ii} = \min_i \max_j u_{ij}$$

but $\min_i u_{ij}$ cannot be equal to u_{jj} and hence $\max_j \min u_{ij}$ cannot be equal to $\min_i \max_j u_{ij}$. Hence pure strategy saddle point solutions do not exist. However since the strategies are finite, if follows by von Neumann's minimax theorem that saddle point solutions exist in mixed strategies.

Remark 5.1

Let there be only two choices for each player and let N(ij) = M(ij) = I, an identity matrix, then the probabilities π_1, π_2 can be determined from

$$\pi_1 = 1 - \pi_2 = \frac{u_{22} - u_{21}}{(u_{11} - u_{12}) + (u_{22} - u_{21})}; \quad u_{ij} = c(i)'x(j)$$

These probabilities may be used to construct mixed strategy saddle point solutions. Note that π_1, π_2 would be strictly positive, $0 < \pi_i < 1$ by condition (9.3).

Remark 5.2

With only two choices for each player define u_{ij} in terms of the conventional LP model:

$$u_{ij} = c(i)'x(j) - y(i)'A(i)x(j) + y'(i)b(i) \quad i,j = 1,2$$

where c, A, b are the parameters of the LP model (1.1), (1.2). Player I uses strategies x(j) while player II uses (c(i), y(i), A(i), b(i)). Player I chooses x(1), x(2) so as to equate the expected return in the two cases i.e.

$$\pi_1 u_{11} + (1 - \pi_1)u_{21} = \pi_1 u_{12} + (1 - \pi_1)u_{22}$$

from which one gets

$$\pi_1 = (u_{22} - u_{21})[(u_{11} - u_{12}) + (u_{22} - u_{21})]^{-1}$$

By using (9.3), $0 < \pi_1 < 1$.

Theorem 6

A Nash equilibrium point $(c^o, | x^o)$ exists fo the two-person game defined by (9.2) and (9.1), where

$$g_1(x) \leq g_1(x^o) = \max_x g_1(x) = \max_x g_1(x|c^o), \ x \varepsilon R_1$$

(10.1)

$$g_2(c) \leq g_2(c^o) = \max_c g_2(c) = \max_c g_2(c|x^o), \ c \varepsilon R_2$$

Proof

The functions $g_1(x) = g_1(x|c)$, $g_2(c) = g_2(c|x)$ defined by (9.2) are continuous in x and c and $g_1(x|c)$ is concave in x for every fixed c and $g_2(c|x)$ is concave in c for every fixed x. By assumption the constraint sets R_1 and R_2 are convex compact sets in finite dimensions. Consider an enlarged strategy space $R = R_1 \times R_2$ wehre R is a coupled constraint set from which the palyers choose their strategies. Then define the point-to-set mapping $x \varepsilon R \rightarrow \phi(x) \subset R$ given by

$$\phi(x) = \{y \mid \max_{c \varepsilon R} g_1(x|c) = g_1(x, y)\}$$

The mapping ϕ is upper semicontinuous, since $g_1(x, y)$ is continuous and concave in y for every fixed x and it maps each point of the convex compact set R into a closed convex subset of R. Then by Brower-Kakutani fixed point theorem [5], there exists a point $x^o \varepsilon R$ such that $x^o = \phi(x^o)$. The fixed point x^o is an equilibrium point satisfying (10.1). Similarly, the existence of the equilibrium point c^o can be established. In general, define $\psi(x, c) = g_1(x) + g_2(c)$ and the point-to-set mapping $x \varepsilon R \rightarrow \phi(x) \subset R$ given by

$$\phi(x) = \{\gamma \mid \max_{c \varepsilon R} \psi(x, c) = \psi(x, \gamma\} \qquad (10.2)$$

By the fixed point theorem there exists a point $x^o \varepsilon R$ such that $x^o = \phi(x^o)$. This fixed point x^o is a Nash equilibrium point satisfying (10.1).

Remark 6.1

If the constraint sets R_1, R_2 in (9.1) are not empty, the Nash equilibrium point must satisfy the conditions:

$$s_j \sum_i \pi_i\ c(i)'M(ij) - 2\lambda_j x(j) = 0,\ \lambda_j \geq 0$$

$$\lambda_j(x(j)'x(j) - 1) = 0,\ j = 1, 2, \ldots, J \qquad (10.3)$$

$$\pi_i \sum_j s_j N(ij)x(j) - 2r_i\ c(i) = 0,\ r_i \geq 0$$

$$r_i(c(i)'c(i) -1) = 0,\ i = 1, \ldots, I$$

These conditios [5] are the necessary Kuhn-Tucker conditions.

Remark 6.2

If the probabilities π_i, s_j are equal in the sense $\pi_i = \pi_o\ 1/I$ and $s_j = s_o = 1/J$ and $M(ij)$, $N(ij)$ are constant matrices M_o and N_o and the optimal Lagrange multipliers λ_j^o, r_i^o are positive, then (10.3) implies the following

$$\frac{2\lambda_j^o}{s_o}\ \bar{x} = \bar{c}'M \text{ and } \frac{2r_i^o}{\pi_o}\ \bar{c} = N\bar{x}$$

where $\bar{c} = \sum_i \pi_i c(i)$, $\bar{x} = \sum_j s_j x(j)$ are mixed strategies. Therefore the strategies

$\bar{c}$, $\bar{x}$ are interdependent.

Theorem 7

The search game defined by the payoffs (9.5) possesses a Nash equilibrium point under the constraints (9.1). If the constraint sets R_1, R_2 are nonempty, the Nash equilibrium point must satisfy the following conditions:

$$\pi_i M'(i)c(i) - 2\lambda_i x(i) = 0, \ \lambda_i \geq 0$$

$$\lambda_i(x'(i)x(i) - 1) = 0 \qquad (10.4)$$

$$s_j N(j)x(j) - 2r_j c(j) = 0, \ r_j \geq 0$$

$$r_j(c'(j)c(j) - 1) = 0$$

where i, j = 1, 2, ..., I and I = J. If the optimal Lagrange multipliers λ_i, r_j are positive and the states guessed are mutually consistent in the sense that c(j) = c(k) when x(i) = x(k), then the optimal strategies must satisfy the complementary eigenvalue problems in θ:

$$[M'(k)N(k) - \theta I]\ x(k) = 0$$
$$[N(k)M'(k) - \theta I]\ c(k) = 0 \qquad (10.5)$$

where $\theta = 4\lambda_k\ r_k/(s_k\ \pi_k)$ is the maximum eigenvalue of the product matrix M'(k)N(k).

Proof

The existence of the Nash equilibrium point can be proved by methods used in Theorem 6 which utilize Brower-Kakutani fixed point theorems. The payoff function $g_1(x)$ is continuous and concave in x for every fixed c and likewise $g_2(c)$ is concave in c for even fixed x. Hence the Kuhn-Tucker necessary conditions (10.4) must hold.

When the optimal Lagrange multipliers λ_k, r_k are positive for c(k), x(k) satisfying the first and third equation of (10.4), we have, on combining these equations, the complementary eigenvalue problems (10.5) where the maximum eigenvalue θ has to be chosen because it corresponds to Nash equilibrium i.e., it corresponds to a point where the two players reach their maximum payoff simultaneously.

Remark 7.1

For any nonnegative λ_k, r_k and positive π_k, s_k where $0 < \pi_k$, $s_k < 1$ the first and third equations of (10.4) may be written as a set of linear reaction functions:

$$\begin{bmatrix} -2\lambda_k I & \pi_k M'(k) \\ s_k N(k) & -2r_k I \end{bmatrix} \begin{bmatrix} x(k) \\ c(k) \end{bmatrix} = \begin{bmatrix} 0 \\ 0 \end{bmatrix}$$

If the coefficient matrix is nonsingular, then x(k) = c(k) = zero, which implies that $\tilde{x}(k)$ and $\tilde{c}(k)$ equal the reference points x_o, c_o. If the coefficient matrix is singular, then the strategies x(k) and c(k) are interdependent and the complementary eigenvalue problems (10.5) characterize the Nash equilibrium.

Remark 7.2

The equilibrium strategies $x(k) = x^{\circ}$, $c(k) = c^{\circ}$ which satisfy the complementary eigenvalue problems (10.5) define an optimal Stackelberg strategy [10] for player I in the following sense:

$$\max_{x} g_1 = \pi_k c(k)'M(k)x + \lambda_k(1 - x'x) \tag{10.6}$$

subject to

$$s_k N(k)\, x - 2r_k c(k) = 0$$

Likewise for the second player's equilibrium strategy.

Remark 7.3

The interpretation of (10.6) as an optimal Stackelberg strategy of player I suggests that he can be a leader with the other player being a follower. This of course assumes that the leader knows the parameters of the follower's strategy. If this knowledge is imperfect, other variants of Stackelberg strategies [10] are possible.

It is clear now that for the remaining game model specified by (9.6) and (9.7), the optimal Nash equilibrum strategies may be specified under conditions analogous to (10.5) as follows:

$$M_o'\bar{c} - 2\lambda\bar{x} = 0 = N_o\bar{x} - 2r\bar{c}$$

which lead to the eigenvalue problems:

$$(M_o' N_o - \theta I)\bar{x} = 0 = (N_o M_o' - \theta I)\bar{c} \tag{10.7}$$

where $\theta = 4r\lambda$ is the maximum eigenvalue of the matrix $M_o'N_o$.

However (10.7) presumes that player I's guess $\bar{c}$ about his rival's strategy and his rival's guess $\bar{x}$ about his strategy are mutually satisfied at the equilibrium point. If such guesses are not mutually fulfilled, a trial and error process begins, e.g., with past observations a guess $\bar{c}_{t-1}$ at time t-1 is made for computing an optimal solution $\bar{x}_t^*$ at time t; likewise for player II. This generates the system:

$$M_o' \bar{c}_{t-1} - 2\lambda_t \bar{x}_t^* = 0$$

$$N_o \bar{x}_{t-1} - 2r_t \bar{c}_t^* = 0 \qquad (11.1)$$

The fact that $\bar{c}_{t+k}$ does not equal $\bar{c}^*_{t+k}$ for different $k > 0$ may be observed by the first player and he may want to predict his rival's mean strategy $\bar{c}$ with a correction factor which incorporates the observed dispersion of rival's strategy around the mean strategy i.e. he may set up a modified payoff function $f_1(\bar{x})$ to reflect a possible inaccuracy of his forecast:

$$\max_{x} f_1(\bar{x}) = \bar{x}' M_o'(\bar{c} - \beta_1 V_c \bar{x})$$

$$\text{subject to } \bar{x}'\bar{x} - 1 = 0$$

Here V_c is the variance of past strategies of his rival and $\beta_1 > 0$ is a positive weight indicating the importance of the variance term. If $\beta = 0$, it means that the prediction of mean strategy $\bar{c}$ is very accurate, so there is no need to improve accuracy by observing the dispersion of second player's perturbed strategies around the mean estimate.

Likewise for the second player we may set up the NLP problem as:

$$\max_{\bar{c}} f_2(\bar{c}) = \bar{c}' N_o(\bar{x} - \beta_2 V_x \bar{c}) \qquad (11.3)$$

$$\text{subject to } \bar{c}'\bar{c} - 1 = 0$$

Here V_x is the variance of past strategies of player I as perceived by player II and β_2 is a positive weight.

Theorem 8

If the payoff $f_1(\bar{x})$ is concave for every $\bar{c}$ and $f_2(\bar{c})$ is concave for every $\bar{x}$, then the optimal Nash equilibrium strategies $\bar{c}^o$, $\bar{x}^o$ must satisfy the complementary eigenvalue problems:

$$[N_o - \beta F]\, \bar{x} = 0 = [M_o' - \beta H]\, \bar{c} \qquad (11.4)$$

where $\beta = \beta_1\beta_2$, $F = (N_oV_x + V_xN_o' + 2rI)M_o'^{-1}\,(M_o'\,V_c + V_cM_o + 2\lambda I)$

and $H = (M_o'V_c + V_cM_o + 2\lambda I)N_o^{-1}\;(N_oV_x + V_xN_o' + 2rI)$ provided the inverses M_o^{-1}, N_o^{-1} exist.

Proof

The existence of Nash equilibrium strategies is apparent. By direct application of the necessary conditions of Kuhn-Tucker theorem, which are also sufficient by the assumption of concavity, we obtain (11.4) by substitution. If M_o, N_o are symmetric, then F and H take simpler forms,

$$F = 4(N_oV_x + rI)\ M_o^{-1}\ (M_oV_x + rI)$$

$$H = 4(M_oV_c + \lambda I)N_o^{-1}\ (N_oV_x + rI)$$

Remark 8.1

If the constraints $\bar{c}'\bar{c} < 1$, $\bar{x}'\bar{x} < 1$ are not binding in the sense that λ and r equal zero and M_o, N_o are symmetric, then the complementary eigenvalue problems (11.4) become

$$N_o(\theta I - V_xV_c)\bar{x} = 0 = M_o(\theta I - V_cV_x)\bar{c}$$

where $\theta = (4\beta_1\ \beta_2)^{-1}$ is the eigenvalue of the product matrix V_xV_c. But since the variance-covariance matrices V_x, V_c are symmetric and positive definte, all the eigenvalues θ are positive and real.

Remark 8.2

Since by setting the weights β_1, β_2 equal to zero, we would get back the optimal strategies of (10.7). The optimal strategies from (11.4) may be compared with those from (10.7). Such comparisons would indicate the value of perturbed optimal strategies of each player according to (11.4).

4. Concluding Remarks

The system description (1.1), (1.2) which we started our formulation is in static terms. By it needs pointing out that this description may, with suitable modification apply to dynamic systems also. For discrete time situations, linear quadratic control problems can be viewed as quadratic programming problems, though in higher dimensions and the approach of linear decision rules of control problems [9] may be compared with the linear optimal strategies proposed here.

Second, we have not specifically differentiated between cooperative and non-cooperative solutions. It is clear however that to every Nash equilibrium point, a cooperative solution through joint cooperation of the two players may be characterized.

References

1. Charnes, A., M. Kirby and W. Raike: Chance-constrained games with partially controllable strategies, Operations Research, 16, 1968, 142-149.

2. Chernoff, H.: The efficient estimation of a paramater measurable by two instruments of unknown precision, in J.S. Rustagi, ed., Optimizing Methods in Statistics, Academic Press, New York, 1971, 1-27.

3. Dresher, M.: Games of Strategy, Prentice-Hall, Englewood Cliffs, NJ, 1961.

4. Kolbin, V.V.: Stochastic Programming, Reidel Publishing, Dordrecht, Holland, 1977.

5. Rosen, J.B.: Existence and uniqueness of equilibrium points for concave N-person games, Econometrica 33, 1965, 520-533.

6. Rosenfeld, J.L.: Adaptive competitive decision, in M. Dresher et. al. eds., Advances in Game Theory, Princeton University Press, Princeton, 1964.

7. Sengupta, J.K.: Constrained games as complementary eigenvalue problems, Journal of Mathematical Analysis and Applications, 73, 1980.

8. Sengupta, J.K.: Constrained nonzero sum games with partially controllable strategies, Journal of Optimization Theory and Applications, 31, 1980.

9. Sengupta, J.K.: Decision Models in Stochastic Programming, North Holland, American Elsevier, ca. 1981.

10. Simaan, M. and J.B. Cruz, Jr.: On the Stackelberg strategy in nonzero sum games, Journal of Optimization Theory and Applications, 11, 1974, 533-555.

11. Zoutenjijk, G.: Mathematical Programming Methods, North Holland, Amsterdam, 1976.

CHAPTER 7
RESEARCH TRENDS AND PROBLEMS

Need for optimal decision rules under uncertainty has been increasingly felt in several fields both new and old. Old fields are operations reserach, economics of planning, portfolio models in finance and insurance theory of risk business. New fields include management information systems, team decisions and differential games, market research and systems science. Methods of signal detection, remote sensing and search, optimal reliability analysis in engineering and biomedical systems have components that are common to the theory of optimal decisions under uncertainty.

From an applied viewpoint, the most useful lines of advance in the theory are likely to be generated in the different applied fields, where new techniques and decision rules are constantly needed due to the inadequacy of current model formulations. Conceptually, the following new areas appear in the forefront of current and future research in the field:

A. Methods of characterizing and computing efficient solution vectors in stochastic environments. We have reviewed in earlier chapters some of the existing methods and their limitations. Considerable scope exists for their generalizations in several aspects e.g., (a) probability structure of the feasible set may be known in a parametric or a nonparametric form, (b) sharing of information through communication may be possible when there are two or more members in a team, and (c) the concept of a core in many-player differential games may be explored.

B. Multivariate measures of risk aversion and their applications in operational models of private and public decision-making. As we have analyzed in our critical survey of risk aversion measures in Chapter 3, the multivariate measures basically consider risk aversion as a vector or a matrix and hence the distance between two vectors or two matrices representing different degrees of risk aversion. In the theory of collective risk as applied to insurance businesses, it is presumed that there are different risk classes, to which different individuals in an aggregate belong; hence the individual risk aversion may be very different from the collective one, unless appropriate insurance markets can be developed and implemented. The implications of alternative insurance contracts and arrangements offer an open field of research. These implications may indirectly suggest the various imperfections of the competitive market structure for contingent claims and allocation of risk-bearing securities in the Arrow-Debreu world.

C. Discrimination and classification of alternative potential solutions. We have seen in our treatment of stochastic LP models, that a particular basic feasible solution may remain optimal only in a restricted domain of variations of the stochastic components. This emphasizes the need to analyze the distance between two potential optimal solutions. Such an analysis may be helpful in two ways. First, as in statistical discriminant function approach, it provides a classification of the entire set of basic feasible solutions (or potential solutions) into homogeneous strata, for each of which production response coefficients may be efficiently estimated. Second, a vector comparison can be made in respect of a given goal. Thus, one could ask: which of the two potential solution vectors is closer to the preassigned target or goal. The latter for example may denote a cooperative solution, whereas the two potential solutions may denote noncooperative equilibria.

D. Informational evaluation of policies and decision rules. Our treatment of informational aspects of decision rules under uncertainty, either in stochastic controls or in stochastic allocation rules have paid very inadequate attention to some aspects which are wide open for future research, e.g., (a) integration of search and information theory in the building of a decision model and its decision rules, (b) incorporating qualitative dimensions of information e.g., reducing the number of dimensions of an information vector, applying subjective weights and inside information as in fuzzy systems, (c) building information retrieval and learning rules along with the structure of decision rules which are conditional on information channels presumed and (d) the nature of operation of hypothetical market systems or games where information of different sorts can be bought and sold in terms of price (or other incentives) or costs (or other disincentives).

E. Nonconvex problems ad the role of mixed strategy solutions. It is known that for nonconvex objective functions arising in inventory control and stochastic LP models, a pure strategy solution which minimizes the objective function may not exist. Moreover, if the objective function is partly convex in one domain and partly concave in another domain, a mixed strategy also called randomized solutions may be preferable over a pure strategy solution. Thus, the failure of convexity (concavity) in minimization (maximization) problems may necessitate the need for exploring randomized solutions.

Several open questions arises here:

a. What are the implications for stochastic LP models, when the convexity of the feasible set fails to hold, due to te presence of stochastic components?

b. If the failure of convexity of the objective function can be measured in terms of a parameter, how could then one incorporate the influence of this parameter in transforming a stochastic LP model into a suitable deterministic form?
Would it be possible to develop Bayesian methods of using the prior and posterior distributions of this critical parameter?

c. Methods of embedding nonconvex functions or sets in a larger set, that is minimal convex may be explored to see if an approximate solution may be obtained which is either easier to compute or closer to a pure strategy.

F. Methods of empirical validation of the optimal solutions obtained from N sample data points say. We have discussed several econometric tests for comparing optimal solution vectors with the actual observed. However these tests usually require a large number of samples or cross-section data, normality in the underlying probability distributions and an assumption about comparability. Several open questions remain to be explored e.g.,

a. The statistical tests may be applied either to output vector or to the vector of shadow prices and the associated market prices but the results may be different. Thus, optimal outputs may be very close to the actual observed but the optimal shadow prices may differ considerably from the observed input prices.

b. How to test the change in the size and shape of the constraint set, generated by the stochastic components of the environment?

c. How to devise a test for the aggregate model to see if the N units or firms satisfy the requirement of a competitive resource allocation process?

d. How to devise a test when there are more than one distribution generating the observed data points?

Thus there exist several areas wide open for future research. From the trend of progress of current research, it may be hoped that in the next decade or so, we would observe new attempts and newer solutions to most of the problems outlined above.

Vol. 83: NTG/GI-Gesellschaft für Informatik, Nachrichtentechnische Gesellschaft. Fachtagung „Cognitive Verfahren und Systeme", Hamburg, 11.–13. April 1973. Herausgegeben im Auftrag der NTG/GI von Th. Einsele, W. Giloi und H.-H. Nagel. VIII, 373 Seiten. 1973.

Vol. 84: A. V. Balakrishnan, Stochastic Differential Systems I. Filtering and Control. A Function Space Approach. V, 252 pages. 1973.

Vol. 85: T. Page, Economics of Involuntary Transfers: A Unified Approach to Pollution and Congestion Externalities. XI, 159 pages. 1973.

Vol. 86: Symposium on the Theory of Scheduling and its Applications. Edited by S. E. Elmaghraby. VIII, 437 pages. 1973.

Vol. 87: G. F. Newell, Approximate Stochastic Behavior of n-Server Service Systems with Large n. VII, 118 pages. 1973.

Vol. 88: H. Steckhan, Güterströme in Netzen. VII, 134 Seiten. 1973.

Vol. 89: J. P. Wallace and A. Sherret, Estimation of Product. Attributes and Their Importances. V, 94 pages. 1973.

Vol. 90: J.-F. Richard, Posterior and Predictive Densities for Simultaneous Equation Models. VI, 226 pages. 1973.

Vol. 91: Th. Marschak and R. Selten, General Equilibrium with Price-Making Firms. XI, 246 pages. 1974.

Vol. 92: E. Dierker, Topological Methods in Walrasian Economics. IV, 130 pages. 1974.

Vol. 93: 4th IFAC/IFIP International Conference on Digital Computer Applications to Process Control, Part I. Zürich/Switzerland, March 19–22, 1974. Edited by M. Mansour and W. Schaufelberger. XVIII, 544 pages. 1974.

Vol. 94: 4th IFAC/IFIP International Conference on Digital Computer Applications to Process Control, Part II. Zürich/Switzerland, March 19–22, 1974. Edited by M. Mansour and W. Schaufelberger. XVIII, 546 pages. 1974.

Vol. 95: M. Zeleny, Linear Multiobjective Programming. X, 220 pages. 1974.

Vol. 96: O. Moeschlin, Zur Theorie von Neumannscher Wachstumsmodelle. XI, 115 Seiten. 1974.

Vol. 97: G. Schmidt, Über die Stabilität des einfachen Bedienungskanals. VII, 147 Seiten. 1974.

Vol. 98: Mathematical Methods in Queueing Theory. Proceedings 1973. Edited by A. B. Clarke. VII, 374 pages. 1974.

Vol. 99: Production Theory. Edited by W. Eichhorn, R. Henn, O. Opitz, and R. W. Shephard. VIII, 386 pages. 1974.

Vol. 100: B. S. Duran and P. L. Odell, Cluster Analysis. A Survey. VI, 137 pages. 1974.

Vol. 101: W. M. Wonham, Linear Multivariable Control. A Geometric Approach. X, 344 pages. 1974.

Vol. 102: Analyse Convexe et Ses Applications. Comptes Rendus, Janvier 1974. Edited by J.-P. Aubin. IV, 244 pages. 1974.

Vol. 103: D. E. Boyce, A. Farhi, R. Weischedel, Optimal Subset Selection. Multiple Regression, Interdependence and Optimal Network Algorithms. XIII, 187 pages. 1974.

Vol. 104: S. Fujino, A Neo-Keynesian Theory of Inflation and Economic Growth. V, 96 pages. 1974.

Vol. 105: Optimal Control Theory and its Applications. Part I. Proceedings 1973. Edited by B. J. Kirby. VI, 425 pages. 1974.

Vol. 106: Optimal Control Theory and its Applications. Part II. Proceedings 1973. Edited by B. J. Kirby. VI, 403 pages. 1974.

Vol. 107: Control Theory, Numerical Methods and Computer Systems Modeling. International Symposium, Rocquencourt, June 17–21, 1974. Edited by A. Bensoussan and J. L. Lions. VIII, 757 pages. 1975.

Vol. 108: F. Bauer et al., Supercritical Wing Sections II. A Handbook. V, 296 pages. 1975.

Vol. 109: R. von Randow, Introduction to the Theory of Matroids. IX, 102 pages. 1975.

Vol. 110: C. Striebel, Optimal Control of Discrete Time Stochastic Systems. III. 208 pages. 1975.

Vol. 111: Variable Structure Systems with Application to Economics and Biology. Proceedings 1974. Edited by A. Ruberti and R. R. Mohler. VI, 321 pages. 1975.

Vol. 112: J. Wilhelm, Objectives and Multi-Objective Decision Making Under Uncertainty. IV, 111 pages. 1975.

Vol. 113: G. A. Aschinger, Stabilitätsaussagen über Klassen von Matrizen mit verschwindenden Zeilensummen. V, 102 Seiten. 1975.

Vol. 114: G. Uebe, Produktionstheorie. XVII, 301 Seiten. 1976.

Vol. 115: Anderson et al., Foundations of System Theory: Finitary and Infinitary Conditions. VII, 93 pages. 1976

Vol. 116: K. Miyazawa, Input-Output Analysis and the Structure of Income Distribution. IX, 135 pages. 1976.

Vol. 117: Optimization and Operations Research. Proceedings 1975. Edited by W. Oettli and K. Ritter. IV, 316 pages. 1976.

Vol. 118: Traffic Equilibrium Methods, Proceedings 1974. Edited by M. A. Florian. XXIII, 432 pages. 1976.

Vol. 119: Inflation in Small Countries. Proceedings 1974. Edited by H. Frisch. VI, 356 pages. 1976.

Vol. 120: G. Hasenkamp, Specification and Estimation of Multiple-Output Production Functions. VII, 151 pages. 1976.

Vol. 121: J. W. Cohen, On Regenerative Processes in Queueing Theory. IX, 93 pages. 1976.

Vol. 122: M. S. Bazaraa, and C. M. Shetty,Foundations of Optimization VI. 193 pages. 1976

Vol. 123: Multiple Criteria Decision Making. Kyoto 1975. Edited by M. Zeleny. XXVII, 345 pages. 1976.

Vol. 124: M. J. Todd. The Computation of Fixed Points and Applications. VII, 129 pages. 1976.

Vol. 125: Karl C. Mosler. Optimale Transportnetze. Zur Bestimmung ihres kostengünstigsten Standorts bei gegebener Nachfrage. VI, 142 Seiten. 1976.

Vol. 126: Energy, Regional Science and Public Policy. Energy and Environment I. Proceedings 1975. Edited by M. Chatterji and P. Van Rompuy. VIII, 316 pages. 1976.

Vol. 127: Environment, Regional Science and Interregional Modeling. Energy and Environment II. Proceedings 1975. Edited by M. Chatterji and P. Van Rompuy. IX, 211 pages. 1976.

Vol. 128: Integer Programming and Related Areas. A Classified Bibliography. Edited by C. Kastning. XII, 495 pages. 1976.

Vol. 129: H.-J. Lüthi, Komplementaritäts- und Fixpunktalgorithmen in der mathematischen Programmierung. Spieltheorie und Ökonomie. VII, 145 Seiten. 1976.

Vol. 130: Multiple Criteria Decision Making, Jouy-en-Josas, France. Proceedings 1975. Edited by H. Thiriez and S. Zionts. VI, 409 pages. 1976.

Vol. 131: Mathematical Systems Theory. Proceedings 1975. Edited by G. Marchesini and S. K. Mitter. X, 408 pages. 1976.

Vol. 132: U. H. Funke, Mathematical Models in Marketing. A Collection of Abstracts. XX, 514 pages. 1976.

Vol. 133: Warsaw Fall Seminars in Mathematical Economics 1975. Edited by M. W. Loś, J. Loś, and A. Wieczorek. V. 159 pages. 1976.

Vol. 134: Computing Methods in Applied Sciences and Engineering. Proceedings 1975. VIII, 390 pages. 1976.

Vol. 135: H. Haga, A Disequilibrium – Equilibrium Model with Money and Bonds. A Keynesian – Walrasian Synthesis. VI, 119 pages. 1976.

Vol. 136: E. Kofler und G. Menges, Entscheidungen bei unvollständiger Information. XII, 357 Seiten. 1976.

Vol. 137: R. Wets, Grundlagen Konvexer Optimierung. VI, 146 Seiten. 1976.

Vol. 138: K. Okuguchi, Expectations and Stability in Oligopoly Models. VI, 103 pages. 1976.

Vol. 139: Production Theory and Its Applications. Proceedings. Edited by H. Albach and G. Bergendahl. VIII, 193 pages. 1977.

Vol. 140: W. Eichhorn and J. Voeller, Theory of the Price Index. Fisher's Test Approach and Generalizations. VII, 95 pages. 1976.

Vol. 141: Mathematical Economics and Game Theory. Essays in Honor of Oskar Morgenstern. Edited by R. Henn and O. Moeschlin. XIV, 703 pages. 1977.

Vol. 142: J. S. Lane, On Optimal Population Paths. V, 123 pages. 1977.

Vol. 143: B. Näslund, An Analysis of Economic Size Distributions. XV, 100 pages. 1977.

Vol. 144: Convex Analysis and Its Applications. Proceedings 1976. Edited by A. Auslender. VI, 219 pages. 1977.

Vol. 145: J. Rosenmüller, Extreme Games and Their Solutions. IV, 126 pages. 1977.

Vol. 146: In Search of Economic Indicators. Edited by W. H. Strigel. XVI, 198 pages. 1977.

Vol. 147: Resource Allocation and Division of Space. Proceedings. Edited by T. Fujii and R. Sato. VIII, 184 pages. 1977.

Vol. 148: C. E. Mandl, Simulationstechnik und Simulationsmodelle in den Sozial- und Wirtschaftswissenschaften. IX, 173 Seiten. 1977.

Vol. 149: Stationäre und schrumpfende Bevölkerungen: Demographisches Null- und Negativwachstum in Österreich. Herausgegeben von G. Feichtinger. VI, 262 Seiten. 1977.

Vol. 150: Bauer et al., Supercritical Wing Sections III. VI, 179 pages. 1977.

Vol. 151: C. A. Schneeweiß, Inventory-Production Theory. VI, 116 pages. 1977.

Vol. 152: Kirsch et al., Notwendige Optimalitätsbedingungen und ihre Anwendung. VI, 157 Seiten. 1978.

Vol. 153: Kombinatorische Entscheidungsprobleme: Methoden und Anwendungen. Herausgegeben von T. M. Liebling und M. Rössler. VIII, 206 Seiten. 1978.

Vol. 154: Problems and Instruments of Business Cycle Analysis. Proceedings 1977. Edited by W. H. Strigel. VI, 442 pages. 1978.

Vol. 155: Multiple Criteria Problem Solving. Proceedings 1977. Edited by S. Zionts. VIII, 567 pages. 1978.

Vol. 156: B. Näslund and B. Sellstedt, Neo-Ricardian Theory. With Applications to Some Current Economic Problems. VI, 165 pages. 1978.

Vol. 157: Optimization and Operations Research. Proceedings 1977. Edited by R. Henn, B. Korte, and W. Oettli. VI, 270 pages. 1978.

Vol. 158: L. J. Cherene, Set Valued Dynamical Systems and Economic Flow. VIII, 83 pages. 1978.

Vol. 159: Some Aspects of the Foundations of General Equilibrium Theory: The Posthumous Papers of Peter J. Kalman. Edited by J. Green. VI, 167 pages. 1978.

Vol. 160: Integer Programming and Related Areas. A Classified Bibliography. Edited by D. Hausmann. XIV, 314 pages. 1978.

Vol. 161: M. J. Beckmann, Rank in Organizations. VIII, 164 pages. 1978.

Vol. 162: Recent Developments in Variable Structure Systems, Economics and Biology. Proceedings 1977. Edited by R. R. Mohler and A. Ruberti. VI, 326 pages. 1978.

Vol. 163: G. Fandel, Optimale Entscheidungen in Organisationen. VI, 143 Seiten. 1979.

Vol. 164: C. L. Hwang and A. S. M. Masud, Multiple Objective Decision Making – Methods and Applications. A State-of-the-Art Survey. XII, 351 pages. 1979.

Vol. 165: A. Maravall, Identification in Dynamic Shock-Error Models. VIII, 158 pages. 1979.

Vol. 166: R. Cuninghame-Green, Minimax Algebra. XI, 258 pages. 1979.

Vol. 167: M. Faber, Introduction to Modern Austrian Capital Theory. X, 196 pages. 1979.

Vol. 168: Convex Analysis and Mathematical Economics. Proceedings 1978. Edited by J. Kriens. V, 136 pages. 1979.

Vol. 169: A. Rapoport et al., Coalition Formation by Sophisticated Players. VII, 170 pages. 1979.

Vol. 170: A. E. Roth, Axiomatic Models of Bargaining. V, 121 pages. 1979.

Vol. 171: G. F. Newell, Approximate Behavior of Tandem Queues. XI, 410 pages. 1979.

Vol. 172: K. Neumann and U. Steinhardt, GERT Networks and the Time-Oriented Evaluation of Projects. 268 pages. 1979.

Vol. 173: S. Erlander, Optimal Spatial Interaction and the Gravity Model. VII, 107 pages. 1980.

Vol. 174: Extremal Methods and Systems Analysis. Edited by A. V. Fiacco and K. O. Kortanek. XI, 545 pages. 1980.

Vol. 175: S. K. Srinivasan and R. Subramanian, Probabilistic Analysis of Redundant Systems. VII, 356 pages. 1980.

Vol. 176: R. Färe, Laws of Diminishing Returns. VIII, 97 pages. 1980.

Vol. 177: Multiple Criteria Decision Making-Theory and Application. Proceedings, 1979. Edited by G. Fandel and T. Gal. XVI, 570 pages. 1980.

Vol. 178: M. N. Bhattacharyya, Comparison of Box-Jenkins and Bonn Monetary Model Prediction Performance. VII, 146 pages. 1980.

Vol. 179: Recent Results in Stochastic Programming. Proceedings, 1979. Edited by P. Kall and A. Prékopa. IX, 237 pages. 1980.

Vol. 180: J. F. Brotchie, J. W. Dickey and R. Sharpe, TOPAZ – General Planning Technique and its Applications at the Regional, Urban, and Facility Planning Levels. VII, 356 pages. 1980.

Vol. 181: H. D. Sherali and C. M. Shetty, Optimization with Disjunctive Constraints. VIII, 156 pages. 1980.

Vol. 182: J. Wolters, Stochastic Dynamic Properties of Linear Econometric Models. VIII, 154 pages. 1980.

Vol. 183: K. Schittkowski, Nonlinear Programming Codes. VIII, 242 pages. 1980.

Vol. 184: R. E. Burkard and U. Derigs, Assignment and Matching Problems: Solution Methods with FORTRAN-Programs. VIII, 148 pages. 1980.

Vol. 185: C. C. von Weizsäcker, Barriers to Entry. VI, 220 pages. 1980.

Vol. 186: Ch.-L. Hwang and K. Yoon, Multiple Attribute Decision Making – Methods and Applications. A State-of-the-Art-Survey. XI, 259 pages. 1981.

Vol. 187: W. Hock, K. Schittkowski, Test Examples for Nonlinear Programming Codes. V. 178 pages. 1981.

Vol. 188: D. Bös, Economic Theory of Public Enterprise. VII, 142 pages. 1981.

Vol. 189: A. P. Lüthi, Messung wirtschaftlicher Ungleichheit. IX, 287 pages. 1981.

Vol. 190: J. N. Morse, Organizations: Multiple Agents with Multiple Criteria. Proceedings, 1980. VI, 509 pages. 1981.

Vol. 191: H. R. Sneessens, Theory and Estimation of Macroeconomic Rationing Models. VII, 138 pages. 1981.

Vol. 192: H. J. Bierens: Robust Methods and Asymptotic Theory in Nonlinear Econometrics. IX, 198 pages. 1981.

Vol. 193: J. K. Sengupta, Optimal Decisions under Uncertainty. VII, 156 pages. 1981.

Ökonometrie und Unternehmensforschung
Econometrics and Operations Research

Vol. I	Nichtlineare Programmierung. Von H. P. Künzi und W. Krelle unter Mitwirkung von W. Oettli. Vergriffen
Vol. II	Lineare Programmierung und Erweiterungen. Von G. B. Dantzig. Ins Deutsche übertragen und bearbeitet von A. Jaeger. – Mit 103 Abbildungen. XVI, 712 Seiten. 1966. Geb.
Vol. III	Stochastic Processes. By M. Girault. – With 35 figures. XII, 126 pages. 1966. Cloth
Vol. IV	Methoden der Unternehmensforschung im Versicherungswesen. Von K. H. Wolff. – Mit 14 Diagrammen. VIII, 266 Seiten. 1966. Geb.
Vol. V	The Theory of Max-Min and its Application to Weapons Allocation Problems. By John M. Danskin. – With 6 figures. X, 126 pages. 1967. Cloth
Vol. VI	Entscheidungskriterien bei Risiko. Von H. Schneeweiss. – Mit 35 Abbildungen. XII, 215 Seiten. 1967. Geb.
Vol. VII	Boolean Methods in Operations Research and Related Areas. By P. L. Hammer (Ivănescu) and S. Rudeanu. With a preface by R. Bellman. – With 25 figures. XVI, 329 pages. 1968. Cloth
Vol. VIII	Strategy for R & D: Studies in the Microeconomics of Development. By Th. Marschak. Th K. Glennan Jr., and R. Summers. – With 44 figures. XIV, 330 pages. 1967. Cloth
Vol. IX	Dynamic Programming of Economic Decisions. By M. J. Beckmann. – With 9 figures XII, 143 pages. 1968. Cloth
Vol. X	Input-Output-Analyse. Von J. Schumann. – Mit 12 Abbildungen. X, 311 Seiten. 1968. Geb.
Vol. XI	Produktionstheorie. Von W. Wittmann. – Mit 54 Abbildungen. VIII, 177 Seiten. 1968. Geb.
Vol. XII	Sensitivitätsanalysen und parametrische Programmierung. Von W. Dinkelbach. – Mit 20 Abbildungen. XI, 190 Seiten. 1969. Geb.
Vol. XIII	Graphentheoretische Methoden und ihre Anwendungen. Von W. Knödel. – Mit 24 Abbildungen. VIII, 111 Seiten. 1969. Geb.
Vol. XIV	Praktische Studien zur Unternehmensforschung. Von E. Nievergelt, O. Müller, F. E. Schlaepfer und W. H. Landis. – Mit 82 Abbildungen. XII, 240 Seiten. 1970. Geb.
Vol. XV	Optimale Reihenfolgen. Von H. Müller-Merbach. – Mit 45 Abbildungen. IX, 225 Seiten. 1970. Geb.
Vol. XVI	Preispolitik der Mehrproduktenunternehmung in der statischen Theorie. Von R. Selten. – Mit 20 Abbildungen. VIII, 195 Seiten. 1970. Geb.
Vol. XVII	Information Theory for Systems Engineers. By L. P. Hyvärinen. – With 42 figures. VIII, 197 pages. 1970. Cloth
Vol. XVIII	Unternehmensforschung im Bergbau. Von F. L. Wilke. – Mit 29 Abbildungen. VIII, 150 Seiten. 1972. Geb.
Vol. XIX	Anti-Äquilibrium. Von J. Kornai. – Mit 31 Abbildungen. XVI, 382 Seiten. 1975. Geb.
Vol. XX	Mathematische Optimierung. Von E. Blum, W. Oettli. IX, 413 Seiten. (davon 75 Seiten Bibliographie). 1975. Geb.
Vol. XXI	Stochastic Linear Programming. By P. Kall. VI, 95 pages. 1976. Cloth.

GPSR Compliance

The European Union's (EU) General Product Safety Regulation (GPSR) is a set of rules that requires consumer products to be safe and our obligations to ensure this.

If you have any concerns about our products, you can contact us on ProductSafety@springernature.com

In case Publisher is established outside the EU, the EU authorized representative is:

Springer Nature Customer Service Center GmbH
Europaplatz 3
69115 Heidelberg, Germany

Batch number: 10844827

Printed by Printforce, the Netherlands